INTERGENERATIONAL PROGRAMS

INTERGENERATIONAL PROGRAMS
Past, Present, and Future

by

Sally Newman
Christopher R. Ward
Thomas B. Smith
Janet O. Wilson
James M. McCrea

with
Gary Calhoun and Eric Kingson

Taylor & Francis
Publishers since 1798

USA	Publishing Office:	Taylor & Francis 1101 Vermont Avenue, N.W., Suite 200 Washington, DC 20005-3521 Tel: (202) 289-2174 Fax: (202) 289-3665
	Distribution Center:	Taylor & Francis 1900 Frost Road, Suite 101 Bristol, PA 19007-1598 Tel: (215) 785-5800 Fax: (215) 785-5515
UK		Taylor & Francis Ltd. 1 Gunpowder Square London EC4A 3DE Tel: 0171 583 0490 Fax: 0171 583 0581

INTERGENERATIONAL PROGRAMS: Past, Present, and Future

1 2 3 4 5 6 7 8 9 0   B R B R   9 8 7

This book was set in Times Roman. The editors were Christine Williams and Kathleen Sheedy. Cover design by Michelle Fleitz.

A CIP catalog record for this book is available from the British Library.
∞ The paper in this publication meets the requirements of the ANSI Standard Z39.48-1984 (Permanence of Paper)

Library of Congress Cataloging-in-Publication Data

Intergenerational programs: past, present, and future/by Sally
    Newman . . . [et al.].
      p.   cm.
    Includes bibliographical references.

    1. Age groups—United States.   2. Intergenerational relations—
United States.   3. United States—Social policy.   4. Social work
with children—United States.   5. Social work with the aged—United
States.   I. Newman, Sally.
HM131.I544   1997
305.2—dc21   97-10289
                                                                          CIP
ISBN 1-56032-420-1 (case)
ISBN 1-56032-421-X (paper)

Contents

II
BACKGROUND AND DESCRIPTIONS OF INTERGENERATIONAL PROGRAMS

III
RESEARCH AND EVALUATION OF INTERGENERATIONAL PROGRAMS

IV
PUBLIC POLICY AND THE FUTURE
OF INTERGENERATIONAL PROGRAMS

Acknowledgments

The authors would like to acknowledge the Generations Together staff contribution to the preparation of this book—Sandra Harris, for her tireless efforts in maintaining updated and corrected versions of the book chapters, and Heidi Streetman and Nancy Palumbo for their library work and literature reviews.

We also appreciate the contributions of the organizations who provided the case study models used to demonstrate the diversity of existing intergenerational programs:

- Care Castle,
- The Community Intergenerational Program,
- The Full Circle Theater Group,
- Generations,
- Neighborhoods 2000,
- Self-Esteem Through Service, and
- The Senior Citizen School Volunteer Program.

A special thank you goes to our families, whose support enabled us to spend the extra time needed to complete this book. We also owe a debt of gratitude to many unnamed colleagues, who helped us pool our strength and collaborate in the development of a book that we hope will make a difference in the intergenerational field.

Finally, a heartfelt thanks to Elaine Pirrone, a former senior acquisitions editor at Taylor & Francis, who was patient, supportive, and understanding throughout the process of creating this book.

Preface

The term *intergenerational* is appearing more and more frequently in descriptions of human service programs addressing a wide range of contemporary social concerns. The intergenerational idea reflects the relationships that define families, and the word describes the basic mechanism by which persons of different generations collaborate to nurture and support each other. Ideally, within a family system, the older adults pass along their acquired wisdom, perspective, and understanding to the youngest generation. The older generations benefit as well, receiving nurturing themselves from the family's young.

In the real world, however, families experience varying degrees of success in providing connections across multiple generations. Particularly in the last 50 years, rapid and accelerating changes in Western cultures have increasingly inhibited this mutually satisfying arrangement. Industrial-age nuclear family lifestyles create conditions that limit and devalue the role of the family's older adults (grandparents, great-grandparents, older aunts and uncles) and restrict the ability of families to care for their older members. The increasing complexity of modern culture has created gaps in the traditional two-way links between the generations.

These gaps may take the form of actual geographical separation. Adult children move away from their parents to raise their own families. Older adults themselves often move away from younger family members. There are many reasons, both positive and negative, for these separations, for example, changing professional expectations, shifting economic pressures, and health needs. Social pressures create other kinds of gaps, too, as these age cohorts spend less time interacting with each other. The opportunities for interaction have become fewer as the members of each age group have become more and more highly segregated. Children congregate with each other in child-care centers, schools, and youth-oriented groups. Younger adults tend to work and socialize with others of similar age. Older adults often frequent social centers designed exclusively for senior citizens and are increasingly residing in communities with people their own age where the regular presence of younger people may be limited or unacceptable.

In the 1970s, observers of social trends took note of the widening physical gap between the generations and began to connect this phenomenon with the appearance of social and emotional gaps. Members of the younger and older generations, for example, began to misperceive each other, almost as though they were too far apart to see each other clearly. The 1960s and 1970s saw the growth of some specific negative attitudes and stereotypes, a result of the absence of family experience in which it is natural and expected to observe life from womb to tomb. During this period, professionals noted an appearance of behaviors among the young and old that may have been related to disconnectedness within the family units: loneliness and depression among older adults distanced from their younger family members; feelings of insecurity, dependency, and fear of the future among the young separated from their elders.

CLOSING THE GAPS

In response to this increase in family fragmentation, the concept of an *intergenerational program* appeared. Social scientists began to suspect that, for members of both age groups, ideal and appropriate psychosocial development required intergenerational connections. Some of these intergenerational pioneers theorized that closer, more frequent contact between the generations could help them see each other more realistically and receive from each other the kind of mutual support typically available in the family structures of an earlier period. Deliberate attempts were begun, through specific program activities, to create opportunities for purposeful and ongoing interactions between nonbiologically linked members of these two age cohorts, with the intent of fostering connections akin to those within a multigenerational family unit.

During the 1970s, as these early intergenerational programs emerged and evolved, their developers began to notice and document outcomes that went beyond anticipated changes in attitudes and perceptions. Participants in these programs, both children and older adults, reported positive internal changes in their self-esteem, their sense of purpose and usefulness, and their sense of being connected to the cycle of life in their communities. These changes were significant enough to generate a new set of hypotheses about the benefits of, and uses for, intergenerational programming. Program designers began to move away from projects that focused narrowly on the reconstruction of intergenerational connections and began to consider other, broader social goals.

Other emerging social factors helped to shape this modification in focus. As the initial intergenerational program outcomes were being studied, a new role for these programs had become apparent. During three decades of program development, social pressures in the United States have shifted. An awareness of urgent social needs and issues—poverty, violence, drug and alcohol abuse, and the related decay of families and entire communities—has surfaced or expanded. These pressures have had a profound effect on the generations that seem to be most vulnerable: children, youth, and older adults. In many communities, members of these age groups have become the primary victims of deteriorating social structures.

The question currently posed, then, is whether there is a way to harness the power of intergenerational programming to address the impact of these growing social concerns. An early answer to this question would appear to be yes, as intergenerational components are increasingly included in intervention programs addressing contemporary social issues.

THE FIELD OF INTERGENERATIONAL STUDIES

A clear relationship between intergenerational programs and positive societal change has not been measured. A growing need for more documentation and harder information has driven an emerging intergenerational field into its current phase of development. The rapid increase in intergenerational programming has also led to a rapid expansion in the body of data, as researched and as reported by the practitioners. As this emerging field finds its shape, this data must be built into program performance standards and drawn on as models for replication are developed.

Intergenerational programming, then, is evolving into an intergenerational field that incorporates intergenerational studies as well as programs and related data-gathering and advocacy activities. The practitioner-oriented model is finding a place within a larger academic discipline that embraces knowledge and skill development related to programs, evaluation, research, and public policy. This book, by combining academic information with comprehensive information about the past, present, and future of intergenerational programs, illustrates the relationship between theory and practice.

FORMAT OF THE BOOK

This book is meant to be used by a variety of professionals, academics, and students involved in or considering an intergenerational field as an area for study or for practice. The information presented in this book will be useful to

- the intergenerational professional who wants to formally study the theoretical insights that undergird the field;
- the academic who wants to examine the relationship between theory and practice in an emerging intergenerational field;
- the student considering a human service career with possible intergenerational components;
- the human service professional interested in enhancing his or her intergenerational skills and knowledge; and
- the policymaker who needs to understand both theoretical and practical implications of the intergenerational concept.

For professionals, students, and academics interested in this work, there is a need to understand the evolving field's conceptual framework, its direction for the future, and the social forces that shape and power the intergenerational initiative. This book addresses these elements of the intergenerational field and their relationship to each other, providing a comprehensive overview. Specific chapters focus on various aspects of the topic.

The book begins with a presentation of the fundamental rationale for the intergenerational field and of the information that professionals will need to become familiar with the foundations and characteristics of the field. The chapters in Part I present both a foundation and a context for intergenerational programming. Chapter 1 reviews basic human development theory as it relates to intergenerational connections. Chapter 2 describes the societal forces and problems that have shaped the field, and chapter 3 focuses on those issues that lend themselves most clearly to successful intervention strategies for connecting older adults with children or youth.

Part II begins with chapter 4, which presents an historical perspective of the intergenerational field in response to developmental and social forces. It continues with a chronology of events that reflect the changes and status of this field from the 1960s to the 1990s. Chapter 5 presents an analysis of actual intergenerational program types and models. There is no need for modern professionals to reinvent the wheel when they can study the struggles and successes of their predecessors. The models examined in chapter 5 represent three basic program types; the presentation format emphasizes the common elements of program models and enables a quick comparison across models and populations served. This chapter describes what makes programs work, elements that contribute to their success, and some keys to successful replication. There is also an examination of program outcomes that reflect the impact of intergenerational programming. In chapter 6, programs representing the three basic intergenerational types are discussed in detail with a case history design.

The intergenerational field is dominated by programs and programmatic concerns. These concerns have fueled a steadily increasing emphasis on evaluating outcomes and on providing a professional knowledge base through applied research efforts. In Part III, chapters 7 and 8 deal with concepts, issues, and results of intergenerational evaluation and research. Chapter 7 includes approaches to program evaluation and insights that have been gained to date from systematic evaluation efforts, and chapter 8 presents an overview of questions addressed and information acquired through research initiatives.

Part IV focuses on the public policy implications of this growing field. It begins in chapter 9 with an examination of the interrelationship between intergenerational programs and the shape of public policy. Chapter 10 continues the analysis with a look at broader trends and influences. The section concludes in chapter 11 with a discussion of ideas, questions, and considerations for the future of the intergenerational field.

The final portion of the book is devoted to helping readers develop their own methods of finding and using resource materials. In the appendix, readers are introduced to the unique challenges involved in accessing intergenerational information with standard library resources such as literature reviews. The appendix also contains a variety of other search strategies appropriate to the characteristics of the field. Here also the reader will find lists of intergenerational resources to assist administrators and practitioners: organizations, manuals, newsletters, journals, media, and databases. These resources are available nationally and can help to link people, systems, and information.

CONCLUSION

Intergenerational Programs was conceived, and largely written, by current and former staff members at Generations Together, an intergenerational studies program at the University of Pittsburgh. Generations Together is a one-of-a-kind intergenerational program with a 20-year history of leadership in developing and promoting the intergenerational concept.

As a leader in the new emerging field of intergenerational studies, Generations

Together's mission is twofold: to promote intergenerational activity as a positive force in society and to establish criteria for measuring the success of professionals in this field.

Intergenerational Programs, then, combines the experience, insights, and knowledge of the authors, professionals who have been involved in the shaping of the field from its programmatic inception to its now more comprehensive academic, programming, and public policy configuration. Their active participation in the evolution of the field has contributed to the comprehensiveness of this book's content and shaped the convictions expressed therein.

By sharing their experience with the readers, the authors hope to create competent, trained professionals whose skills will continue to shape the future of the intergenerational movement. This book is dedicated to those professionals in the hope that it will support their efforts to build and shape an exciting new human service field and academic discipline.

I

RATIONALE FOR INTERGENERATIONAL PROGRAMS

1

Developmental Theories as the Basis for Intergenerational Programs

Sally Newman, PhD, and Thomas B. Smith, MLS

Grow old along with me!
The best is yet to be,
The last of life, for which the first was made
Our times are in his hand.

—Robert Browning

During the past 20 years, the term *intergenerational* has been used to describe a social phenomenon that brings together the nation's oldest and youngest generations. Intergenerational programs have been emerging as a new form of human service that provides for systematic and deliberate interaction between persons at the opposite end of the human age continuum.

Such programs offer a mechanism by which persons of different generations purposefully collaborate to support and nurture each other. In this collaboration, older adults, children, and youth each assume a special role, designed to have a positive and mutually beneficial impact. Intergenerational programs owe their existence to the convergence of a number of social, economic, and political factors, as well as to a unique synergy that seems to exist between older adults and young people.

Such programs offer effective methods for confronting a wide range of modern concerns, especially those of older adults and young people. Intergenerational programs have been successful over the years in beginning to address

- social problems, such as isolation, inadequate support systems, and the disconnectedness of both generations from each other and from their communities;
- economic problems, such as inadequate employment opportunities for the young and old; and
- political problems, such as the competition for shrinking human service funds.

In reflecting on these successes and reviewing a plethora of intergenerational programs, it is clear that the intuitive sense of the program designers and implementers has proved to be reliable. With the increase in number and variety of intergenerational programs, practitioners and administrators have begun to see themselves as members of a special new and growing profession: the intergenerational human service field.

The intergenerational concept is now appearing as an element of human service programs that address a diverse range of the social issues affecting today's families and communities, issues such as school dropout rates, teen pregnancy, inadequate child care, isolation of older adults, and substance abuse among all generations. The concept is embodied in programs that involve planned, ongoing interactions between nonbiologically linked children, youth, and older adults. Such programs engage these groups in activities that benefit both the young and the old. The younger participants, who may be identified as mainstream, at risk, having special needs, or gifted, include infants through college-age youth. Participating older persons include well, high-functioning independent elders as well as elders who are dependent, lower functioning, and at risk.

As this new field matures, it becomes increasingly important to examine its fundamental premises. When professionals recognize and appreciate these premises, they can understand the reasons for the successes of intergenerational programming and will be equipped to make a more compelling case for its continuation and expansion.

FAMILY ROOTS

At the foundation of the intergenerational concept is a relationship that is as old as the institutions of family and community. Its roots can be seen in the connections that link specific generations within families—the elder and younger members. Ideally, while living their own lives, elders—the oldest family members—have acquired wisdom, skills, insights, and perspectives that can be passed on to the family's younger generations. Historically, elders have formed special relationships with the younger members of their families. They are nurturers, positive role models, and communicators of culture, knowledge, and values.

This transfer of knowledge and values through intergenerational bonding has a long-term impact on the learning, growth, and security of a family's children and youth. Such bonds are equally important for the family's elders, affecting their sense of purpose, well-being, and life satisfaction. The intergenerational bonds within the family enable its older and younger members to become aware of each other's needs across the life span and to recognize their roles in meeting these needs for each other (Kingson, 1989). The young provide understanding and support for their elders as they move from an independent to a more dependent stage of life; the elders offer understanding and support to the young from babyhood through adolescence and in many cases into young adulthood.

Within a family, the bonding between the youngest and oldest members arises from their mutual and compatible needs and often results in the development of strong synergistic relationships. This unique synergy is natural and appropriate, and it is an underlying element of the intergenerational concept now spreading throughout the human services.

The basic structure of extended human families, then, led to an intuitive understanding that created the notion of intergenerational programming. In this chapter, that intuition will be examined in terms of its relationship to accepted theories that identify the development and needs of young children, youth, and older adults. To this end, sections of the chapter describe basic child and older adult development theories, highlighting those aspects that are particularly relevant to the inter-generational concept. In a concluding section, the theoretically delineated character-istics of the two age groups are compared and connected in ways that begin to explain the special synergy of intergenerational programming. The theories are pre-ceded by a discussion of the nature and importance of theoretical constructs in attempting to describe and predict the forces that shape human personalities.

UNDERSTANDING HUMAN GROWTH

From the moment of conception, the human organism is engaged in a process of change and growth. While the physiological changes that characterize human growth are obvious to any observer, the changes that occur internally—in learning, for example, and in personality—are much less visible and much more mysterious as a result. Careful observation and experimentation has been necessary to clarify the mystery that is the lifelong development of a human being and to build the capacity for explaining and predicting behavior.

These explanations are part of a rich tradition; human beings have always been curious, searching for ways to better understand their environment and themselves. The quest for information about the environment through scientific inquiry has spawned increasingly complex models as isolated observations are connected into larger and larger explanations. These explanations of the way the universe works are theories, ways of systematically organizing information in an attempt to describe the operations of invisible mechanisms and relationships.

Human beings are dynamic creatures, and theoretical explanations of their be-havior require information about the way people grow and change. The study of humans, then, led to the study of human learning and of other internal aspects of development. This branch of psychology is focused on the ways in which humans acquire skills and knowledge, emphasizing and attempting to explain the causes and outcomes of change within the human personality. Human growth scientists create developmental and educational theories, schemes by which their observations of the changes that characterize the internal growth of a human being can be explained, organized, quantified, and given meaning.

Theoretical explanations of internal human growth are valuable when they can accurately predict the types of changes people will experience during their lifetimes and their responses to life events along the way. This ability to make accurate predictions is important to human service practitioners, who by definition are inter-ested in using theoretical explanations to help them keep an individual's develop-ment on its normal track. Programs intended to help people grow must apply theo-retical concepts in ways that assist positive development or at least lessen the negative influences on development.

Practitioners, then, use theoretical concepts to help them design effective pro-grams and to help them gauge the success of their models. Modern child-care providers depend on theories that offer useful explanations for behavior in develop-mental stages. For example, the standards of developmentally appropriate practice, developed and disseminated by the National Association for the Education of Young Children (Bredekamp, 1987), prescribe self-guided experiences of exploration and discovery (for children in preschool through third grade) that reflect theories about the way in which young people absorb and utilize information most readily. The rationale for creating classroom curricula and procedures for school-age children is based on a body of knowledge built by theorists such as Maria Montessori, John Dewey, Lev Vygotsky, and Erik Erikson; their developmental and educational theories, described later in the chapter, offer insight into the way children and youth learn and grow.

Similarly, professionals involved with the aging population use theories of adult development to help them design appropriate services and programs for their constituents. The work of theorists such as Malcolm Knowles, Robert Butler, K. Warner Schaie, L. Rosenmayr, and Robert Atchley, for example, clarifies the functional levels of older adults in a variety of settings. The adult-learning and socialization theories described later in this chapter provide a foundation for the programmatic structure of senior centers and adult and long-term care environments.

The quality of a specific human service, then, can be assessed by examining its relationship to relevant theory. A sound theoretical foundation for practice also enables judgments to be made about the professionalism of an individual's approach to human service and underscores the importance of creating a professional field through the application of theory to practice.

Competent intergenerational professionals need to examine and understand the developmental theories that describe and explain the characteristics of children, youth, and older adults. It seems likely that these largely separate bodies of knowledge can potentially be combined into a comprehensive theory that reflects elements common to both child and adult development, explains intergenerational interactions, and provides a tool with which intergenerational practitioners can predict and evaluate program outcomes.

BUILDING INTERGENERATIONAL THEORY

The work of combining these theories remains to be done; there is as yet no formal and specific intergenerational theory to guide practitioners in this new field. Intergenerational professionals borrow from child development, adult development, and other disciplines as they attempt to define the synergy that seems to exist between older adults and children. They are especially interested in theoretical explanations for the ways in which normal human development is positively influenced by connections between members of the "separated" generations.

It is not the intention of this chapter to formulate a complete intergenerational theory; rather, this chapter will highlight some of the ways in which currently accepted theories of human development interrelate to suggest a possible theoretical framework for intergenerational programming. Concepts can be seen in the work of leading child and older adult developmental theorists—embedded within their well-accepted theories—which when matched, compared, and linked together support intergenerational policies and programs. These concepts, linked across the age spectrum, describe the dynamics, issues, and underlying human characteristics that make up the uniqueness of intergenerational exchange. They suggest directions for further study toward the development of a comprehensive intergenerational theory.

AN OVERVIEW OF SIGNIFICANT OR PROMINENT
HUMAN GROWTH THEORIES

Since the 19th century, developmental and educational theorists have exercised an expanding influence on the understanding of the growth, development, and social behavior of the country's young and old. Many of the ideas generated by these theorists are integral to intergenerational concepts.

The Development of Children

The theories described in the following section represent a spectrum of concepts that describe the ways children grow and develop and that embody ideas that undergird intergenerational programs.

Maria Montessori (Kramer, 1976; Standing, 1959). One of the earliest and most influential early childhood theoreticians was Maria Montessori. Born in Italy in 1870, Montessori devised a theory-based educational system for young children that had a powerful impact on the early childhood field. Despite the 19th-century barriers against women achieving professional status, Montessori pursued and received a medical degree and became an instructor of psychiatry. Because of her work with retarded children in this capacity, she was given an opportunity to organize a school system for residents of a tenement housing project. The programs she designed, implemented, and studied at this school, the Casa Dei Bambina, provided ideas and models that are still seen and practiced today, in Montessori schools and in many early childhood programs.

Montessori's educational theory is built on the notion of respect for the child, a radical idea in the late 19th century. She stressed the need for individualized, child-oriented education and paid particular attention to the importance of a learning environment that truly supports learning. Her observation that children learn primarily through experience and experimentation led to the formation of the concept of *autoeducation,* which focuses on children's capacity for educating themselves.

The portions of Montessori's work that are most relevant to intergenerational professionals are found primarily in her concern with the social context of growth and development. An important component of Montessori programs is a *compassionate teacher,* an adult who is available and ready to provide guidance without pushing, demanding, punishing, or doing the work a child should be doing. Montessori's theory emphasizes children's need for nurturing and guiding adult facilitators who know and understand them as individuals, who can recognize the sensitive periods when a child is most ready to learn a particular task or subject and who can then organize the child's environment to support that learning. According to Montessori, adults also provide a framework of acceptable options within which the child has free choice of activities.

Older adults, because of their learning experiences and developmental characteristics (discussed later in this chapter) are especially appropriate for these necessary roles in a child's life; in fact, Dr. Montessori herself was a mature adult when she created the Casa Dei Bambina.

John Dewey (Boydston, 1970; Campbell, 1971; Dewey, 1938). While Maria Montessori's theories were shaping early childhood practice in Italy, an American philosopher and educator was exercising a similarly powerful influence on the nature of the

American education system. John Dewey's theories about the way children learn and the way they ought to be educated became known as *progressivism* and stressed educational techniques that deemphasized traditional subject matter. In progressive schools, teachers were trained and encouraged to build connections with individual children and, using a child-centered curriculum, emphasize the value of their interests.

Dewey's curriculum was less formal than was common at that time in history. It consisted of four primary components: *physical activities* (active play), *using tools and objects* (provided through normal daily life or special crafts activities), *cognitive tasks* (inquiry and discovery), and *social interaction*. Socializing, a key component of Dewey's theory, was ideally provided through contact with other children and adults in a classroom with a nonauthoritarian atmosphere.

Within this framework, Dewey insisted that the ultimate design of an educational curriculum depended on the interests of the individual children in each classroom. The adults' responsibility is to build in—and take advantage of—natural ways to thread traditional subject matter into and through the chosen activities of the children. He also advanced the complementary notions of the educated society and the socially useful education. Instead of preparing children for a far-off adult future, Dewey's ideas focused on the development of skills with immediate applications in the life of the child.

Dewey also discussed the philosophy of education in broader ways, which have intergenerational implications. For example, he recognized the need for society to provide children with an educational environment. As society's most experienced and learned members, older adults are a critical element in the creation of this environment. Children need adults in other ways, Dewey suggested: to teach them the skills they need to cope with the realities of their daily lives and to provide role models for success. Again, older adults are uniquely appropriate as critical informal teachers and as the positive role models who have successfully negotiated the realities of life. Interactions with older adults have a significant impact on children in both formal and informal learning experiences.

Lev Vygotsky (Miller, 1993; Wertsch, 1985; Yaroshevsky, 1989). At about the same time that Montessori and Dewey were developing their theories, a third pioneer, working in a more obscure part of the world, was also studying children's growth and development. Lev Vygotsky was an educated Russian intellectual, born near the end of the 19th century. Although he did acquire a law degree and dabbled in a wide variety of other professions, he was best known as a brilliant psychologist, widely recognized for the contributions he made to this field at an early age. His work is relatively new to the Western world, having become available through translation only as recently as 1962. One reason for the long delay was the active suppression of his work by Russian and Soviet officials; his theorizing was somewhat political in nature, primarily because he fully intended to transform society through new ideas and applications of psychological theory.

His contributions to the understanding of child development have received considerable attention in recent years. Many child development theories are focused primarily on individual, internal processes of development. Vygotsky, however, built his theories around the notion that "the mind extends beyond the skin" (Wertsch, 1985, p. 90) and that children's interaction with others in social settings is a crucial factor in shaping their thinking. In this model, adults are responsible for sharing their knowledge with children, and their knowledge is key to the development of the child. He suggests that this knowledge includes information about one's culture as well as about typical academic subjects such as reading, arithmetic, and science.

Because of his emphasis on culture, Vygotsky's theory has been described as contextualist. According to Vygotsky, all humans are embedded in a culture, which provides a context for behavior and learning and which must be considered when attempting to understand it (Miller, 1993, p. 223).

Adults are a crucial element of a notion that is central to Vygotsky's theories: the *zone of proximal development*. This term describes a set of tasks that an individual child is not capable of performing alone, but which he or she can manage with the help of someone more skilled (often an adult). The interaction within this zone, which shifts as an individual child masters more complex tasks, is responsible for academic learning as well as enculturation and social behavior. These ideas were first applied to child development practice in subject areas such as reading and mathematics; more recently, practitioners have used Vygotsky's theories to explain and support curriculum areas such as make-believe play.

Vygotsky's ideas about the needs of developing children contain clear intergenerational implications. In his view, the essential child-rearing tasks of adults are those of sharing knowledge and culture with children and of providing assistance within the zone of proximal development. These tasks are highly appropriate for older adults, who bring their own life experience, their cultural insights and roots, and their unique developmental characteristics.

Erik Erikson (Erikson, 1959, 1963; Erikson, Erikson, & Kivnick, 1986). Another European whose ideas have contributed greatly to the understanding of human growth is Erik Erikson, a German psychoanalyst who was strongly influenced by Sigmund Freud and the psychoanalytic movement. Born in 1902, Erikson believed that environment and interactions influence the course of development and that children also have an active role in shaping their experiences.

In his theoretical view, development over the entire course of a person's life occurs in a series of stages, each stage contributing to and influenced by the ones preceding and following it. The tasks of a particular stage are never fully resolved but appear in some form throughout development.

He assigned rough age boundaries to each stage and described each stage in terms of a "crisis" with a duality of possible negative and positive outcomes: trust versus mistrust (birth–1 year), autonomy versus shame and doubt (1–3 years), initiative versus guilt (3–5 years), industry versus inferiority (6 years–puberty), and identity versus identity diffusion (adolescence). Successful resolution at each stage yields positive dominant outcomes. Some carryover from unresolved crises at an earlier stage may persist, but there is always potential for resolution in a subsequent stage, later in the life of the individual.

The resolution of the crisis at each of Erikson's early stages requires the assistance of adults who are sensitive to the conflicts and the issues of each stage. Older adults, with special characteristics that include a wealth of life experience, sensitivity, and understanding, are well suited to provide this assistance. Intergenerational experiences can also help to resolve critical issues of legacy and generativity for the older adult (discussed later in this chapter), offering a mechanism for passing along values, culture, and unique life skills to members of a succeeding generation. Similarly, service to the frail elderly offers young people a natural opportunity to provide real and meaningful service in the context of a supportive relationship with a dependent elder. Such service can provide a powerful boost to a young child's self-esteem or provide an adolescent with a positive role to add to his or her coalescing sense of identity.

Erikson's theorizing has more significant intergenerational implications, however, because of his life-span approach to the question of development or growth. Unlike many child development theorists, Erikson's model continues through adulthood. His sixth stage (young adulthood), for example, incorporates the concept of intimacy and solidarity versus isolation, a conflict faced by the newly integrated personality emerging from adolescence (and later revisited as an older adult). Stages seven and eight describe middle and late adulthood; the relationship between the developmental characteristics of these stages and those of early life are of great importance to the intergenerational concept and will be discussed later in this chapter.

Summary of child development theories. Modern early childhood and education practitioners draw freely from all of these ideas (and others) as they attempt to design programs that meet the needs of the children they serve. The theories are perhaps stronger in conjunction with one another than they are as separate models, providing widely divergent lenses through which the processes of growth and learning may be viewed. There are some commonalities, however. All of these developmental and educational theories reflect a connection between the cognitive and affective aspects of growth. They also suggest the importance of firm connections between the child, older adults, and society as a whole.

Older Adult Development Theories

The early years of life are important, as a foundation is constructed that will determine the characteristics of an adult human being and the shape of his or her life. For educators, caregivers, social workers, medical practitioners, and parents, accurate information about children's growth is critical; as a result, the study of child development has received more attention than the study of the later years. Still, as the average life span increases, and older adults make up a steadily increasing proportion of the human community, the need to achieve a deeper understanding of the nature of aging has become more compelling. Perhaps as a result of this pressure, the later years of human life have recently been studied with vigor equal to that applied to the earliest years. Such studies have contributed greatly to an understanding of the processes of aging.

For the most part, older adult theorists have not focused on the creation of overarching developmental constructs. More often, theories about older adult development represent attempts to understand and quantify the physiological, social, and emotional development of the older adult in the context of their peers, their families, and society at large. Driven by the needs of an aging population, theorists look for answers that will help aging individuals cope with

- physiological aging (changes in appearance, changes in health),
- social aging (changes in life roles, changes in available income), and
- emotional aging (multiple losses, adjusting to a changing world).

Considerations of aging usually fall into one of these three developmental domains. Theories of adaptation attempt to describe relationships between the domains (e.g., the impact of an older person's reaction to physiological changes on his or her emotional development) and are discussed later in this chapter.

Physiological aging. Development within these three domains is an ongoing process, with significant differences appearing among three chronological age groups of older adults: the young-old, the old-old, and the very old. The term young-old refers to high-functioning older adults, 65–75 years of age. The old-old category includes persons 75–90 who may be more dependent and require some care. The very old are those persons over 90, many of whom require a great deal of care on a consistent basis. It is important to note that these age boundaries are approximate; as the number of high-functioning older adults increases, for example, the typical age of the young-old population is moving beyond 75.

For older adults in all three of these chronological groupings, aging involves physiological change. Functions that are affected include the senses (sight, hearing, touch, taste, and smell), memory, and problem-solving capability. Researchers have noted that most young-old, at least, can rather easily adapt to these physiological changes and that only minor changes in productivity and social performance can be directly attributed to the physiological process of aging (Clark & Spengler, 1980).

In fact, it has been demonstrated that the capacity for learning and growth is not significantly diminished by advancing age (Schaie & Willis, 1986; Schuetz, 1988). Malcolm Knowles, who used the term *andragogy* to describe the unique characteristics of adult education, sets no upper age limit on the capacity to learn, given appropriate forms of instruction (Knowles, 1978). Skills in organization, and the presentation of information in meaningful contexts, can totally compensate for any losses in speed or memory (Haslerud, 1972). Older adults learn best, for example, in social situations, giving information to and getting information from other participants as well as from the teacher (Schuetz, 1988).

The aging process itself is influenced by environmental factors; physical exercise, mental activity, and social contact have all been shown to reduce or slow its impact (Rosenmayr, 1980). As seen in examples presented in later chapters of this book, the young people who enter an older adults' environment through intergenerational programming can delay the aging process by offering a natural incentive to exercise, think, and interact.

Social aging. The aging process produces other characteristics that relate to and are manifested in social interactions. Aging adults experience changes in their emotional range and response, related to alterations in their perspectives and priorities. These include a tendency toward isolation, feelings of worthlessness, and a somewhat lower level of adaptability (Schuetz, 1988).

It is difficult to clearly identify the roots of these alterations. The interrelationship between the very real changes associated with aging and the influence of society's perspective is almost impossible to sort out. At the very least, it is possible that generally accepted, widespread perceptions of the elderly intensify an aging individual's natural physical and emotional changes.

The notion of social roles is useful in attempting to understand this interrelationship. As an individual ages, he or she outgrows a series of roles, some of which last for decades before they are no longer relevant. The role of spouse disappears when one's husband or wife dies; the role of career worker ends with retirement. Some roles, such as those of parent or sibling, become ambiguous, the expectations less clear. Skills related to previous roles are no longer useful, and information becomes outdated or irrelevant (Hooyman & Kiyak, 1991). New information, if it contradicts the things an older adult has "always" known to be true, may create conflicts that must be resolved before the information can be assimilated (Dance, 1988). Finally, these role shifts must be accomplished with very little external support; contemporary society offers few guidelines, and fewer role models, to its aging members.

Specific governmental policies have also played a part in creating—or at least reinforcing—the social separation and marginalization of the elderly. This separateness is then easily interpreted as a normal developmental characteristic, and new policies are built on this erroneous conclusion. The normal developmental characteristics of older adults, then, seen in this social context, might actually change or improve under the influence of policies that reshape social institutions (such as the labor market) to assume life-span participation (Estes, 1979).

Other ways of describing the interrelationship between older adults and their larger society involve the notion of relative power (Dowd, 1980). Partly because of social perceptions and policy, aging individuals experience a steady decrease in their ability to influence their environment. Older adults have less of the stuff by which contemporary society measures success and power: money and possessions, physical attractiveness, strength, health, and mental quickness.

This "inferiority" is only partly the result of the natural aging process. For example, the opportunities to develop and maintain relationships (an important source of social influence) are diminished largely by social isolation and marginalization imposed from without. Perhaps the clearest source of self-worth for older adults is the respect that they have earned through decades of living and learning. Such respect is also, of course, heavily dependent on social attitudes; these might be adjusted through changes in social policy, including an increased focus on expanding intergenerational interaction. The young people who participate in intergenerational programming often experience a positive change in attitude toward the older adult participants and toward older adults in general. Social policy that supports and fosters the growth of such programs, therefore, can ultimately affect broad societal perspectives.

Emotional aging. Other typical characteristics of older adults are less easily compensated for. Gerontologists have not been able to completely unravel the complex developmental and environmental factors that contribute to an older person's feelings of worthlessness and isolation. The impact of the environment, as embodied in myths and stereotypes about aging and the aged, is probably as significant as an older individual's internal struggles. Certainly, socially reinforced feelings of worthlessness and inadequacy do not make those struggles any easier. The myths exert a powerful influence in part because they are largely based on exaggerations of the actual changes brought on by the aging process.

More often than not, widely held cultural beliefs about the nature and consequences of aging are, on investigation, substantially incorrect. These beliefs are the root of many destructive stereotypes because they are used to make inferences or draw conclusions. Obviously, if one's beliefs are faulty, so too will be one's conclusions. It is estimated that about half of the common assumptions about aging are incorrect or doubtful, and it is these misconceptions that provide justification for overt discrimination against older persons (Atchley, 1988).

For example, the existence of negative workplace stereotypes is well documented. In an early study, Rosen and Jerdee (1976) reported that, in comparison with their younger counterparts, older workers were *seen* as more accident prone, not as productive or efficient, and unreceptive to new ideas; in general, they were seen as less adaptable and less versatile. The problem of discrimination is compounded by company managers, who tend to act on socially accepted beliefs about older workers rather than on their actual performance (Lawrence, 1988). A recent study conducted for the American Association of Retired Persons (AARP) suggests that little has changed, noting the persistence of two overpowering stereotypes: a "perceived lack of flexibility" and a "resistance to technology" (American Association of Retired Persons, 1996, p. 2).

The tenacity of these misperceptions and their application is especially troubling given the existence of much evidence to the contrary. As early as 1974, a study conducted by McCormick and Tifflin found that older workers are, in truth, *less* accident prone and *more* productive, efficient, and enterprising.

The disparity between the real abilities of older adults and the perceptions of employers has an obvious and immediate impact on their employment prospects. Perhaps more important, theorists have postulated and researched more subtle effects. In their work, Kuypers and Bengston (1973) described the interaction between an unaccepting environment and an older adult's self-concept as a classic vicious cycle in which the elderly, seen as incompetent and inferior, begin to live down to these expectations.

Some theorists suggest that this aspect of older adult development, the tendency toward low self-esteem, is subject to successful external intervention. "In order for the elderly to feel good about themselves," said Charles Zastrow, "they need feedback from others that they are worthwhile, competent, and respected" (Zastrow & Kirst-Ashman, 1994, p. 596). Perhaps the cycle will be reversed. As the number of capable, contributing older adults grows and their contributions are recognized, social perceptions of aging may change as well, changes that could well have a positive impact on the self-images of individual elders. By encouraging and training older adults to participate meaningfully in their community and their world, society can communicate to them a sense of being valued, combating the pervasive feelings of uselessness (Botan, 1988). Intergenerational programs, such as those described later in this book, offer training, motivation, and meaningful activities, which can produce significant gains in participants' self-esteem. Such programs can positively impact the quality of life for older adult participants from all chronological age groups.

Engagement and disengagement. This strategy of social intervention through participation stands in direct opposition to the so-called disengagement theory (Cumming & Henry, 1961). Cumming and Henry's model suggests that older adults have a developmental need to turn away from society and the world at large, to be left alone. Application of this theory suggested that social institutions ought to support this need; aging individuals were encouraged to withdraw from the community, and society was encouraged to let them go. Through further research, this model was largely discredited; in the words of Robert Atchley, "disengagement is neither natural nor inevitable and . . . most cases of disengagement result from a lack of opportunities for continued involvement" (Atchley, 1988, p. 246). Disengagement theory has been replaced by theories of adaptation and social intervention that draw radically different conclusions and offer the opposite recommendations.

An older adult's ability to remain active and engaged is seen as critical, exerting a powerful positive influence on physical well-being, mental health, and productive aging. Healthy, independent members of the young-old (60–75 years old) find it relatively easy to participate in activities to make connections and to remain valued members of the community. The creation of intergenerational programs is steadily expanding their opportunities for productive engagement in society. For the frail elderly, the possibilities for active engagement are more limited. For a frail, more dependent older adult with physical and cognitive limitations, therefore, intergenerational programs represent one of only a few ways to build and maintain ongoing connections. As noted earlier, visiting and service-providing programs for frail elders also offer special benefits to the participating children and adolescents—including a greater understanding of and respect for older adults.

Adaptation. The theories of adaptation that ultimately replaced the disengagement model strongly support the value of social connections and postulate the mechanisms and significance of older adults' integration into contemporary society. This theoretical construct takes note of the significant changes, described earlier, that occur as an individual ages: physiological changes, changes in social roles, the reorganization of one's self-perception and the modification of others' perception of oneself, all in the context of transformation in the surrounding world.

Adaptation theories consider two separate but related phenomena: the ability to adopt new activities and the adapting of old activities as a compensation for the shift in social roles that occurs as one leaves middle age. These theories, then, are attempts to describe the process by which an individual accommodates to change and continues to fit into his or her world. One theory, developed by Klaus Riegel (1976), suggests that the older adult personality emerges from a struggle between various ongoing influences: biological, psychological, cultural–sociological, and environmental. Adult development is seen as a complex interaction between the self and its social and physiological environment. Refining this theory, Susan Krauss Whitbourne (1985) suggested a developmental model that focuses specifically on adaptation; that is, the ongoing effort to preserve one's psychological well-being and physiological health (Kimmel, 1990).

Atchley (1988, p. 245) suggested that the most important adaptation task is that of coping with the loss of roles and activities. As individuals lose their familiar roles (through retirement, reduced functioning, loss of spouse, etc.) and their ability to engage in habitual activities, they can cope by

- *replacing* the lost activities and roles with new, more suitable ones,
- *shifting* the focus of time and energy toward the roles and activities that remain, and
- *disengaging*, which, while no longer viewed as the normal state of an aging adult, may still be seen in individuals who lack the ability or opportunity to exercise one of the other two options.

The outcomes of successful adaptation to internal change could be described as satisfaction with one's life (past and present), functional autonomy, and a sense of personal continuity. An older adult who has successfully adapted to external changes is one who continues to participate in the world and who is compensated in some way for his or her participation.

Successful preservation of functionality, then, depends much on the older adult's ability to live with, learn about, and accept the younger generations' new spectrum of behaviors and values. One key factor in successful adaptation is the ability to accommodate and to grow from this accommodation; as detailed in this book, inter-generational programming offers unique opportunities for the kind of contact and dialogue that facilitates such growth.

Life review. Other theories of older adult development focus more on internal states and processes than on the impact of social attitudes. For example, some researchers have observed the importance of life review as a major developmental task of the aging process. This theory, according to Butler and Lewis (1977), suggests that older adults must somehow come to terms with the events and activities of their lives, putting them into perspective and balance. If older adults are successful at this task, they achieve a sense of having lived a worthwhile life; an unresolved or negative life review indicates and fosters serious self-image problems and possibly real pathology. A key component in the life review process is an appraisal of an individual's lifetime in the context of ongoing interaction with members of succeeding generations. In fact, such interaction may be an essential element of a successful life review.

The work of life review also figures prominently in the ideas of Erik Erikson, whose early childhood theories were discussed earlier in the chapter. As noted there, he was one of the first developmental theorists to describe the later stages of life within a developmental framework. According to Erikson's theories, the life review task in the final stages of development is part of a larger struggle, the conflict between integrity and despair. Integrity refers to an individual's ability to accept the shape his or her life has taken and the capacity to bravely face its ending. Despair is Erikson's term for the sense of guilt, regret, and remorse that accompanies a concern with unfinished business and that makes it impossible to peacefully accept the end of life (Erikson et al., 1986).

Erikson's discussion of life review overlaps with the notion of legacy. The sense of having created a future, of leaving behind something worthwhile, is a positive outcome of the eighth stage of life. Butler and Lewis (1977, p. 28) also noted that older adults experience an increasing need to leave something of themselves behind when they die, and they suggested several possible causes: a desire to be remembered, an altruistic giving of oneself, a less altruistic yearning to stay in control even beyond one's death, and the urge to tie up the loose ends of one's life. A legacy provides a sense of continuity, allowing an older person to feel that he or she will continue to participate in the life of the world.

The desire to leave a legacy is also linked to a phenomenon that Butler and Lewis (1977, p. 28) refer to as the *elder* function of an older adult. This term refers to the natural tendency of the old to share their special knowledge and experience with those who are younger; an urge that stimulates the development of links between generations. Such connections can have a profound impact on the self-esteem of older adults; they also have a similar impact on youth (and self-image is an important issue in the earlier developmental stages). An older adult who experiences the satisfaction of acknowledgment from a younger person is much more likely to see his or her life, in review, as interesting and therefore worthwhile. This mutually beneficial process of transfer and affirmation between the oldest and youngest generations is a fundamental intergenerational concept, and as can be seen in the examples presented in this book, it is present in the design and implementation of every intergenerational program.

Because of the complexity of the interaction between these needs, desires, and social environments, Erikson's somewhat simplistic dualities have been challenged. The results of a study of older adults that was conducted in the late 1960s (Buhler, 1968) suggest that, although the notion of a life-stage struggle with paired opposite outcomes offers a useful conceptual framework, most older adults approach the end of their lives with mixed feelings that are never resolved with the kind of clarity Erikson postulated. People's lives are filled with both satisfactions and regrets, and Buhler's data suggests that the likeliest resolution of this conflict is best described as a state of resignation. The study also suggests that the outcomes of this life review process are not firmly tied to the realities of the past but can be influenced and shaped by current events in the life of an older adult.

Summary of older adult development theories. These theoretical constructs strongly suggest the importance of interaction between generations as a critical element in sustaining the physiological, emotional, and psychological functionality of the nation's aging population. They are directly applicable to human service practice because opportunities for meaningful intergenerational experiences powerfully affect the ability to have a productive and successful old age and to live out the final stages of life with peace and dignity.

IMPLICATIONS FOR INTERGENERATIONAL PRACTICE

A formal theory of organized intergenerational activity is not directly expressed in either child development or older adult theory alone. However, a strong rationale emerges when the two bodies of thought are considered together and the needs and characteristics of these generations are compared and matched.

Intergenerational Components of Growth Theories

Child development theorists agree that there is a need for an adult presence in the lives of children, to fulfill a variety of roles that change as the child grows into a youth. Examples of this include:

- the importance of children's interaction with a variety of adults, to acquire knowledge, skills, and cultural awareness (Vygotsky; see Wertsch, 1985, and Yaroshevsky, 1989);
- the need for society as a whole to provide an educational environment for children (Dewey, 1938); and
- the need for mature adult facilitators who know and understand children (Montessori; see Kramer, 1976, and Standing, 1959).

Adult development theorists enlarge the understanding of older adults in modern society and describe the ways in which intergenerational links enhance the quality of life for members of this generation. For example,

- the role of cross-generational social interaction in reducing or slowing the impact of aging (Rosenmayr, 1980);
- the importance of adaptation to the loss of roles and activities and the need for mechanisms to find new and meaningful roles (Atchley, 1988); and
- the function of younger generations in supporting the critical task of life review (Butler & Lewis, 1977).

The life-span approach of Erikson, whose work includes all generations, describes developmental tasks for the oldest and youngest age groups that parallel each other as life crises are reworked in succeeding stages. These parallel structures reflect Erikson's basic premise that the issues of each life stage are never fully resolved but reoccur throughout life in increasingly mature and complex forms. The repetitive and parallel structure of an individual's life stages reinforces the argument for intergenerational exchange. The side-by-side consideration of these life tasks shown in Table 1 strongly suggests that the members of each age group have much to offer each other across the span of generations.

Table 1 Parallel life stages

Children	Adults
Sense of basic trust	Capacity for intimacy
Sense of autonomy	Ego integrity
Sense of industry	Sense of generativity
Basic identity	Leaving a legacy

Note. A basic sense of trust develops in children in their first year of life, through the emerging bond between baby and parent. This fundamental relationship is recapitulated in later life, as seen in the bonds that characterize the shared lives of people—friends, family, and spouses—who have been together across the years. Children's sense of autonomy develops as they experience their ability to function independently of others, especially their parents. In older adults, ego integrity enables the continued sense of independence despite the life changes precipitated by advancing age. Children's sense of industry is constructed when they learn that they can learn: new facts, ideas, and skills. An older adult's sense of generativity is related to this achievement, modified by the additional need to review the accomplishments and completed tasks of a fulfilled lifetime. The adolescent's task of developing a sense of identity is begun through his or her ties to the family, community, and peers. The completion of this task, in late life, involves a purposeful effort to leave a legacy of ideas, skills, and values for one's family, community and society.

Reciprocal and Shared Needs

By extrapolating further, from Erikson and the other human growth theorists, and by factoring in observations of social structure and changes, intergenerational professionals can build a table of reciprocal and shared needs as a developmental framework for their efforts. The reciprocal needs described in Table 2 demonstrate the interdependence of these two unique yet linked populations. Accompanying these reciprocal needs is another set of needs that are shared by these generations. These needs are common to both the young and the old, are related to the placement and role of these generations within the life continuum, and reflect treatment of the young and the old by the larger society:

- to feel secure,
- to have a place or role in society,
- to be valued, and
- to be accepted.

Human growth theories also suggest that the fit between the youngest and oldest members of society is not constrained by age or physical abilities. A newborn infant, for example, can provide a satisfying role and a sense of purpose for the older adult who becomes its caregiver. Less clear cut, but no less powerful, is the example of an interaction between, say, a young teenage boy and a frail, physically limited older man. Older adults in this situation can, through an intergenerational experience, re-solve some issues of legacy and life review by communicating to a youth their values, culture, and life skills. The developmental characteristics of a young person (which may include curiosity, vitality, creativity, and interest in service) may make him or her well suited to meet the physiological and emotional needs of the older adult, and the interaction may improve the young person's self-image by enabling him or her to function as a provider of meaningful service. For a young person, becoming a caregiver for the elderly provides insights, understanding, compassion, and humanity, qualities essential for a productive life.

CONCLUSION

The intergenerational approach to addressing the needs of children, youth, and older adults is based on the developmental characteristics of these populations.

Table 2 Reciprocal needs directly linking the generations

Older adults' needs	Children's needs
To nurture	To be nurtured
To teach	To be taught
To have a successful life review	To learn from and about the past
To share cultural mores	To have a cultural identity
To communicate positive values	To have positive role models
To leave a legacy	To be connected to preceding generations

Through mutual interaction, people across the life span from one another can contribute to each other's growth and development while enhancing their own lives. These interactions reflect a unique synergy between the two age groups that enables growth and provides the kind of purposeful existence that is important to human development.

This synergy is reinforced further by the interdependence of these generations and the familial need for intergenerational caregiving. The strong bonds between the generations within an individual family, the genesis of the current intergenerational initiative in the United States, exemplify a caregiving exchange that was traditionally accepted and preferred throughout the family's life. In his examination of family structure, Kingson (1986, p. 51) stated that intergenerational caregiving within the family is so common and natural that it is hardly noticed—until it ceases. In today's society, people are increasingly aware of this absence and are feeling the need to recreate the unique bonds of mutual family caregiving.

The need to reenergize intergenerational caregiving is closely linked to the recognition of the developmental needs of the populations in question. Intergenerational programming has long-term implications not only for individuals but also for the collective values and behaviors of the younger and older populations. These factors together fuel the drive to meet the needs of both young and old in today's society and create a social imperative for intergenerational programming.

Caring, communication, collaboration, learning, positive role modeling, and positive relationship building—all of these benefits are inherent in the intergenerational exchange, and all extend to the community at large, affecting values and behaviors and helping to shape a society that is respectful of the developmental and social needs of all its generations.

2

The Context of Intergenerational Programs

Christopher R. Ward, PhD

Children are the living message we send to a time we will not see.
                                                            —Unknown

The intergenerational programs of the last several decades developed in the context of the changing social, cultural, and political forces that have prevailed in the United States since World War II. This chapter examines these changes as they relate to intergenerational programs and some of the social problems that these programs address.

The chapter begins with social, demographic, and cultural changes, including age characteristics, economic status, retirement, family ties, health, and the segregation of age groups. Broader political and ideological trends have also been an important part of the context for developing intergenerational programs. Among these trends are the increasing emphasis on group rights and the relations among groups, the increased scope of the federal government since World War II, the intergenerational conflict debate, and changes in generational images and attitudes.

The chapter concludes with a discussion of how intergenerational programs are being used to address social problems. The problems they address are many and diverse, including isolation of the elderly, grandparents serving as parents, ageism, increasing divorce and single-parenthood, the growing demand for quality child care, the abuse and neglect of children, and the increased need for academic and social support for school-age children.

This chapter covers the period from approximately 1950 to the 1990s for several reasons. First, the years immediately after World War II saw many changes in the United States that relate to the intergenerational movement. Among these changes were a rapid increase in the birth rate, increased mobility in American society, and new attention to the rights of all groups. Second, by including data from as early as 1950, the chapter shows how trends developed for several decades prior to the growth of the intergenerational movement.

SOCIAL, DEMOGRAPHIC, AND CULTURAL CHANGES

The Aging Population

The size and shape of the United States' population has changed dramatically since 1950. During these years, the nation grew by 100 million people, and the median age increased from just over 30 years to 34 years (Treas, 1995, p. 6). Although the baby boom—the dramatic rise in the birth rate from 1945 to 1960—temporarily slowed the increase in the 1960s, the aging trend reasserted itself by 1970. Moreover, the median age will continue to rise, reaching at least 43 years in the year 2050 (U.S. Bureau of the Census, 1992, sec. 2-1).

In considering the development of the intergenerational movement, the changes in the nation's age distribution are even more important than the increase in the average age. From World War II through the 1950s, the United States' population expanded at both ends, growing larger at the older end (due to a high birth rate earlier in the century) and also growing larger at the younger end (due to the baby boom).

The age distribution statistics for the 1950s show the growth of the older and younger populations very clearly. In 1950, 8.5% of the U.S. population was 65 years of age and older; in 1960 that figure had risen to 9.2%. The under 20 group grew in the same 10 years from 33% to 40% of the total population (Caplow, Bahr, Modell, & Chadwick, 1991, p. 6). These changes meant that by the 1970s there were many more potential participants, both young and old, for intergenerational programs.

In coming decades, the growth in the number of elderly (persons 65 years of age and older) will mean that the current gap between the percentage of children in the population and the percentage of elderly will narrow. In 1980, 28% of Americans were children and 11% were older adults; by 2030 the two groups will each constitute about 22% of the total population (U. S. Department of Health and Human Services, 1991, pp. 8–9). This trend will undoubtedly have implications for intergenerational programs.

Moreover, the country's age distribution is now changing in new ways. Even as changes in the age distribution provide growing pools of older and younger persons for intergenerational programs, an increase in people's longevity is also more evident. Between 1950 and 1992, the life expectancy for all persons in the United States at birth increased from 68.2 years to 75.8 years (U.S. Bureau of the Census, 1992, sec. 3-1; U.S. Bureau of the Census, 1995, p. 87). Longer life-span means more time for older adults to seek volunteer, employment, and educational opportunities. It also means increased demand for services to the elderly, including the kinds of services—friendly visiting, for example—that young people can provide through intergenerational programs.

Because a population's average life expectancy is heavily influenced by infant mortality, life expectancy from a later age is a better measure of increase in longevity than is expected life-span from birth. Using this measure, it can be seen that in the four decades from 1940 to 1981 the life expectancy of older adults in the United States increased considerably. Just before World War II, a 70-year-old man could expect to live 9.5 more years; in 1981—when the intergenerational movement was emerging—a man of the same age could expect to live 11.5 more years; and in 1992, he could expect to live 12.4 more years. For 70-year-old women, the increase was from 10.6 years to 15.1 years to 15.6 years, respectively (Caplow et al., 1991, p. 39; U.S. Bureau of the Census, 1995, p. 87).

In the last few decades, the most rapid growth in the older population has occurred among those 85 years and older. Between 1960 and 1987, the life expectancy at age 85 rose by 33% (U. S. Department of Health and Human Services, 1991, p. 11) and in 1992 stood at 6.2 years (U.S. Bureau of the Census, 1995, p. 87). The number of Americans age 100 or older tripled between 1980 and 1995 (Treas, 1995, p. 6). The growth in the very old population (85 years of age and older) has meant that it is ever more likely that persons in their 60s or 70s, once considered the oldest of the population, now have at least one surviving parent. These changes challenge intergenerational programs to reach new groups and to face new situations. For example, caregiving responsibilities for very old parents may be a barrier preventing some older adults from easily participating in intergenerational programs. Increased poverty and greater likelihood of living in a nursing home also increase with age.

Geographic Dispersion and Mobility

One important demographic issue is the absolute size of the elderly population in a given location. In 1994, over half (52%) the country's older adults lived in just nine states (California, New York, Florida, Pennsylvania, Texas, Illinois, Ohio, Michigan, and New Jersey). Each of these states had over 1 million residents 65 years of age or older (Treas, 1995, p. 10). Not coincidentally, some of these states were the location of many of the early intergenerational efforts and continue to be centers for intergenerational activities.

A second issue is the percentage of the population that is elderly, irrespective of its absolute size. The five states with the highest percentage of older adults are Florida, Pennsylvania, Rhode Island, West Virginia, and Iowa, each having 15% or more of their population over 65 years of age. The national average is 12.7% (Treas, 1995, pp. 12–13).

Concentrations of older adults have occurred primarily because of the emigration of younger persons from one region to another, as is the case in four of the five states cited above (Florida being the exception). Some areas of the country— especially rural areas of the Midwest and industrial cities like Pittsburgh and their environs—are becoming older because young people are leaving, primarily for economic reasons. By 1990, nine cities in the United States had 100,000 or more residents aged 65 or older (U.S. Bureau of the Census, 1992, p. 33).

A highly visible but less common reason for the increase in the concentration of elderly in a particular area is the migration of older adults to new retirement homes in other parts of the country. Older adults who move tend to be well educated and affluent and tend to move with their spouse. Many retire to Sunbelt states: southern California, Arizona, Texas, and Florida. Others retire to locations with particular cultural or physical attractions such as the Ozarks of Arkansas, the coast of New England, or the Puget Sound area of Washington (U.S. Bureau of the Census, 1992, sec. 5-1).

The migration of older adults has coincided with some intergenerational program development—Florida, for example, was an early leader in utilizing older adult volunteers in schools. At the same time, migration has also been the cause of separation of children from grandparents, who move away. To some degree, postretirement migration has spawned the growth of housing patterns that separate older adults and children. Older adults often move to retirement communities designed and marketed for people their age where there are few families with children.

Several other issues related to mobility and the concentration of young and old are linked to intergenerational programs. Over the last 4 decades, technological developments have increased the possibility of building and maintaining relationships in spite of geographical distance. Telephones and computers mean that people can communicate and visit regularly even if they live far from each other. As an example of the possibilities for this type of communication, intergenerational programs have used telephone reassurance programs, pen pal clubs, and electronic mail to bring young and old together. Specific initiatives such as those carried out by the computer organization SeniorNet support this kind of intergenerational activity.

At the same time, other societal developments have limited mobility and interaction among the generations. The growth of the suburbs in the 1950s and 1960s has recently meant that more older adults—having aged in place—find it difficult to get around in environments that assume car ownership and the ability to drive a car day and night. For example, in 1950 only 17.6% of the elderly in New York, Connecticut, and New Jersey lived in the suburbs. By 1990, 56.1% lived in the suburbs. For those persons who lack transportation or who are physically unable to participate fully in all the suburbs offer, the single-family dwellings and open spaces that attracted them to the suburbs now interfere with their day-to-day lives and make interaction with younger generations less likely (Fein, 1994).

Economic Status

The economic status of the elderly is more varied than that for any other group. Although the number of very poor older adults has decreased dramatically since 1950, many older Americans remain close to poverty. Between 1966 and 1974, the poverty rate for the elderly was cut in half from 28.5% to 14.6%. In contrast, the decline for the under-65 adult population for the same period was much more modest, from 10.5% to 8.3%. Increases in Social Security benefits between 1969 and 1972 accounted for much of the decrease in poverty for the elderly in this period (U.S. Department of Health and Human Services, 1991, p. 43). In 1993, 12% of the elderly population was considered poor. In comparison, 23% of children were poor in that year and 12% of working age (16 to 64 years of age) persons were poor (Treas, 1995, p. 26).

Elderly persons are more likely than other adults to be poor. However, because children are the most likely of any age group to be poor, when children are included in the calculations, the elderly are somewhat less likely to be poor than the population as a whole. At the same time, although the elderly are less likely to be below the poverty level, they are much more likely than other adults to be among the near poor (when near poor is defined as having an income of 100–150% of the poverty level). The elderly are also less likely to be economically mobile than are younger members of the population. For example, unlike other adults, most older persons do not have the option of increasing their income by getting a better job. Moreover, few older adults are likely to improve their economic status through marriage.

In 1993, the median income of families headed by a person 65 years of age or older was $17,751. For persons under 65, it was $35,956. For persons not living in families, elderly individuals had an income 46% that of nonelderly individuals (Treas, 1995, p. 27). These figures do not reveal, however, the problems faced by particular groups of elderly: those who are older, who are female, or who are racial or ethnic minorities. To cite several examples of such problems:

- Income declines with age. In 1993, for both families headed by elderly and for single elderly, those 85 years of age and older had incomes less than three quarters of those 65 to 74 (Treas, 1995, p. 27).
- Elderly women are poorer than elderly men. In 1993, the median income of women over 65 living alone was only $9,980, compared with $13,896 for men over 65 living alone (Treas, 1995, p. 27).
- Blacks and Hispanics have similarly lower incomes than Whites. In 1993, for example, the median income of elderly Black householders was $11,926, compared with $13,284 for elderly Hispanic householders and $18,471 for elderly White householders (Treas, 1995, p. 27).

Particularly in the last decade, the intergenerational field has recognized the importance of programs that bring the expertise and support of older adults to bear on the problems of poor children and that address the needs of specific groups of low-income older adults. For example, work in intergenerational child care and the Foster Grandparent Program both provide opportunities for the elderly—including those who are members of some of the groups most at risk for poverty—to supplement their incomes while serving children. Practitioners have also become more aware of the great variation in the economic status of older adults and its implications for intergenerational programs. For example, program components such as stipends, reimbursements for meals and incidental expenses, and assistance with transportation may vary widely depending on the economic status of the older adults involved in the program.

The question may not be whether elders or children are poorer, but the implications of contemporary changes for the future of today's young. For example, those who cannot buy a house will spend resources for rent that they will not have later in life in the form of home equity.

Retirement

Changes in retirement patterns since World War II—combined with increased longevity—have greatly increased the number of years when older adults seek new activities, including intergenerational involvements. These changes have added to the resources available to children and youth through intergenerational programs, such as those that bring retired professionals into high schools and colleges to assist students through specialized tutoring or curriculum enhancement.

In 1950, men in the United States spent, on average, 15% of their life in retirement. By 1980, men were spending 19% of their life in retirement (U.S. Department of Health and Human Services, 1991, p. 87). In somewhat different terms, a 20-year-old man in 1950 could anticipate spending 7.5 years in retirement. By 1980, a 20-year-old man could anticipate spending twice as much of his life—15 years—in retirement (Caplow et al., 1991, p. 37).

Although Congress abolished age-based mandatory retirement for most positions in 1986, voluntary retirement before age 65 is increasingly common. Most persons apparently retire when they feel they can afford to do so. The growing trend toward early retirement can be seen in the changing male labor force participation rates. In 1950, nearly 46% of men 65 years of age and older were still working; by

1994 this figure had dropped to 16.8%. In contrast, there was almost no change for women 65 and over during the same period. Their labor force participation rate dropped from 9.7% to 9.2% (U.S. Bureau of the Census, 1992, sec. 4-1; U.S. Bureau of the Census, 1995).

In addition to the change in the labor participation rate, the nature of work changed over the last four decades. Of those working at age 65, more men were working part-time in 1989 (48%) than were working part-time in 1960 (30%). For women at age 65, the increase in those working part-time was from 44% to 59% (U.S. Department of Health and Human Services, 1991, p. 102). Because women's work experience has been different than men's experience, it is harder to determine trends for women. However, it appears that over the decades after 1950, the participation of women between age 55 and 64 in the labor force increased, whereas participation after age 65 decreased (Caplow et al., 1991, p. 37).

For intergenerational programs, changes in retirement patterns have meant a greater number of active older adults available for program participation. In particular, the drop in the labor force participation rate for older men means that there is a pool of potential volunteers who can be recruited with properly designed programs and focused recruitment campaigns. The continued participation of older women in the labor force has translated into interest in intergenerational program efforts such as the training of older adults for child-care employment.

Family Ties

The trend over the past 4 decades has been for less extended family living and thus for the elderly and children to have less day-to-day contact. As one sign of these changes, the percentage of the population living in families dropped from 94% in 1950 to 86% in 1988 (Caplow et al., 1991, p. 55). Moreover, by the early 1980s, families without a child under 18—either because they were childless or because older children had moved elsewhere—had become the rule rather than the exception.

This increase in nonfamily living, combined with a decrease in the birth rate after the baby boom, has meant that in the last several decades adults have had less overall experience with children and child rearing. Equally important for the development of intergenerational programs, children are also less likely to grow up with a variety of related persons in the same household, including older adults. This trend has been one of the most frequently cited rationales for intergenerational programs.

On a more positive note, although grown children apparently live farther from elderly parents than they have lived in the past, they still maintain close contact with them. Most families in the United States have patterns of mutual aid between generations, and there is little evidence to support the existence of widespread isolation of the nuclear family or widespread ignoring of elderly parents by their families, despite the tragic and well-publicized cases of elder abuse (Caplow et al., 1991, p. 49).

Research on the geographical distance of adult children and older parents has produced mixed findings. Studies of parents in 1957 and 1975 suggested a growing spatial separation of adult children and their parents. In 1957, the nearest child of

15% of elderly parents lived more than 30 min away; in 1975 that percentage had increased to 25%. However, in contrast to these findings, the results of studies of grown children done from the 1960s to the 1980s showed little change in the distance they lived from their parents (Caplow et al., 1991, pp. 48–49, 56).

Research carried out for the National Institute on Aging and the American Association of Retired Persons in the early 1990s also confirmed a generally positive assessment of family relations in the United States. These studies showed that Americans take care of their elderly parents, help their grown children, and help their grandchildren. For persons 80 and over, up to 85% see or speak to their children two to seven times a week (Kolata, 1993).

At issue for the future, however, and clearly related to intergenerational programs, is the question of who will provide support for the growing number of people who do not have children as they age. Preparing children for an adulthood in which they may have to care for or provide other support for their parents, and also care for their parents' childless peers, is a challenge for intergenerational programmers. Moreover, despite overall positive relations and generally strong family ties, there remain substantial numbers of older adults and children who lack regular, positive contact with other generations.

Health

The majority of the growing numbers of elderly Americans are vigorous and healthy, comprising a pool of persons who can be called on to serve, or to serve with, the young in intergenerational programs. Although they are at risk for more diseases than younger persons, they rate their health as satisfactory (Hooyman & Kiyak, 1991). The activities of daily living (ADLs) measure a person's ability to function independently. Only 5% to 8% of the noninstitutionalized elderly population receive help with one of the following ADLs: bathing, dressing, moving out of beds and chairs, toileting, and eating (U.S. Bureau of the Census, 1992).

Some elderly persons do require long-term care. To provide this care, nursing homes developed after World War II in the United States. The enactment of Medicaid in 1965 provided the greatest boost to the growth of long-term care. Also important were the general growth in the older population (especially the female population) and the movement of traditional caregivers into the workforce (Hooyman & Kiyak, 1991). The growing number of older adults living in nursing homes has become a focus of intergenerational programs.

However, less than 5% of all older adults live in institutions. Of persons 65 to 74 years of age, 1.2% live in nursing homes; for persons over 85 the percentage is 23.7 (Hooyman & Kiyak, 1991). For many older adults, programs built on the notion of aging in place supply important support. These programs, in which older adults continue to live in the community with services provided to keep them in their own homes, have been a natural focus for intergenerational efforts, with friendly visiting and chore services among the benefits provided by younger persons. In other cases, families need respite from caregiving for older adults who continue to live at home. Adult day services have been established to meet this need, sometimes in conjunction with child care, creating an intergenerational center in which both age groups benefit.

Segregation of Age Groups

The media and the related advertising and marketing industries play important roles in shaping public perceptions and opinion in the United States. In the last 4 decades, as television has become commonplace across America, increased age segregation has contributed to the isolation of generations and the need for inter-generational programs.

The baby boom bulge in the population helped to create not only a distinct youth culture in the 1960s but also an emphasis on marketing goods and services to particular age segments, whether it be toys to children on Saturday morning television, clothing to teens on MTV, or vitamins to adults over the age of 50. The growing affluence of the elderly drew media and marketing interest in the 1980s. By 1990, advertising geared to older adults, including ads that featured persons who were clearly aging, was becoming more common.

Today it is possible for the young and the old living close together to be served almost exclusively in worlds of their own with magazines, consumer products, and other items targeted at their age group. Moreover, much of American public recreation and social life is now marketed to specific age groups, resulting in age-segregated films, concerts, restaurants, and other public events. For example, in recent years both the experience of arts organizations and surveys of arts audiences have found significant generational differences in the types of arts events that each generation is interested in and will attend and support (Rothstein, 1996).

For intergenerational programs, these changes present challenges as well as opportunities. The need to bring young and old together is more important than ever. At the same time, the effects of age segregation can mediate against cooperation and collaboration. Youth accustomed to MTV may have little experience in more interactive activities with older persons; older adults living in housing areas geared toward persons of their own age group may be hesitant at first to come into schools or into other youth-oriented community settings.

POLITICAL AND IDEOLOGICAL TRENDS

Group Rights

Intergenerational programs emerged in an era of social change that emphasized both increased group rights and increased interaction between groups. From the 1960s through the 1990s, ethnic and racial minorities, women, the disabled, and gay and lesbian groups fought for greater recognition for their rights. Out of the Civil Rights movement and related struggles grew a new emphasis on group rights and an interest in how groups relate to one another in politics, education, and human services (La Belle & Ward, 1994).

By the 1960s and into the 1970s and 1980s, Americans began to consider it entirely reasonable that older persons, as a group, and young persons and children, as a group, should be accorded the resources and respect that other age groups receive. Likewise, the emphasis on positive intergroup relations and improving communications between groups encouraged the development and growth of the intergenerational movement. An important aspect of a national intergenerational movement was convincing aging and youth advocacy organizations to collaborate to promote the mutual interests of their constituencies. The collaboration took the form of Generations United, a policy and networking group based in Washington, D.C.

Increased Government Role

A second major political impetus to the intergenerational movement—and an important source of funding throughout the development of the field—was the growing federal government support for social welfare programs of all sorts and for programs to aid children and older adults in particular. The federal government first began large-scale assumption of welfare responsibilities in the 1930s as part of the New Deal. Between 1964 and 1966, the administration of Lyndon Johnson brought another round of increased federal interventions and the creation of many new federal agencies in health, education, the arts, and other fields. Overall, in the 40 years after World War II, expenditures for social welfare grew under both Democratic and Republican administrations. For example, total Social Security benefits paid increased from $22 billion in 1970 to $204 billion in 1987 (Caplow et al., 1991, pp. 266–268).

The establishment of Medicare and the passage of the Older Americans Act marked the beginning of a federal role in aging. For children, Head Start symbolized the new federal activism, as did various federal programs that provided aid to education and support for child care. A few programs were directly intergenerational (e.g., the Foster Grandparent Program), and various federal agencies such as the Administration on Aging and the Department of Education periodically supported intergenerational programs. Federal job training program monies designated for older adults became a source of funding to train older persons for intergenerational work in child care. Support for this activist federal role continued into the 1990s but began to slow after the 1994 Congressional elections.

Generational Conflict

Throughout the growth of intergenerational programs, fringe political movements have emphasized conflict between generations rather than mutual benefit and cooperation. Some of the "generation gap" tension in the 1960s appears to be of this sort, although the term is used primarily to refer to the relationships between individual parents and college-age children. A more substantial debate, and one which involved some of the institutions and individuals that were related to the intergenerational movement, were the intergenerational equity conflicts of the 1980s and 1990s. The issues in these debates often centered around who would benefit—or not benefit—from government entitlement programs. Unfortunately, too little attention was paid to truly understanding the wide range of giving across the age span, from monies passed down within families to the informal service rendered by neighborhood and church youth to older persons in their communities.

Throughout this period, in contrast to the rhetoric, studies tended to show little real conflict among citizens of various ages. At the same time, with both sides marked by defensiveness and exaggeration, the debate sometimes seemed to get in the way of needed discussion about intergenerational issues.

Perhaps a more important issue from an intergenerational perspective has been the relative strength of the political power and involvement of youth and the elderly. Although the voting participation by the elderly in national elections has remained relatively consistent, voting by those who are younger has declined. For example in 1964, 64% of those 65 and over voted, as did 54% of those 22 to 24. In 1992, 70.1% of the older group voted, but only 45.7% of the younger group did (Caplow et al., 1991, p. 237; U.S. Bureau of the Census, 1995, p. 289).

Cultural Changes

The context for the rise and growth of intergenerational programs has included a number of broad changes in the way that most Americans view the world. Though more difficult to specify than the demographic, economic, or political changes discussed above, cultural changes have certainly contributed to the growth of the intergenerational movement. A few of the important changes are discussed in the following paragraphs.

Search for meaning. Americans are putting an increased emphasis on searching for meaning over a longer life span. For many older persons freed from absolute poverty and major health restraints, living a fulfilling, meaningful life has become more important. Intergenerational programs seem to have arisen, in part, because they provide a sense of meaning to people through service, through contact with the young, and through passing on a piece of oneself to the next generation. The widespread use of intergenerational programs and activities in religious organizations and congregations may be related to the importance of personal meaning and the possibilities that intergenerational programs offer for finding this meaning.

Privatized experience. Since World War II, Americans have increasingly privatized experience. There is at least a perception that the public and communal sharing of ideas and experiences has lost ground to much more personal approaches— a Saturday evening may now focus on take-out food and a video instead of a church supper and related social activities. Many view the support for intergenerational programs, with their emphasis on person-to-person contact by people who would not otherwise interact, as a healthy and needed reaction to the privatization of experience. Intergenerational programs, with their emphasis on mutual benefit, the breaking down of group barriers, and service to others present a positive alternative for those concerned about a growing societal self-centeredness.

Lifelong growth. Beginning in the 1950s and accelerating in the 1960s, the human potential movement emphasized the importance of continued growth throughout a person's life. Intergenerational programs arose in the context of more and more Americans, of all ages, adopting some values of the human potential movement. Particularly in the early years, and to a large extent through the 1990s, intergenerational programs have drawn on the human potential movement for ideas such as the need to develop self-esteem and the value of lifelong education.

Decline in confidence. Even as many persons came to value personal change and growth, the national mood in the United States began to grow less optimistic after the 1960s. The confidence and sense of growth of the postwar era gave way to a sense of defeat and decline after Vietnam and Watergate. By the 1980s, many Americans were no longer sure that life would be better for their children than it was for them. The decline of many cities only served to confirm this view. Thus, for some persons, the intergenerational movement may very well offer a means to counter pessimism and to help the next generation cope with coming changes. Through intergenerational programs, older adults can pass on to the young a positive, powerful vision of the potential for life, in which national crises are bumps along the road, not detours to despair.

Dissatisfaction with modern society. Finally, throughout the era under consideration, a major cultural theme (widely seen in literature and the arts) has been the growing dissatisfaction with the alienation, complexity, and discontinuities of modern, industrial societies. In an age when there is no society-wide consensus about religious faith, the notion that life derives meaning from the connections between the generations has offered an attractive alternative for many Americans. Intergenerational programs have come to offer personal, nonbureaucratic venues for both young and old to move beyond themselves and any one set of problems to serve others for a widely recognized and valued good.

SOCIAL PROBLEMS

In the last decade, advocates of intergenerational programs have increasingly offered them as a means to address a wide variety of social problems related to a correspondingly broad context of social, cultural, economic, and political forces. A few examples of the many problems that intergenerational programs may be called on to address follow.

Elderly

Isolation. By the late 1980s, about 30% of all Americans over 65 lived alone; more than 80% of these older adults were women. Although living alone is satisfying to many people, for others it is neither satisfying nor voluntary (widowhood, for example). Living alone is often associated with difficulties and lower life satisfaction. Intergenerational programs have addressed the isolation of older persons in several ways. Friendly visiting programs are common, as are programs that provide help with household tasks, where social interaction is an important adjunct to carrying out the chores. The involvement of older adults who live alone as volunteers in intergenerational programs also has the potential for benefits. One survey, for example, found that older adults who live alone and who do volunteer find it very satisfying (Kasper, 1988).

Grandparents as parents. Since 1981, the number of children living with relatives other than parents has increased 16% (U.S. Bureau of the Census, 1993). In the 1990s, the intergenerational movement focused heavily on the issues grandparents faced as the widespread use of crack cocaine increased both the number of small children who needed homes and the number of grandparents suddenly thrust again into parenthood. This issue is one for which some have suggested the intergenerational movement has both a program role and a policy role. Among the efforts in the program role are intergenerational programs in which older adults provide respite care for grandchildren, aiding both the grandchildren and their grandparents, who are in need of a well-deserved break. In the policy role, intergenerational advocates can help to ensure that grandparents not only get interpersonal support but also are the beneficiaries of fair treatment by legislators and bureaucrats.

Ageism. Since the 1950s, there has been concern about the attitudes and knowledge of younger persons toward and about the elderly. In part, the concern has to do with personal relationships. However, it also has to do with concern that young people will devalue older adults, implementing unwanted cutbacks in services and using the political power of youth for their own generation's interests. For some, a related issue has been a concern that minority youth will assimilate the majority culture's attitudes toward older adults at the expense of their own groups' traditional values. Attitudes and knowledge about older adults, including the attitudes and knowledge of minority youth about their elders, have been addressed through many intergenerational programs of varying degrees of size and complexity.

Children and Families

Marriage and divorce. The propensity to marry at some point in life has actually increased over the last 4 decades. In 1950, among men age 55 to 64, 8.4% had never married. That figure decreased to only 4.2% by 1983. For women of the same age, the drop was from 7.9% to 4.4%. However, since 1970, there also seems to be a trend among the young not to marry (Caplow et al., 1991, p. 112).

Divorce has increased over the past 4 decades but with some particular ups and downs. The number of marriages with children that end in divorce has increased. The divorce rate for married women immediately after World War II was 1.4%. It declined through the 1950s to under 1% in 1960 and reached a high in the late 1970s (2.3% in 1979) before dropping slightly and leveling off (Caplow et al., 1991, p. 120). Intergenerational programs have addressed the problems raised by increasing divorce by providing positive, nurturing relationships with older adults for children who are emotionally affected or who may have reduced contact with grandparents.

Decline in two-parent families. The proportion of their first 18 years that children spend with two parents in the household has decreased since World War II. The cohort of White children who were born between 1950 and 1954 spent 92% of their time with two parents in the household. This percentage declined to 81% for those born from 1965 to 1969. For African Americans, the decline between the two cohorts was from 78% to 56% (Caplow et al., 1991, p. 122).

Census figures show that the percentage of children living with both parents has declined over the last 2 decades. In 1970, 85% of children lived with both parents. By 1994 this figure had declined to 69%, including 76% for White families and 33% for African American families (U.S. Bureau of the Census, 1995, p. 66).

Out-of-wedlock births. The rate for births outside of marriage increased quite dramatically from 1950 to 1986. In 1950 just under 4% of all births were outside of marriage; in 1992 that figure had risen to more than 30%. There has been a large difference by race, with the rates in 1992 being 22.6% for Whites and 68.1% for African Americans (Caplow et al., 1991, p. 111; U.S. Bureau of the Census, 1995).

Since 1975, households headed by women have been more likely than other households to have children. From the 1950s to the 1980s, the portion of female-headed households rose from 1 in 10 to 1 in 6 (Caplow et al., 1991, p. 83).

Overall, the changes in marriage, divorce, two-parent families, and out-of-wedlock births have presented a number of problems amenable to intergenerational solutions, from mentoring of mothers-to-be on how to take care of children to programs in which older men fill the need for young boys to have responsible male role models.

Working women and the need for child care. Among the most dramatic societal changes during the post-World War II era has been the rapid increase in labor force participation by married women with young children. In 1950, only 12% of women with children under age 6 were in the labor force. By 1994, that rate had jumped to 57% (Children's Defense Fund, 1995, p. 104). This change has had a huge effect on the need for child care, particularly for center-based child care and the related demand for trained caregivers to staff these centers.

In 1958, for children under 5 with employed mothers, only 5% were in group care in centers. In 1985, that figure had risen to 28% (Caplow et al., 1991, p. 84). This rapid growth in center-based care has expanded the need for well-trained, responsible workers. Intergenerational child care has been a major response as older persons are being trained for a variety of paid positions and as volunteers in child-care centers.

Education. Since World War II, schooling has become far more universal and extended. For example, by the early 1960s, entry into high school and passage on to its second year was almost universal. Likewise, part-time employment has become increasingly part of the experience of adolescents in the last 40 years, especially for girls (Caplow et al., 1991, pp. 32–33).

Society became better educated during the period following World War II. In 1950, only 6% of Americans over the age of 25 had four or more years of college (Caplow et al., 1991, p. 243). By 1986, that figure had reached 22.2%. Figures for high school graduates over the same years rose from 34% to 75% (U.S. Bureau of the Census, 1995, p. 158).

The baby boom and the push for universal education contributed to large increases in the number of elementary students in the 1950s and into the 1960s; the growth continued with the bulge of baby boomers moving on to expanding high schools in the 1960s. In the 1970s and 1980s, declining enrollments were offset by improvement in the dropout picture. The percentage of 16- to 24-year-olds who are high school dropouts declined somewhat between 1970 and 1993 from 12.2% to 9.2% (U.S. Bureau of the Census, 1995, p. 174).

The opportunities for future generations are closely linked to the level of education of their parents. There is a clear relationship between parents' education level and children's poverty. In 1989, the poverty rate for children under 6 whose parents had less than a high school education was 62%. For those whose parents had more than a high school education, the rate was 7% (National Center for Children in Poverty, 1991).

The growth in schooling and the clear link between the outcomes of schooling and a person's chances in life mean that it is imperative that all children succeed. However, limited resources mean that school districts have had to look to volunteer sources for much of this help. In response, schools have been a major location of intergenerational programs over the last three decades, offering assistance to all levels of students and to special populations. The wide range of activities, including activities like art and science, mean that older adults from a wide range of backgrounds can participate as intergenerational volunteers.

During the 1980s and into the 1990s concern grew about the school-to-work transition for non-college-bound youth. With youth poorly prepared for work, companies shy away from hiring them. This leads to high unemployment figures for teenagers, especially minority teenagers. Among the recommendations to improve the transition that could be addressed by intergenerational programs is providing more applied learning experiences for students, with the help of older adults.

Community

An important issue that intergenerational programs have targeted is a general decline in the quality of life in communities of all sizes and locations. For example, the past several decades have seen a rise in violent crime. In 1983, the reported murder rate in the United States was 19.3 per 100,000; by 1993, it had risen to 24.5 per 100,000 (U.S. Bureau of the Census, 1995, p. 199).

Accompanying the decline in the quality of life is a trend for many persons to withdraw support for social and educational services for their poorer neighbors. The manifestation of this trend can be seen since the 1970s in California, where a tax revolt began the process of that state's education system from the envy of the nation to mediocrity. In the mid-1960s, California was fifth in the nation in spending per pupil; in 1995, it was 42nd, with the third worst dropout rate in the country and among the lowest standardized test scores for fourth graders in the United States (Sterngold, 1995). A benefit of many intergenerational programs is the involvement of the community's older adults in projects that bring them into the schools and other institutions that serve all residents, including the poor. Such involvement has the potential to counteract the decline in support for public institutions.

For some, the decline in community has come from a decline in social capital—the efforts by unrelated individuals to intervene in positive ways in the lives of the community's young. Persons who volunteer to lead Boy Scout troops or who serve as role models for neighborhood girls contribute social capital, an element necessary to the development of a community. The growth in intergenerational programs may reflect a wide recognition of this shortage of social capital and the need for organized ways to bring non-kin older adults into the lives of children and youth.

Other Concerns

The aforementioned problems are only a few of the many that have been suggested as amenable to intergenerational solutions. Additional problems include those that are primarily cultural, such as the growing loss of tradition and culture by both majority and minority communities as first-generation immigrants age and die. Intergenerational art and oral history projects have been addressing these problems for several decades.

Also, children and youth have many unmet needs ranging from abuse and neglect to the potential for later alcohol, tobacco, and drug abuse. Older adults have been and will continue to address these needs through intergenerational programs.

Finally, special needs populations and children with chronic illness are other youth who can benefit from older adults in special intergenerational programs.

CONCLUSION

Intergenerational programs and the growing field that supports them did not arise spontaneously. At the same time, no single trend paralleled their growth and development, nor did they spring from one event. Rather, in combination with the ideas found in chapter 1, the field emerged from a dynamic, changing society in the years that followed the end of World War II. This chapter has reviewed some of these economic, cultural, social, and political forces and linked them to intergenerational programs. The next chapter focuses in detail on specific issues within these broad trends and problems.

3

Social Issues Addressed by Intergenerational Programs

James M. McCrea, MPW, and Thomas B. Smith, MLS

The way we treat our children in the dawn of their lives and the way we treat our elderly in the twilight of their lives is a measure of the quality of a nation.
—Hubert Humphrey

The social trends that were described in chapter 2 have reshaped the structure of the American community and given a new profile to the families within it. In the contemporary world, the lives of individuals are influenced by a rapidly shifting context that requires almost constant adaptation to new concepts, attitudes, and social structures.

The quality of an individual's life depends on interactions between three levels of social structures—community, family, and individuals—connected in a complex give and take of contribution and support. Communities provide shelter and support for families, which connect and nurture the individuals within them. To provide shelter and support, a healthy community in turn requires active participation from its component families and individuals.

There are some critical dynamics associated with this delicate interdependence. When the shape of a community begins to change, the shape of the families within it changes as well. When basic family structures are altered, there is all too often a failure of that family's ability to meet the basic needs of its individual members.

Because of its roots in family interactions, intergenerational programming has a positive impact on all three of these levels. By supplementing, recreating, or replacing the basic familial connections that now seem to be crumbling in many American communities, such programs can have a direct impact on the quality of an individual's life. They also help to rebuild the community itself by establishing vital links between its older and younger members. In addition, by helping to meet an individual's basic needs, intergenerational programs can free his or her time and energy, encouraging and enabling additional efforts to rebuild and maintain community functioning.

This chapter examines the impact of social, political, and economic trends on the quality of individual lives and on the ability of communities and families to meet basic individual needs. The specific needs that will be discussed are

- the need for safety and security,
- the need for care,

- the need for stability,
- the need for quality education,
- the need to be productive, and
- the need for contact between the generations.

These fundamental human needs share three important characteristics:

- They cut across social, economic, and age distinctions.
- They have been magnified by modern social trends.
- They are amenable to intergenerational solutions.

Each of these needs is discussed in its own section, and each section concludes with a review of some ways in which intergenerational programming can meet these needs at a personal level and thereby strengthen the families and communities in which individuals live and work.

THE NEED FOR SAFETY AND SECURITY

Several trends occurring in the past 40 years have had a significant impact on the ability of children, youth, and older adults to be safe and secure. The need to be safe refers to both real safety, such as being physically safe in one's community, school, or workplace, and to the perception of safety, such as the fear that an older adult may feel about neighborhood youth. This fear may be grounded in stereotypes about youth, but the feeling of being unsafe is real nonetheless. Feelings of insecurity, though somewhat more subtle than feelings of being unsafe, can also be real or based on misperceptions. For example, the need to be secure may refer to economic security, that is, having a job or other income to provide food and shelter, or it may refer to feelings of insecurity such as those a young child may feel when his or her family moves to a new community as the result of a job transfer.

The reasons people feel unsafe or insecure, whether the insecurity is real or not, are complex and may include inadequate support systems for children, youth, and older adults and families in schools, neighborhoods, and institutions; a lack of knowledge of self-protection skills or of how to be safe; a loss of cultural and family links; or economic shifts. Some of these reasons are a direct result of trends occurring over the last 40 years, and others have been exacerbated by these trends.

Two of the trends affecting the need for safety and security are detailed in chapter 2. They are the change in the age structure of the population, resulting in an increase in the number of older adults, especially the oldest of the old (those over 85), and the increase in mobility and dispersion of the population, resulting in large concentrations of older adults in certain areas and the segregation of poor families, especially in urban areas.

The most rapid growth in the population has occurred among those 85 years old and older, largely as a result of increases in life expectancy. For the oldest of the old, these changes have had serious economic and health implications affecting their safety and security. For example, poverty is higher among older people than among other adults, affecting their ability to maintain a comfortable house and home. In

1994, the median income for elderly nonfamily households (persons living alone or with nonrelatives) of all races was only $11,504 (American Association of Retired Persons [AARP], 1995). It was even less for Blacks and Hispanics. Over one fourth of older renters are dependent on publicly owned or subsidized housing, negatively affecting their ability to be secure in providing for their own basic need for shelter. In total, 19% of the older population were poor or near poor in 1994 (AARP, 1995).

The oldest of the old also face the most health challenges. As age increases, so does the likelihood of living in a nursing home. Besides affecting an individual's economic security (most of the elderly in nursing homes are forced to go on Medicaid), life in a nursing facility requires that one give up much of the independence enjoyed throughout life, not to mention changing one's personal residence. When older adults relinquish all that is familiar and safe, their feelings of insecurity increase. Lack of contact with the outside, reliance on staff for meals, bathing, and recreational activities, lack of privacy, and increased dependence on wheelchairs, walkers, and canes all contribute to feelings of insecurity.

Adults over 85 are not the only ones affected by the changes in the age structure. In chapter 2 it was reported that the growth in the older population has increased the likelihood that persons in their 60s and 70s, once considered old, now have at least one surviving parent. This may adversely affect the economic security of these adults, who are often still involved in the lives of their children and grandchildren. In addition, changes in the family structure, such as the growing number of older adults who have never had children, have the potential for serious social and economic implications for the rest of the population, who may need to assume some responsibility for nonkin elders.

Finally, children and youth may experience feelings of insecurity, caused by the changes in the age structure, when parents and grandparents spend an increasing amount of time and money caring for their elderly mothers and fathers. The time and money pressures may cause stress for all family members, especially young people who receive less attention from their parents.

Another trend that has resulted in important social issues, and which affects people's need for safety and security, involves the mobility and dispersion of the population, fueled in part by the mass closing of industries in the 1980s. Certain areas of the country, especially the northeastern Rust Belt states, have experienced an increase in the percentage of older persons because of the outmigration of young people seeking employment in other states and moving away from older family members. This may also cause feelings of insecurity among young people thrust into new schools and communities.

In addition, as a result of increased longevity, early retirement, and technological advances in travel and communication, many older adults have migrated to the warmer climates of the Sun Belt states. These two trends (the outmigration of young people seeking jobs and of older people seeking warmer climates) have affected the safety of older persons left behind and isolated in areas where crime may be on the rise and the tax base is eroding and have also affected the security of children who have been separated from their grandparents because of migration of the nuclear family. Accompanying the migration of young people away from urban areas has been an influx of less affluent and more transient people to many inner cities, causing overcrowding and increased competition for scarce job opportunities, fostering a lack of trust between young and old, and increasing racial tensions.

Poor living conditions and poverty resulting from the lack of employment opportunities have contributed to rising crime rates, the emergence of youth gangs, and an increase in drug use and trafficking—clearly affecting the safety and security of many older Americans living in urban areas. The same is true for many children and youth, who do not feel safe in their own neighborhoods and schools. Their search for security fosters some destructive trends, as more and more young people seek the security offered by gang membership. Other effects of poverty on children, youth, older adults, and their families include the fear of crime and violence (even for those who have not experienced it directly), hunger, substandard housing and homelessness, poor performance in school, and the depletion of savings to pay for long-term health care.

Intergenerational Programs That Address the Need for Safety and Security

Intergenerational programs can begin to address some of the issues affecting the ability of children, youth, and older adults to be safe and secure. Economic security can be addressed through several types of intergenerational programs. For older adults, there is a growing need for trained people to work in child-care centers. Older retired adults are a natural choice for these jobs because they are often part-time, meeting the desire of many older workers for income to supplement Social Security and pensions and because they meet the needs of older adults to nurture and care for the younger generation. Children also benefit from contact with an older adult who may be seen as a surrogate grandparent. Other part-time work options for older adults include mentoring and tutoring programs in which school-age children and youth receive one-on-one or group social and academic reinforcement. Older adults can often earn a minimum wage stipend and travel expenses by participating in these programs. Although part-time minimum wage positions cannot, by themselves, solve economic security issues, they can contribute to the quality of life of a low-income older adult by supplementing his or her pension or Social Security benefits.

For the middle generation charged with the responsibility of caring for elderly parents, intergenerational respite and friendly visiting programs provide needed free time to pursue part-time employment or to have some relief from the pressures of working full-time and caring for a parent after work. These programs also provide health benefits to the elderly by providing stimulation, interaction with a young person, and an increase in feelings of self-worth brought on by a caring child or teen.

For teenagers, intergenerational work-study programs in which students study about aging and caregiving for the frail elderly and then work part-time in a nursing facility give these young adults practical work experience in a growing field, thereby increasing their chances for meaningful future employment.

For at-risk children, youth, and older adults, intergenerational programs can affect real and perceived issues of physical safety. Friendly visiting programs, escort services, and light chore services can reduce the fears of older adults brought on by isolation and can encourage trust and improve relationships between a neighborhood's young and old. Telephone reassurance programs in which young people call isolated senior citizens to check on how they are doing, or in which older adults phone latchkey kids, help to make both generations feel safe while they are home alone.

Community and school-based mentoring programs foster understanding between the generations and provide older adult role models for at-risk children and youth. Focusing on building relationships between mentor and mentee, these programs can have a significant impact on a young person's development, security, and self-esteem, helping to prevent his or her entrance into the world of crime, drugs, and gangs, breaking the cycle of poverty, and creating a safer community.

THE NEED FOR CARE

In the second half of the 20th century, demographic shifts and changes in social attitudes and expectations have created new care requirements for dependent individuals. Children—infants, toddlers, preschoolers, and those of school age—need care during the workday. On the other end of the age spectrum, the increase in the number of older adults who require some level of special attention has reshaped the field of geriatric care. Despite a variety of public and private responses, however, the need for care remains a critical concern for many individuals.

Care for Children

In the post-World War II era in the United States, the most striking change in the life of a child is probably the amount of time he or she spends away from home and family. Almost from birth, young children in ever-increasing numbers spend much of their day away from their parents, in the care of other relatives or with professional child caregivers. The need for care has also lengthened the school day with before- and after-school child care for children between the ages of 5 and 12.

This steadily increasing use of child care is directly related to three of the social and economic trends described in chapter 2:

- the reorganizing economy—a modern family needs two incomes to survive or at least to maintain the standard of living enjoyed by the parents when they were children;
- the changing nature of family—the percentage of children living with both parents has steadily declined because of the increase in divorce and the increase in the number of children born to women who were never married; and
- new perceptions of gender roles—even when income is not an issue, women in the 1990s are much more likely to be trained and oriented toward a profession or career than were women in the 1950s and no longer see homemaking as a completely satisfying life role.

Types of Child Care

In response to the demand created by these trends, a complex network of child-care options has evolved. In many communities, families rely on an informal caregiving system involving relatives, friends, and neighbors. This is probably the oldest type of child care, and it is still the method of choice for one third of American child-care consumers (Children's Defense Fund, 1996). However, some of the social trends under discussion are eroding the availability of this type of community support. The same economic factors that send one mother into the workplace, for example, are likely to affect her neighbors as well. Also, the mobile lifestyle of many young parents, driven by modern economic realities, precludes the formation of strong bonds within neighborhoods. This same mobile lifestyle has also separated many young families from the relatives who might in the past have been available to care for their children.

As a replacement for these vanishing informal possibilities, a professional child-care industry has evolved to accommodate the needs of families with growing children. This new system includes unrelated caregivers, or nannies, who care for a family's children in that family's home. About 7% of American child-care consumers prefer this type of arrangement, which represents a more professional approach to child care than is usually associated with friends and neighbors. Family child-care providers, who watch small numbers of children in their own homes, meet about 25% of the country's child-care needs (Children's Defense Fund, 1996). Center-based care, probably the most visible of the formal child-care possibilities, serves the remaining 32% of working families (Children's Defense Fund, 1996). In this type of care, larger numbers of children are gathered into a school-like center, where they are divided into groups and tended by trained caregiving staff.

Children of all ages can be found in each of these child-care settings, and many families will use all of them during the years when their children require it. Often a particular family manages its child-care needs with a complex arrangement involving several types of care simultaneously. These arrangements require almost constant attention, a fact that creates high levels of stress for parents whose lives are already filled with the demands of parenting and the workplace. Children, too, experience high levels of stress as they are forced to adapt to schedule changes and adjust to new caregivers. Although long-term research has yet to be done, most experts think it likely that the quality of a child-care agency is critical in determining whether child-care attendence supports or impedes the development of children and their families (Carpenter, 1996).

Care for Older Adults

The social and economic factors that were described in chapter 2 are forcing a shift in the type and quantity of care that a community must provide for its older members. The number of older adults living in some type of long-term care facility will continue to increase as the average life span increases. Families are less able to provide this type of care as the traditional caregivers are forced by economic pressure into the workplace. There is also an increase in the number of older adults who have no children to serve in the traditional caregiving role.

Other types of short-term or respite care are becoming more necessary as a segment of the older adult population finds itself geographically or socially isolated from the younger world. Finally, the increased emphasis on providing meaningful social roles for all members of society adds a new dimension to the need for care.

Types of Care for Older Adults

The kinds of care needed by older adults in contemporary society can be loosely organized into four categories:

Emotional care—for healthy older adults. This type of care addresses the emotional needs of older adults by providing opportunities for them to function in a preferred role, for example, nurturing, communicating with, and transferring knowledge and values to the youngest generation.

Light care—for those older adults who are able to live in their own homes and function independently for the most part. These individuals, however, can still experience isolation caused by a number of factors: lack of contact with their families, the loss of their friends, changes in their neighborhoods, or their inability to replace meaningful social roles. In addition, many of these otherwise capable older adults have trouble with the larger tasks demanded by their independent lifestyle. Limited assistance with chores such as yard work, home maintenance, shopping, or housecleaning can enable such individuals to maintain their independence.

Respite care—for older adults whose families are bearing major responsibility for a high level of care and attention. Many children are understandably reluctant to take the final step of admitting an elderly parent to a long-term care institution but are unable to provide the kind of constant care such an individual might require. The adult children may need to work themselves or may have difficulty juggling the needs of an elderly parent and growing children. In many cases, the aging family member requires specialized medical attention as well as routine caregiving. Adult day-care services designed to provide respite from these demands take many forms. In-home services such as visiting nurses and caregivers can meet the need, and many communities offer adult day care at centers that provide close attention and medical support. All of these services provide an attractive alternative to early institutionalization.

Long-term care—round-the-clock care for ill or frail older adults, usually in a residential setting. As reported in chapter 2, increased life span also increases the likelihood that an individual will spend at least some of his or her life in a setting that provides life-support functions. These range from simple self-help assistance, such as feeding and dressing, to critical medical care. Within such settings, efforts are made to maintain the quality of the residents' lives by providing special programming and activities that satisfy the continuing need for connection, productivity, and meaning.

Intergenerational Programs That Address the Need for Care

Intergenerational programs offer the unique characteristic of simultaneously addressing the needs of both their older and younger participants. The trend of increasing nonparental child care represents an opportunity for healthy, active older adults to receive some of the emotional care they need. Intergenerational programmers also believe that these individuals can help to relieve some of the stress experienced by young children and their parents. The expanding need for child care, for example, coincides with the increased participation of older women in the labor force, and women have provided the vast majority of older child-care employees over the past few decades. There may also be a large number of older men who, with proper motivation and training, can find great satisfaction in exercising their nurturing skills. As noted in chapter 2, a majority of adults over 65 are vigorous and healthy people, fully capable of responding to the demands of active young children.

In fact, there are roles for older adults, relatives and unrelated, within all of the common child-care models. For those working parents whose relatives are nearby, grandparents, aunts, and uncles can provide informal care. Older neighbors, less likely to be working themselves, can fill in for family members if there are none close by. More formally, older adults can receive training for work as nannies or become certified as family child-care providers. Intergenerational programming within the child-care field, however, usually refers to the systematic inclusion of older adults, paid or volunteer, in the everyday programmatic activities of child-care centers.

In addition to numerous volunteer opportunities, older adults can find meaningful employment as staff members in child-care centers. Active older adults are perhaps best suited to the part-time work available in these centers. Certainly, the continuing expansion of center-based care has created a desperate need for competent staff members, a need that is being met by the growing population of older adults.

Either as employees or as volunteers, older adults represent more than just a solution to child-care staffing problems; even frail elders can bring a unique quality to the child-care world. Because young children spend so much time away from their parents and families, child-care centers strive to counteract any negative impact of this separation by providing a family atmosphere. This concept is demonstrated most fully in the growing number of shared-site or colocated older adult–early childhood facilities. Such facilities create opportunities for joint programming, formal or informal, in which each age group provides companionship and support to the other. In these programs, as well as in more traditional settings, the shared experience of older adults and young children helps to create a sense of an extended family that, in the best cases, can substitute for the real experience lacking for both age groups in contemporary society.

Other intergenerational programs, usually involving older children, can help older adults with more intensive care needs. Friendly visiting or chore-service programs, for example, which pair older adults with middle-school or high-school students, can satisfy many light care needs. Such programs provide a sense of connectedness or at least a pair of young hands to perform chores ranging from changing an out-of-reach light bulb to yard work and shopping.

For family members who are caring for an older adult, a regular visit from a teenager can provide a welcome respite from heavy responsibility. The visitor can provide company and attention through talking, sharing a game, reading together, or going for a walk. During this break, the attending family member can attend to necessary errands or simply relax. The quality of care that the family member provides is enhanced by the opportunity to step away, however briefly.

Intergenerational programs in long-term care facilities tend to be more formally structured to fit into the routines and schedules of the institutions. Younger children—preschoolers and school-age children—are not likely to be involved in direct caretaking of the residents. However, visits from and scheduled joint activities with these children have a definite positive impact on the quality of the older adults' lives, bringing a welcome variety to their activities and a sense of connection to the outside world. Older children, too, participate in a variety of programs that structure their visits to long-term care facilities. In addition, some intergenerational programs offer teenagers an opportunity to perform genuine caregiving tasks under the supervision of the facility staff. There may be opportunities for a special kind of community service, often part of a specific school curriculum. They may also be part of a job-training program, designed to prepare teenagers for employment in the older adult caregiving profession.

THE NEED FOR STABILITY

One of the unique and pervasive characteristics of contemporary society is the sense of instability produced by the unprecedented pace and scale of social change. These changes have exerted a powerful debilitating effect on the predictability of the course of an individual's life, and the impact falls most heavily on older adults and young children. For these age groups, destabilization is a negative outcome of almost every trend noted in chapter 2.

Consider, for example, the fact that changes in the economic structure have practically eliminated the notion of employment security as experienced by previous generations. Children suffer when a parent is laid off or when the family is forced to relocate because of a career move. Teenagers face a bewildering array of career possibilities and the certainty that they must somehow prepare for more than one of these. Even discounting forced changes in employment status, the modern economy exerts a destabilizing influence. Many families now require the income produced by two working parents for their economic survival, and there are few social structures and support mechanisms in place to mitigate the stress of this complex and pressured lifestyle.

The effects of this pressure are powerful and disturbing. The impact of single parenthood, divorce, and inconsistent or poor quality out-of-home child care on family stability has been linked to violence and depression as well as a general lack of self-esteem among children (Vincent, 1988). Some of the consequences are even more far-reaching. Research on American males, for example, suggests that family instability during childhood has a profound impact on a male adult's ability to find higher level employment or to move beyond the employment level of his parents (Biblarz, 1993). Through distressed family systems, then, the problems perpetuate themselves.

Even individuals who have not directly experienced any of these changes are affected by their existence. The very fact that these conditions are becoming ever more common in modern American society indirectly creates stress and feelings of instability as children and parents find it more and more difficult to count on the continued stability of their own families.

Economic changes also affect the quality of life for the elderly. Poorer as a group than other adults, many of these individuals are faced with the pressures and stresses that financial insecurity creates, including anxiety about an uncertain future. The same economic concerns affect adult children, male and female, who are likely to be working or distant and therefore less available to provide the care and support that their parents may require.

The changes in family structure (i.e., increased divorce rate and out-of-wedlock births) complicate the lives of children who are being raised by a single parent and create fears in the children of two-parent families, who are forced to consider the realities of broken families in ways that were certainly not common earlier in the century. Increased mobility erodes the structure of communities and reduces the availability of naturally occurring support networks among neighbors and long-term friends.

Changes in educational systems create pressure on parents who are anxious to see their children achieve success and are uncertain about the ability of their schools to guarantee it. The transformation of the American health care delivery system creates unpredictability and anxiety about the quality and affordability of basic medical services, a burden that falls especially on the oldest and youngest members of society.

Finally, a great deal of unpredictability has been introduced into contemporary American society by rapidly improving technology, which has changed every aspect of an individual's life. Many of these changes are positive, of course, but the fact that they are occurring at all, and at an almost unmanageable pace, raises fears related to an individual's inability to see very far—or very clearly—into the future.

Although the ability to cope with change and unpredictability varies from individual to individual, people do seem to require a certain amount of stability. From the moment of an infant's birth, its parents attempt to provide a routine, a predictable structure on which the child supports his or her sense of self relative to the larger world. Throughout their lives, in fact, humans strive to create order out of chaos, seeking novelty only from within a stable framework of predictable events and circumstances. The importance of routine predictability cannot be overstated, and the inability to count on the future, to make reasonable plans, is a source of stress that is very difficult to alleviate.

Intergenerational Programs That Address
the Need for Stability

Perhaps the greatest impact of intergenerational programming on the stability of communities, families, and individual lives will occur at some point in the future. The spread and growth of intergenerational programs, it is hoped, will ultimately generate local and national policy initiatives that will help to solidify communities and provide more stability for families and individuals. These changes might come about, for example, as a result of the considerable long-term impact of intergenerational programming on the attitudes of different age groups toward each other.

At this point in the history of the field, however, individual intergenerational programs will have very little impact on the larger forces that are reshaping the world. Community-based programs that connect the oldest and youngest generations will not have a noticeable impact on the global economy, for example, and the changes it is forcing on the lives of contemporary individuals.

Some research, however, points to coping mechanisms that can be of great value to individuals. One such study, which focused on the effects of multiple life changes on adolescents, strongly suggests that effective coping requires areas of stability and nurturance in at least some segments of one's life (Simmons, 1987). By providing sources of support and stability for families and individuals, intergenerational programs work to offset modern cultural uncertainties and reduce the stress felt by families and individuals. For example,

- Older adults in child-care programs provide stability and predictability for young children while creating in their own lives a sense of routine and value.
- Youths visiting older adults may be preparing for a specific human service career; they are also preparing for their own future, obtaining a sense of what it means to grow older. The lives of the older adult participants gain some predictability and order, and the fear of being unable to cope is lessened.
- Telephone reassurance programs provide a predictable friendly voice for both the child and the older adult participant.
- Tutoring and mentoring programs owe many of their achievements to the fact that, by creating a special routine of visits and sessions, they introduce a measure of stability and predictability into the days of their participants.

There are many more examples; in fact, it might be said that the power and success of any intergenerational program is related at least partly to its positive impact on the stability and predictability of the participants' lives.

THE NEED FOR QUALITY EDUCATION

Chapter 2 illustrates several issues that directly or indirectly affect the need for quality education. For example, the poverty rate directly affects education. Migration of businesses and young people, especially from urban areas, has resulted in the erosion of the tax base, leading to substandard school systems. The influx of poor minorities to inner cities, coupled with the lack of unskilled, high-wage employment, has further complicated the problem. Inadequate educational facilities that produce young people who are unable to find jobs that pay a living wage contribute to the problems of crime, violence, hunger, and poverty facing many communities today. Despite the fact that since World War II some segments of society have become increasingly well educated because of government spending for education, the question of using public dollars for education continues to be debated. The issues depicted above negatively affect the availability of resources for education, exacerbating the need for quality education.

Children, youth, and older adults share common educational needs, which are affected by limited resources. Among them are basic skills to adequately function in the contemporary world. Both generations need to be literate, have adequate computational skills, life skills, survival skills, communication skills, motivation, and an appreciation of the value of lifelong learning. Young people need to prepare for employment in a technical world, to develop social skills, and to develop leadership skills, whereas older adults need continued educational opportunities and opportunities to experience and understand modern technology.

Intergenerational Programs That Address
the Need for Quality Education

Intergenerational programs hold particular promise for positively affecting the need for quality education by tapping unused resources in the community such as the skills, knowledge, and wisdom of older adults and the vitality and enthusiasm of young people in ways that stretch limited resources. One of the most successful ways in which intergenerational programs can positively affect the need for quality education is through tutoring and mentoring programs. In countless numbers of schools in the United States, older adults are volunteering their time—helping teachers in the classroom, working with individuals or groups of students on academic skills, or being a friend to a troubled teen. Older adults can transmit unique work skills, culture, and values to young people. For example, in at least two school districts in Pennsylvania, senior citizens who volunteer in the schools receive a $5.00 per hour credit against their school's property tax. Considering the high percentage of Pennsylvania residents who are over the age of 55 and the fact that fewer than 20% of Pennsylvania households have children in public schools, intergenerational school volunteer programs can positively affect not only students but also the school district and its tax payers. On college campuses, older adults can play a meaningful role in the education of students who may need guidance or remediation in many areas. Given their experience and knowledge of the workplace, the retiree population is invaluable at this level of educational need.

In contrast, young people can serve as tutors to older adults, teaching about new technology such as computer skills or helping older adults learn about nutrition through proper meal planning and preparation. Similarly, older adults can share techniques of "lost arts" such as bread baking. Finally, when young people and elders combine their skills and knowledge, they can work together to provide educational services to others such as preschool children or frail older adults.

Intergenerational programs that positively affect a young person's education are not limited to schools. Many community-based programs enable children and youth to grow and succeed in social situations and family relationships and are successful in preventing self-destructive behaviors among youth, such as drug and alcohol abuse and gang involvement.

Training provided for older adults participating in mentoring and tutoring programs enables them to continue their lifelong and work-related skills and to learn new skills such as classroom management, tutoring, motivational goal setting, and child development.

Intergenerational youth community-service and service-learning programs also help meet the need for quality education. When students are engaged in service to older adults in the community, they are able to apply their classroom instruction in real-world situations, thereby increasing their learning and knowledge about the sociology, psychology, and economics of the older adult population. Students experience an increase in self-esteem, develop a sense of belonging to the community, and are exposed to a wealth of information that older adults can provide. By helping frail elderly, youth can help them maintain a sense of independence and at the same time learn practical skills such as how to balance a checkbook, budgeting, and aspects of medical and legal services. Through participating in a pen-pal or oral history project, older adults are able to pass history, culture, and values on to the younger generation, thereby meeting their own need to share and teach what life has taught them.

Finally, poor communities lacking educational resources are not alone in their need for quality education. Even children of affluent communities can benefit from intergenerational programs. Those experiencing learning problems because of inadequate educational supports at home, lack of discipline, or too many diversions can profit from the experience of older adult tutors, mentors, or role models.

THE NEED TO BE PRODUCTIVE

Child development theories confirm the need for children and youth to actively participate in their own learning. This applies not only to the classroom but also to outside activities. High juvenile crime rates in many areas are associated with the lack of productive educational and recreational opportunities outside of school. With the emergence of the two-worker family mentioned in chapter 2, the need for after-school activities for children and youth is even more evident.

Theories of human development and aging point out the necessity of productive activities for older adults in their retirement years and the relationship of such activities to an individual's physical, mental, and emotional health. For healthy older adults, staying productive and eliminating boredom is increasingly important given the growing trend toward early retirement cited in chapter 2. In long-term care institutions, structured activities are viewed as a crucial elements in the health and well-being of elderly residents. Even highly impaired older adults in the late stages of dementia can benefit from meaningful and appropriate activities.

Intergenerational Programs That Address
the Need to Be Productive

Intergenerational programs provide numerous opportunities for children, youth, and older adults to remain active in their communities and schools. Tutoring, mentoring, and older worker child-care programs provide occasions for older adults to interact with young people in ways that aid in successful growth and development, enhance education, and help prevent self-destructive activity. Young people can participate in after-school recreational or community-service activities with older adults as mentors or by volunteering with frail elderly. Teams of youths and older adults can join together to provide other types of service, such as working with the homeless, gardening, or visiting isolated older adults.

THE NEED FOR CONTACT BETWEEN GENERATIONS

Regular contact between older adults and children was once built into the fabric of their lives. Because of the trends outlined in chapter 2, many children now grow up in an age-segregated world where older adults are unfamiliar, encountered from afar in the community, or glimpsed in brief visits from grandparents. Older adults, too, suffer from this separation of generations, which is both geographical and cultural. Geographical segregation results in far less day-to-day contact between the generations, whereas cultural trends such as focused marketing strategies create separate worlds for older adults and young people, with little natural overlap.

The lack of family contact affects both age groups, in several ways. The ways in which older adults benefit specifically from contact with young children have been exhaustively documented, as shown in the following examples:

- In a survey of intergenerational program staff members, 41% identified intergenerational activities as having a very positive impact on elders (Hegeman, 1985).
- Other researchers interviewing intergenerational program participants and staff have reported a positive impact on older adults (Seefeldt, 1987).
- Long-term-care residents in intergenerational programs are more alert, active, and smile more (Vujovich, 1987).
- Connections to young people foster in older adults a sense of personal continuity (Prosper, 1987).
- Intergenerational contact improves physical, cognitive, and emotional functioning in older adults (Allis, 1989).
- The traditional role of nurturer has been linked to physical health in older adults (Luks, 1988).

Additional evidence, often more anecdotal in nature, suggests that young children also benefit from contact with the oldest generation:

- A child's understanding of the way the world works is broadened by the sharing of an older adult's life experience.
- Young children feel more comfortable with change in general, and with aging in particular, if they are in contact with people of all ages who are enjoying and engaging in productive activities. Children need to understand aging (because everybody ages!).
- Children's fundamental perceptions of the complete life cycle are enhanced through direct experience with older adults.
- Children who develop relationships with older adults acquire the ability to see them as individuals, not stereotypical figures.
- Young children can learn history from older adults, who often represent disappearing cultures and lifestyles.
- Contact with the frail elderly can prepare children for the task of providing care to older adults—their own family members and to others without children of their own.

Other research suggests even more subtle interrelationships between the generations. An increase in child abuse incidents, for example, has been attributed to a lack of strong elder figures in communities and extended families, a contributing factor in the isolation of the contemporary nuclear family (Gutmann, 1986).

Intergenerational Programs That Address
the Need for Contact Between Generations

Of course, by definition, intergenerational programming addresses the need for contact between the generations, breaking down the barriers that modern society has erected between the age groups. Young children whose grandparents live far away can experience the satisfaction of a relationship with an older adult through special programs at their day-care centers. Those same grandparents can work or volunteer at an early childhood program in their own community, staying in touch with the lives and characteristics of young children. Parallel programs in elementary and secondary schools provide similar opportunities for older children and their grandparents.

Even children and older adults who live in the same community face barriers to interaction, as social trends push them into separate worlds. Intergenerational programs that offer the colocation of service facilities help to counteract these forces. They provide children and youth with a broad experience of aging, well beyond the limited contact with active, healthy older adults in caregiving roles or formalized visits with the frail elderly. As members of both age groups experience daily ongoing integration into each other's daily lives, the barriers are broken.

CONCLUSION

The social trends that were discussed in chapter 2 describe a world that has become in many ways less friendly to its communities, families, and individuals. Contemporary social realities are especially burdensome for children and older adults, but the middle generation, often responsible for the care and support of the other age groups, is also feeling the pinch. Intergenerational programs can help to meet the needs of all three generations through efficient solutions that are rooted in organic human family and community structures.

II

BACKGROUND AND DESCRIPTIONS OF INTERGENERATIONAL PROGRAMS

4

History and Evolution
of Intergenerational Programs

Sally Newman, PhD

When you know where you came from—you know where you are going.
—Navajo Proverb

During the past 30 years, professionals in human service fields concerned with the well-being of children, youth, and older adults have been systematically reporting on the impact of a changing society on these generations. Gerontologists reported on the status of older adults, their increase in numbers, the emphasis on early retirement, the change in life expectancy, the change in their roles in the family and in the community, the geographic separation from their families, and their lack of adequate support systems. Child and adolescent development professionals reported on the status of children and youth; inadequate child care and lack of appropriate support systems for young children; and an increase in school drop out, gang involvement, drug abuse, and teen pregnancy for school-age children and youth.

These reports prompted discussions among human service providers for both generations on the common social issues affecting these two populations. They also resulted in the development of spontaneous programs that could address some issues of the young and old. The discussions occurred within small and large groups informally and formally at the local, regional, and national levels. They involved practitioners, direct service providers, and administrators in grass roots and large system programs; developmental specialists working in early childhood, adolescence, and aging; educators concerned with education across the life span; academics in child development, psychology, family studies, and gerontology; and policy strategists concerned with understanding the multigenerational issues confronting American society. In the process of examining the common problems of the young and old, a concept unfolded that could simultaneously address issues and problems of both populations (Tice, 1982; White House Conference on Aging, 1981c). The concept was already being reflected in the spontaneous local programs that were evidenced in some communities.

Intergenerational programs—the emerging concept—would promote sharing of skills, knowledge, or experience between the old and young; and would provide ongoing and planned interactions designed to benefit both populations (Newman, 1986; Ventura-Merkel & Lidoff, 1983).

Intergenerational programs are based on developmental and historical evidence that positive mutually beneficial effects do occur as a result of interactions among older and younger persons. Though traditionally these benefits occur among elder and younger family members, we believe that they can also occur between nonbiologically linked older and younger persons. The challenge to the intergenerational movement, therefore, is: How can intergenerational programs replicate between nonbiologically linked older and younger persons the positive outcomes historically evidenced in familial intergenerational exchange?

During the past several decades, intergenerational programs have accepted this challenge and have become a social movement that involves millions of the United States' oldest and youngest persons. Today, working with these populations are thousands of professionals who are practitioners, administrators, scholars, and policymakers, moving and shaping the direction of intergenerational programs and participating in the emergence of an intergenerational human service field.

This chapter offers an historical perspective of the intergenerational field, its development, its focus over time, its current status, and its projection for the future. It includes an overview of the several components that undergird the past, present, and future of the intergenerational field and that are integral to its growth and development. These components are intergenerational programs, publications, networking, professionalism, and funding. The chapter then presents a chronology of historical events that have helped to shape the intergenerational field. These events parallel the development of the components during the past several decades. Although public policy is a key component and is essential to the history of intergenerational programs, it has had a unique influence on the development of intergenerational programs and is addressed in a separate chapter.

INTERGENERATIONAL PROGRAMS

The intergenerational field is historically grounded in intergenerational programs that bring together both the young and the old to share experiences that benefit both populations. These programs provide a structure on which the field is built.

Intergenerational programs are designed to engage nonbiologically linked older and younger persons in interactions that encourage cross-generational bonding, promote cultural exchange, and provide positive support systems that help to maintain the well-being and security of the younger and older generations.

The historical development of intergenerational programs is divided into two phases; the first phase occurred in the late 1960s and 1970s with programs addressing issues related to generational separation. The second phase, in the 1980s and 1990s, addressed societal problems that emerged in response to the social forces discussed in chapter 2.

The creation of intergenerational programs was motivated by a growing awareness that geographic separation of older and younger family members in many of America's families, a consequence of family mobility, was having negative effects on both generations. Geographic separation of many families resulted in a lack of consistent intergenerational contact and a growth of misperceptions and misunderstanding between the young and old. In some communities, emerging myths, stereotypes, and negative attitudes and behaviors were evidenced between these generations (Kalish, 1969). Lack of contact within families increased feelings of isolation and purposelessness among many older adults, who reported loss of meaningful roles in their families. Lack of contact affected children and youth, who missed the nurturing and positive role models of their grandparents. Caregivers and teachers working with children and youth referred to a disconnection between children and their elderly family members that often resulted in a lack of family continuity (Newman, 1992).

Intergenerational programs in the 1960s and 1970s were created to address issues of generational separation and perceived negative outcomes for both generations. Programs were designed to fill a familial intergenerational void created by the geographic separation that was the norm in 30–40% of American families (Newman, 1980). Intergenerational programs become a vehicle used by human service agencies and systems serving elderly and children to recreate some of the cross-generational interactions absent in families (Thorp, 1985).

The second phase of intergenerational programs, in the 1980s and 1990s, was in response to an increasing number of social issues affecting the old and young. Intergenerational programs in these 2 decades have focused on specific social issues affecting these two vulnerable populations. For youth, intergenerational programs address issues of low self-esteem, school dropout, drug and alcohol abuse, gang involvement, poor school achievement, inadequate child-care support systems, teen pregnancy, and literacy. For the elderly, intergenerational programs address issues of isolation and loneliness, drug and alcohol abuse, low self-esteem, inadequate support systems, literacy, and unemployment. For both young and old, intergenerational programs address the disconnectedness from family and society experienced by both generations (Phillips, 1992).

The shift in focus from generational issues during the 1960s and 1970s to social issues in the 1980s and 1990s resulted in an increased national awareness of the social value of intergenerational programs. Identifying intergenerational programs as a vehicle to address social issues enabled people to see their relevance and importance in communities. The outcome of this awareness is their expansion into many areas and systems. Intergenerational programs are operational throughout the United States in a variety of systems concerned with the education, health, and welfare of the young and the old. They are in urban, suburban, and rural communities across the country and involve children and youth and older adults with diverse backgrounds and needs. Intergenerational programs are in K–12 schools, colleges, adult and child day-care centers, Head Start centers, senior centers and senior high rises, homeless shelters, and long-term care and residential communities.

PUBLICATIONS

Related to the growth of intergenerational programs and a direct outcome of their development is a body of print materials prepared for professionals and the general public. These materials reflect the changes and the evolution of intergenerational programs. They include instructional manuals, papers, and newsletters that present program information and implementation procedures; technical reports that describe program development and outcomes; and research articles that address some fundamental questions related to the issues, impact, and future of intergenerational programs.

Instructional materials, both print and audiovisual, are created to support the maintenance and replication of intergenerational program efforts across the country. They encompass all aspects of program development and maintenance needed to implement and sustain programs over time and reflect the shift in focus and changing structure of intergenerational programs. These materials have become more complex and more detailed as programmers have become more knowledgeable and able to describe program implementation procedures in greater detail. Instructional materials are the tools used to develop and maintain international programs by intergenerational professionals at various job levels, for example, direct service providers, administrators, coordinators, and program developers.

Technical reports serve a different function in this growing field. They inform professionals and the community at large of the effects and implications of these programs. As programs are sustained and replicated, documentation of their effectiveness is reported through these documents. The reports available in the 1970s typically described the development, evaluation, and outcomes of individual local programs. In the 1980s and 1990s, as intergenerational program models expanded nationally, these reports have become more complex, with multiple sections and more elaborate evaluations. Diverse programs focusing on social issues produce technical reports that are comparative and examine similarities and differences among programmatic structure and outcomes. They often examine the effect of national demonstration models in multiple sites across the country. Multisite reports have generated valuable information used to determine the effectiveness of individual and groups of programs and have become a database of information on successful models.

Research articles describing findings in the field examine intergenerational programs from the perspective of understanding the social, behavioral, and attitudinal effects of intergenerational programs. These articles give credence to and reinforce the rationale for further examination of this emerging human service field, which can have a significant effect on U.S. society.

NETWORKING

As intergenerational programs expand across the country, there is an increasing need to share ideas and information. The creation of formal and informal networks beyond the immediate community in which a program is developed has created a dynamic communication system that reinforces and supports intergenerational program initiatives across the country (Newman, 1989a).

During the late 1960s and the 1970s, networking activities began to facilitate informal local agency or interagency communication. Networking expanded as a cross-agency and statewide initiative in the early 1980s and in 1986 became a formal structured national initiative.

In the 1960s and 1970s, with the creation of the Retired Senior Volunteer Program (RSVP), the Foster Grandparents Program (FGP), and schools-based intergenerational programs, networking strategies included local and regional system-sponsored training workshops, informal discussions at agency-sponsored conferences, and system-initiated networking newsletters. ACTION funded the RSVP

Intergenerational Clearinghouse Newsletter to disseminate information on inter-generational programs and issues to the ACTION-sponsored organizations (RSVP, FGP, and VISTA [Volunteers in Service to America]). The clearinghouse newsletter became a forum for information dissemination beyond the ACTION network.

In the 1980s, increased public and private funding for statewide and cross-agency intergenerational programs prompted additional networking activities. The following states created internal networks to share information on intergenerational activities: California, Illinois, Kansas, Massachusetts, New Jersey, New Mexico, Wisconsin, and New York. State and local intergenerational leadership convened statewide training workshops, meetings, and conferences to provide support for existing intergenerational programs and to encourage the creation of additional models within the state. The statewide networks promoted the partnering of social service agencies and participated in public and private funding activities to support the expansion of intergenerational activities within these states.

In 1986, four national organizations, the National Council on the Aging, the Child Welfare League of America, the American Association of Retired People (AARP), and the Children's Defense Fund collaborated in the creation of Generations United, a formal national networking and advocacy agency. This agency promotes statewide and national linkages of systems involved in intergenerational activities and provides a forum for cross-state, regional, and national dialogue. Generations United advocates for intergenerational cross-system linkages and for federal legislation to encourage state and local collaboration of agencies supporting children, youth, and older adults. Generations United has become the catalyst for the expansion of networks in the 1990s.

PROFESSIONALISM

With the development and expansion of intergenerational programs has come an increasing number of professionals working in intergenerational settings. Programmers, planners, administrators, and direct service providers in human service fields are interested in learning about intergenerational program development, management, and evaluation. They are interested in achieving skills that lead to success in this work and in understanding program standards that enable them to measure their success.

In addition to the professional in the intergenerational workplace, academics and students are interested in learning about the concepts, issues, and premises that have given rise to and continue to guide the intergenerational field. Multidisciplinary professionals and academics trained in human service fields and working in intergenerational settings recognize the importance of gaining skills and acquiring knowledge to become competent in this new specialty.

Preparation for professionalizing an emerging field began in the 1980s through intergenerational tracks offered in national conferences such as the American Society on Aging, the National Council on the Aging, the National Association for the Education of Young Children, and Generations United. In addition, state networks in Illinois, Kansas, Massachusetts, and Texas convened specialized skill-building intergenerational workshops for the growing number of persons working in inter-generational settings.

During the 1990s, there has been a consistent increase in the number of persons who do intergenerational work in a variety of human service and educational environments. It is estimated that several thousand people are involved in intergenerational activities as part of their professional responsibilities. Consistent with this increase is an expanding interest in professionalizing the intergenerational field. Training institutes, university courses, and a variety of academic options have been initiated to prepare people to work as intergenerational specialists. Efforts are being directed to promote competency development for these specialists and to begin a dialogue on the creation of standards for intergenerational performance and achievement.

The current interest in this work establishes a climate to examine the timeliness for considering the role of intergenerational specialists in human service fields such as early childhood, education, and aging or the creation of an independent new human service field. In the 1990s, several higher education institutions have begun to explore possibilities for intergenerational studies as an academic experience. They are convening certificate-bearing training institutes, including intergenerational modules within existing academic courses, developing intergenerational courses with a multidisciplinary focus, considering an intergenerational minor in a degree program, and in one college (Wheelock College) offering a degree in intergenerational studies (Larkin, 1995). With the development of these academic options, more multidisciplinary human service professionals will emerge to establish a direction for a growing intergenerational field.

FUNDING

From their inception, the focus, size, and sustainability of intergenerational programs have been a function of their funding. Since the late 1960s, sources of funding have been diverse and unpredictable, reflecting the economic and political climate of the country. Funding for intergenerational programs has come from both the public and private sector and includes support from local, state, and national government agencies and from local, regional, and national foundations and corporations. The following section highlights some of the significant intergenerational funding initiatives during this period and reflects the economic and political change in the United States during the past 30 years. Public policy implications that may be evident in some of these initiatives are addressed in chapters 9 and 10 as part of the discussion on public policy issues.

Though this section focuses on some of the large funding trends, the most consistent and ongoing funding support for intergenerational programs has come from local corporations, businesses, foundations, and community organizations. This section presents a broad picture of these trends, along with additional references to specific funding initiatives, which are described in the chronology section that follows.

In the late 1960s, federal funds were used to initiate three national intergenerational programs that had a significant impact on the development of intergenerational programs. The FGP and the RSVP were formed to create opportunities for older adults to interact with a community's children and youth. The FGP is designed to connect healthy lower income older adults with special or exceptional needs children. The RSVP was funded to enable older adults to provide volunteer service to their community. The National Center for Service Learning was established as an advocate for the development and expansion of student volunteers and service learning programs, with a focus on service to the elderly.

In the 1970s, a variety of diverse intergenerational funding sources became available, including various government agencies and private foundations. State-funded intergenerational efforts were initiated in California with two significant funding efforts. The California Department of Education supported the development and implementation of a curriculum on aging for primary and secondary schools. The state of California and a private foundation collaborated to support the development of three pilot intergenerational child-care sites.

Also in the 1970s, an important national effort by a foundation was initiated with the funding of six large school systems in the United States, which were charged with developing intergenerational programs in schools. Funding for three consecutive years supported the involvement of older adults as volunteers contributing directly to students' growth and learning in school settings. This grant was a catalyst for the largest and most significant intergenerational program model in the United States (older adults as volunteers in schools).

Independent of this multischool district effort, two other volunteers in schools models are noteworthy because they also were replicated in communities across the country. Teaching–Learning Communities in Ann Arbor, Michigan, was funded by the federal government and the local school district and became a national model for intergenerational art experiences in the schools. The Generations Together Senior Citizen School Volunteer Program was funded by a local foundation and local school systems that involved neighborhood elders as classroom resources. This program was introduced in school districts across Pennsylvania and was replicated in other states across the country.

The 1980s saw the emergence of a variety of new funding initiatives that reflected efforts to expand the number of intergenerational programs within states and across the nation. Several states, such as Pennsylvania, New Jersey, Wisconsin, New York, and Massachusetts, funded a variety of intergenerational initiatives, including conferences, demonstration projects, and publications for statewide dissemination. The first federal multiagency intergenerational initiative, coordinated by the Office of Human Development Service, provided discretionary funds to support a variety of intergenerational initiatives that linked agencies serving older adults, children, and youth at the local, state, or regional levels. This initiative continued into the 1990s.

During the 1980s, large-scale, multistate, multisource funding efforts were initiated:

- The Administration on Aging partnered with several local foundations in a public–private initiative to develop and evaluate nine new intergenerational initiatives.
- A multistate partnership began between the National Council on the Aging and the Robert Wood Johnson Foundation. It involves older adults as support persons to families with chronically ill or disabled children. This partnership has continued into the 1990s and has expanded to 35 sites.

- Two federal programs, Title V of the Older Americans Act and the Job Training Partnership Act, that fund training for work programs for older adults joined with local community colleges and local businesses to support the creation of intergenerational older worker programs to train and place older adults into the child-care workplace. This partnership project, which has continued into the 1990s, is being replicated in communities across the country.
- In preparation for the 1981 White House Conference on Aging, the National Council on the Aging received funding for mini workshops in 24 sites across the country to develop strategies for linking the generations (White House Conference on Aging, 1981b).
- A partnership of several foundations provided support to a multiyear research demonstration project linking older mentors with vulnerable youth. This project was implemented in several communities across the country.
- Beginning in the 1980s and continuing into the 1990s, the AARP has assumed a leadership role by producing and disseminating information on intergenerational initiatives. AARP created several publications as resources to the intergenerational field and supported research that contributed to the knowledge base of the effects of intergenerational programs.

Intergenerational funding sources in the 1990s have resulted in several new model initiatives:

- The newly established Corporation for National and Community Service encourages citizens regardless of age, income, or ability to engage in full-time or part-time service. The corporation funds two parallel tracks of service, one that involves youth in programs that benefit the nation and improve their own lives and one for the senior volunteer network (e.g., the RSVP, the FGP, and the Senior Companion Program) to serve entire communities. A funding interest of the corporation is to promote intergenerational projects that link the senior and youth networks.
- The Administration on Aging has funded two major initiatives: an intergenerational awareness and dissemination campaign to identify, select, and disseminate information on intergenerational child-care programs; and the development and evaluation of seven diverse intergenerational projects around the country.
- The Fund for the Improvement of Post Secondary Education, an agency within the U.S. Department of Education, awarded grants to universities to conduct a variety of intergenerational program and research projects.
- A foundation in the state of South Carolina funded a statewide public and private multiyear partnership initiative to develop and evaluate seven rural intergenerational programs across the state that focus on the needs of at-risk children and youth.
- The Brookdale Foundation funded a new national intergenerational initiative that does not represent the typical intergenerational program model of interaction between nonbiologically connected children, youth, and older adults. The Brookdale Foundation model involves grandparents as caregivers and includes a variety of grandparenting programs across the country.

This summary of funding highlights since the 1960s presents a view of the types of funding initiatives and funders that have shaped the course of the intergenerational field and continue to create a national impetus for intergenerational programs. It showcases the large initiatives that tend to involve participants across the country.

It is important to restate, however, that the intergenerational efforts that will be sustained long term and that represent the largest number of participants are the programs that receive local public and private community partnership funding. These programs typically focus directly on a community's needs and strive to improve the quality of life within that community. The evolution and diversity of funding sources for intergenerational programs (public and private at the local, regional, state, and national levels) suggests various options for supporting the expanding initiatives that consider an intergenerational approach to addressing some of the social problems that affect young and old in the United States.

CHRONOLOGY

The previous section of this chapter presented a broad view of the unique development since the 1960s of each component that is integral to the intergenerational field: program development, publications, networking, professionalism, and funding. The following section presents a chronology of events that integrates these components and reflects the changes and status of the intergenerational field from the 1960s to the 1990s.

This section integrates the events chronologically to illustrate the shape of the field's growth so the reader can become familiar with the relationship of the components as they influenced the direction of the field. References in the chronology between 1963 and 1988 are drawn from a chapter written by this author in *Intergenerational Programs: Imperatives, Strategies, Impacts, Trends* (Newman, 1989b).

1963: Adopt a Grandparent Program

The first reported intergenerational program was developed at the P. K. Yonge Laboratory School, University of Florida (Whitley, Duncan, McKenzie, & Sledjecki, 1976). It involved weekly class visits by young children to a neighboring convalescent home. An adaptation of this model was integrated into the programming of the Beverly Nursing Home Network for implementation system wide.

1965: Foster Grandparent Program

In 1965, when the Foster Grandparent Program became a member of the volunteer ACTION network, its focus was described as an intergenerational model concerned with matching lower income, healthy older adults to children with special or exceptional needs.

1967–1969: Serve and Enrich Retirement by Volunteer Experience

This program was established on Staten Island, New York, as a project of the Community Service Society to enable persons over 60 to provide volunteer service to the community. Funded initially with grants from the federal government, local foundations, and the Community Service Society, the program grew from a project with 23 older volunteers working with children and young adults at a residential home for the mentally retarded to a project involving 1,500 senior volunteers working in 90 agencies, of which the majority serve children and their families (Sainer & Zander, 1971).

1969: Retired Senior Volunteer Program

RSVP was created as a national program authorized under Title IV, Part A, of the reauthorization act of the Older Americans Act of 1965. Though not inherently intergenerational, many RSVP programs identified local schools as placement sites for their volunteers and integrated intergenerational opportunities among their volunteer options.

1969: National Center for Service Learning

This center was established as the National Student Volunteer Program and was an advocate for the development and expansion of student volunteers and service-learning programs with a focus on service to the elderly. It offered free training programs, resource materials, and technical assistance for high school and college community service program coordinators (National Center for Service-Learning, 1980). Students from 50 universities in disciplines such as nursing, social work, vocational education, rehabilitation counseling, and so forth provided weekly service to the elderly in their community. The concept of student community service, though in decline during the 1980s, has been introduced as a national initiative in the 1990s with the establishment of the Corporation for National and Community Service.

1970: The Gray Panthers

Maggie Kuhn convened the Gray Panthers as an advocacy group in which younger and older members of society actively collaborated to address social policy issues. Ageism and intergenerational exchange are basic issues addressed by the Gray Panthers.

1975: U.S. Office of Education and U.S. Administration on Aging Establish Guidelines for Creating Opportunities for Senior Citizens

An agreement was signed between these two federal agencies that established guidelines for using the nation's schools to provide a variety of educational, recreational, nutritional, and volunteer opportunities for the nation's elderly. An outgrowth of this federal initiative was a series of memoranda signed between the secretaries of Aging and Education in 14 states. These memoranda fostered regional meetings between members of aging and education networks to develop strategies for providing service to older Americans through their involvement in schools. The regional meetings were convened in several states and continued for several years until there was a political shift in the states' leadership.

1975: Survey by Louis Harris and Associates

Data reported from this survey, "Myths and Reality of Aging in America" (1975), conducted for the National Council on the Aging, estimated that more than 40,000 Americans over 65 years of age were serving as volunteers in public education systems throughout the United States.

1976: California Develops Aging Education Program

With a grant from the Department of Education, the first aging education program was developed and introduced into the curriculum for children in kindergarten through 12th grade in the California public schools. This demonstration project, which included older persons as resources in the classroom, was implemented in 43 classrooms throughout the state (Marshall, 1985).

1976: Teaching–Learning Communities

This intergenerational program was developed as a model to bring elders, their crafts, and their caring into the public schools of Ann Arbor, Michigan. The model has been adapted and replicated in a variety of communities across the United States (Tice & Warren, 1986).

1977–1979: Florida Creates School Volunteer Network That Includes Senior Citizens

Legislation was passed to support the creation of a school volunteer network throughout the state. The network included the community's senior citizens, who became an essential part of the classroom instructional teaching team in early child-hood classrooms (kindergarten through 5th grades; Florida Department of Education, 1979).

1978: The Edna McConnell Clark Foundation Funds Intergenerational Programs

An award of $10,000,000 was made to six major school systems (Boston, Los Angeles, Miami, New York, Seattle, St. Louis) with the charge to develop, over a 3-year period, intergenerational programs that would involve older persons as school volunteers to work directly with students to support the growth and learning of youth in school settings. This grant precipitated the development of the largest and most significant intergenerational program network in the United States.

1978: Messiah Village

The first multicare retirement center that integrated an intergenerational component was Messiah Village in Mechanicsburg, Pennsylvania. The design of Messiah Village included the integration of a child-care center whose daily schedule included interaction between the children and the older residents. This unique intergenerational project became the prototype for other long-term care or retirement centers that integrate the concept of child care.

1978: Generations Together Established at the University of Pittsburgh

This was the first university program dedicated to the concept of intergenerational programs and related issues. Still a leader in the intergenerational field, Generations Together develops intergenerational program models, assists other groups in program development, researches the outcomes of intergenerational programs, and disseminates information on program development and research.

1979: Intergenerational Child-Care Centers Developed in California

The California Intergenerational Child Care Act of 1979 supported the development of two intergenerational child-care centers, which were modeled after a 1976 intergenerational child-care center funded by the state and the Elvirita Lewis Foundation (Johnson & Siegel, 1980). These successful intergenerational child-care models prompted the preparation of the California Intergenerational Child Care Act of 1980, which passed the legislature unanimously but was vetoed by the governor.

1980: *Close Harmony*

This first intergenerational video presented the evolution of a unique program model. *Close Harmony* (Learning Corporation of America, 1980) effectively described the development of an intergenerational choir whose participants, members of a senior center and students at a private school, developed important and meaningful relationships through making music together.

1980: National Council on the Aging Sponsors Mini Conferences

A national effort to foster an intergenerational program network was initiated by the National Council on the Aging. It convened a series of mini conferences throughout the United States to develop strategies for linking the generations. The outcome of this effort was the preparation of a position paper, "Strategies for Linking the Generations," that was presented at the 1981 White House Conference on Aging (National Council on the Aging, 1981).

1981: The White House Conference on Aging

Conferees of the White House Conference on Aging prepared and submitted to Congress two position papers related to intergenerational interaction: (a) "Challenging Age Stereotypes in the Media," a document that reported on a World Health Organization mini conference in which media experts and anti-ageist advocates worked together to develop a strategy for improving the representation of older persons in all aspects of the media (White House Conference on Aging, 1981a), and (b) "Older Americans as a National Growing Resource," a report from the World Health Organization Technical Committee that described existing opportunities for older persons as active participants in society and recommended strategies for the government, the private sector, and the volunteer sector for maintaining this national resource (White House Conference on Aging, 1981c).

1981: Intergenerational Clearinghouse Newsletter

The RSVP chapter in Dane County, Wisconsin, was funded by ACTION to establish a national clearinghouse newsletter on intergenerational programs and issues. The newsletter is still being published, reporting information on RSVP, the FGP, VISTA, and other programs that link the generations. The newsletter receives local funding, appears two times annually, and has become a forum for the exchange of information in the intergenerational program network. It has been a significant force in the creation of the Wisconsin Intergenerational Network ("Intergenerational programming development in Wisconsin," 1987).

1982: State Departments of Aging and Education
Sign Memorandum of Understanding

A memorandum of understanding was signed between the Departments of Aging and Education in California, Florida, and Pennsylvania. It addressed the need to provide educational experiences that promoted an understanding of the aging process and that provided opportunities for exchange between the generations.

1982: The World Assembly on Aging in Vienna

The final report of this international meeting expressed a deep concern regarding the alienation and generational discontinuity in societies accepting Western models of industrialization, bureaucratization, and occupational and organizational complexities and recommended "the encouraging of activities and programs to enhance generational solidarity" (Oriol, 1982, p. 56).

1982: Office of Human Development Services Solicits Proposals

A request for proposals was announced through the Coordinated Discretionary Funds Program of the Office of Human Development Services. Funds for this program were provided by a collaborative effort between the following government departments: the Administration on Aging; the Administration for Children, Youth, and Families; the Administration on Developmental Disabilities; and the Administration for Native Americans. The proposals focused on intergenerational solutions to some of the issues concerning the constituencies served by these government agencies. Requests for proposals continued throughout the 1980s and into the 1990s. Funded proposals included intergenerational child care, partnerships between schools and local aging organizations (RSVP and AARP), intergenerational initiatives in Native American communities, statewide community and school mentoring projects, youth volunteering with isolated or institutionalized elderly, and intergenerational immunization projects that involve grandparents and other older adults with young children.

1982: National School Volunteer Program

The association surveyed several thousand urban, suburban, and rural school systems throughout the country to determine the number of older adults volunteering in schools. The survey reported an estimated 2,000,000 older adults involved in a variety of direct-service volunteer roles within the surveyed public school systems (National School Volunteer Program, 1983). In 1988, the National School Volunteer Program became the National Association of Partners in Education.

1984: AARP Parent Aide Program

AARP received a coordinated discretionary grant from the Office of Human Development Services to develop a demonstration intergenerational program, "Older Volunteers in Partnership With Parents to Prevent Child Abuse and Neglect." This demonstration was implemented in five child abuse projects and involved 40 volunteers working with 135 children in 63 families.

1985: Intergenerational Legislation Introduced in Congress

Congressman Ed Roybal and Senator Carl Levin introduced the Intergenerational Education Volunteer Network Act of 1985 into the 99th Congress. The bill was known, respectively, as House Bill 1587 (1985) and Senate Bill 1022 (1985). It was cosponsored by Republicans and Democrats in both houses, and would have established a tutorial network made up of senior citizen volunteers in public school systems. It would have provided opportunities for senior citizens, through RSVP, AARP, and other aging networks, to work in elementary and secondary schools and in homes with educationally disadvantaged children and their families. The bill was referred to committee and remained there through the term of the 99th Congress with no further action.

1984: Intergenerational Program Surveys Conducted

Several surveys reported on the status of intergenerational programs in the United States. The surveys presented profiles of representative programs at the state and the national levels and were made available to local, state, and national organizations (Murphy, 1984; Pennsylvania Department of Aging, 1984; Ventura-Merkel & Parks, 1984; California State Department of Education, 1984).

1983–1993: Curricula Development

Curricula were developed to introduce aging issues to children, youth, and young adults and to introduce issues related to children and youth to older persons preparing to work in intergenerational settings. A national leader in this work has been the Center for Understanding Aging, created in 1983. The center develops and disseminates curricula and is a resource for curricula prepared by other groups. A list of the variety of curriculum materials available that includes the publications of the Center for Understanding Aging appears in *Intergenerational Readings/Resources* (Wilson, 1994). Examples of the available curricula include *Schools in an Aging Society: Curriculum Series* (Couper, 1992); *Curriculum on Aging: An Intergenerational Program for Grades K–6* (Meany, 1982); *Perspectives on Aging: Bridging the Generation Gap* (Pratt, Miksis, & Trapp, 1986); *Learning from the Past: A Guide to Using Bi-Folkal Productions in Schools and Other Intergenerational Settings* (Bi-Folkal Productions, 1991); *On Growing Older: Curriculum Guides—Grades 1–6* (Lyons, 1982); *Intergenerational Adventure: A Training Curriculum for Older Adult Caregivers Working With School Age Children During the Hours After School* (Fink, 1985); *Share It with the Children: A Preschool Curriculum on Aging Instructional Guide* (Mack & Wilson, 1988); *Linkage—Bringing Together Young and Old* (Leon, 1990); *Generations Together: A Job Training Curriculum for Older Adults in Child Care* (Smith, Mack, & Tittnich, 1993); and *Jobstart: The Road to Independence—Family Friends Training Curriculum* (National Council on the Aging, 1992a).

1984–1989: Statewide Networks Established

Intergenerational statewide and regional networks were created in California, Kansas, Illinois, Massachusetts, New Jersey, New Mexico, New York, Pennsylvania, and Wisconsin. The structure and direction of these networks was based on their membership and the source of the leadership in each state. The networks fostered collaboration between local and state agencies and systems representing aging, education, and child care, consortiums of intergenerational programs, and the business and foundation community.

California—1984–1986. With funding from Luke B. Hancock and other foundations and corporations, several workshops were convened to support the work of intergenerational programs in northern California and to establish the Northern California Intergenerational Program Network ("Update on," 1985). Still in existence, this network is maintained through scheduled meetings and a newsletter.

Illinois—1987. The Illinois Department of Aging held a series of seminars in the spring of 1987 with 11 universities and the volunteer sector. The seminars were designed to address the issue of generational equity and the new generation gap. The seminars, titled "Interdependence of the Generations," presented recommendations to the state on how to mobilize support for a productive state policy that would unite the generations and move toward family policies across the age spectrum (Illinois Department of Aging, 1987). Since 1987, several Illinois intergenerational networks have developed:

- The Illinois Intergenerational Initiative is a statewide network of coalitions that meet to share ideas, increase awareness, and promote intergenerational activities. The initiative publishes a newsletter that is circulated statewide.
- The Chicago Metropolitan Network is a regional network that supports and provides technical assistance to intergenerational programs in northern Illinois. Its members are individuals who meet bimonthly and attend conferences and workshops that focus on intergenerational programming and networking issues.
- The Dupage Consortium is an intergenerational task force that encourages program development, provides technical assistance, and schedules skill-building workshops.
- The governor's Project Success initiative is one of the state's Human Service Reform efforts to provide expanded service to children and their families. This intergenerational effort focuses on building a network of state agencies, local service providers, and schools who will develop activities that are designed to meet the needs of the community's families. A significant statewide intergenerational model within Project Success is Illinois READS (Retirees Educating and Assisting in the Development of Students), a mentoring project coordinated by the Illinois Department of Aging that utilizes retired people as volunteers to help kindergarten though third-grade children with reading and related classroom activities.

Kansas—1989. The Kansas Intergenerational Network was formed with funding from the United Methodist Consortium. The network sponsors training, technical assistance, and conferences designed to increase the numbers and quality of intergenerational programs across the state. Its service includes a resource and information lending library, a quarterly newsletter (*Connections*), and a speakers bureau.

Massachusetts—1987. Following several months of planning by a group representing numerous organizations, the Massachusetts Intergenerational Network was formally established as a membership organization. It is a statewide coalition of people of all ages who believe that intergenerational cooperation among generations contributes to the good of individuals and the well-being of society ("Massachusetts network," 1987).

New Jersey—1985. The Division on Aging in the Department of Community Affairs promoted the concept of intergenerational programs to statewide education and social service agencies and to community-based organizations. As an intergenerational program advocate, the department convened workshops on program development and was a resource for print and media materials. It supported the development of intergenerational programs by funding three demonstration projects, which were subsequently sustained through private or public funds.

New York—1986–1989. The New York State Board of Regents adopted a policy statement that challenged educators to develop a comprehensive strategy to mobilize the capacity of the educational system in addressing the multiple needs of the aging population in the context of existing social and economic conditions. Major policy recommendations advanced by the state were to foster administrative and community intergenerational cooperation and exchange; to enhance the coordination of services for the elderly by strengthening the links between education, aging, and other state-level agencies; to involve the elderly as active participants in society;

and to educate students at all levels about aging (University of the State of New York, 1986). Consistent with this initiative, the New York State Intergenerational Network was created in 1989 as a consortium of agencies interested in promoting support and advocating for intergenerational programs and policies at local, state, and national levels.

Pennsylvania—1982–1988. The Pennsylvania Department of Aging promoted the development and networking of intergenerational programs through several initiatives:

- by funding annually the development of intergenerational demonstration models, each of which prepared a manual to be used for dissemination and replication activities;
- by preparing a 1982 department recommendation for all area agencies on aging, which encouraged their involvement in the development of intergenerational programs;
- by signing a memorandum of understanding in 1982 with the Pennsylvania Department of Public Welfare and the Pennsylvania Association of Non-Profit Homes for the Aged encouraging collaboration in the development of intergenerational programs; and
- by preparing a 1984 resource guide describing 73 existing examples of intergenerational programs in the commonwealth. The guide was designed to promote networking throughout the commonwealth.

In 1984, Generations Together received a coordinated discretionary grant from the Office of Human Development Services to facilitate the development of intergenerational child-care programs linking the child-care and aging network in the commonwealth of Pennsylvania ("Introducing Joining Together," 1986). Through this effort, over 60 intergenerational child-care models emerged that involved collaboration among a variety of child-care and aging network agencies (e.g., child-care centers, Head Start programs, senior centers, and nursing homes).

The Erie Intergenerational Network was formed in 1984 as a voluntary association of aging and youth service agencies and programs in the Erie area. It was initiated by Greater Erie Community Action Center as an outgrowth of an intergenerational collaborative project with Generations Together of the University of Pittsburgh. It comprised representatives from senior centers, volunteer programs, public and private child day care, religious organizations, nursing homes, public schools, and the business community. Informal annual sharing meetings during the initial 5 years have been replaced with biannual structured meetings using a workshop format. In addition, between 1991 and 1995, the network convened several areawide conferences that involved the participation of approximately 100 agencies.

In 1985, Governor Richard Thornburgh issued a public policy statement that encouraged the Departments of Aging, Public Welfare, and Education to work together to increase the availability of child-care services through models involving senior citizens.

In 1986, the Center for Intergenerational Learning (a program of Temple University's Institute on Aging) created the Delaware Valley Intergenerational Network with funding from the Philadelphia Foundation ("Delaware Valley," 1986).

This network brings together agencies serving youth, the elderly, and religious and volunteer sectors to prioritize their needs and identify gaps in their service delivery.

In 1987, the Pennsylvania State Assembly reviewed "Intergenerational Teaching Programs," an amendment to Public School Code Bill 1949 designed to provide funds to education systems (primary, secondary, and higher) for innovative teaching strategies that would result in intergenerational programs in schools. The amendment was introduced in November, referred to committee for review, and was not resubmitted for discussion or a vote in the Assembly.

In 1988, Governor Robert Casey initiated a plan for establishing on-site day-care centers for children of state employees and encouraged the use of intergenerational program models in these sites.

Wisconsin—1981–1987. In 1981, a meeting between community education, public education, and the Department of Aging was held to initiate a discussion on intergenerational efforts in the state.

* In 1984, intergenerational workshops were held throughout the state involving the aging and public school networks.
* In 1985, a consortium of Wisconsin agencies assumed the leadership in the Wingspread Intergenerational Conference held in Racine, Wisconsin. This conference involved the participation of intergenerational programs throughout the country and produced a "how to" guide book to assist local organizations in the development of intergenerational programs (Thorp, 1985).
* In 1986, a statewide Intergenerational Network Conference was convened involving schools and aging and community groups. A conference follow-up was the preparation and distribution of a survey to determine the kind of intergenerational activities and programs available in the state.

1985–1987: Intergenerational Program Manuals Published

Manuals were published to support the development of intergenerational programs and were made available to the intergenerational program networks throughout the country. They described procedures for implementing generic and specific intergenerational program models (e.g., preschoolers, children, and youth with older adults in long-term care settings; older adults with children and youth in school settings; older adult caregivers to children in early childhood settings; youth with the frail elderly in adult day-care and at-home settings; and older adults supporting families of children with chronic illness; Wilson, 1994).

1986: Administration on Aging/National Public–Private Intergenerational Initiative

A contract was signed between the Administration on Aging and the Elvirita Lewis Foundation to support the development of a variety of intergenerational projects in nine communities from Massachusetts to California. Each project was selected and funded by a local foundation, with matching funds from the Administration on Aging contract. The project administration and coordination was assigned to the Elvirita Lewis Foundation, which functioned as the initiative secretariat with the assistance of a consortium of the local collaborating foundations. State and regional meetings were convened to support and review the local projects. Project evaluation was conducted by Generations Together (Schreter, 1989).

1986: Generations United Created

The National Council on the Aging, the Child Welfare League of America, the Children's Defense Fund, and AARP collaborated to create and cosponsor Generations United, a national advocate organization for public policy and programs that recognize the interdependence of children, youth, families, and the elderly. One hundred organizations were the initial members of Generations United, supporting and participating in a variety of advocacy and networking activities. Generations United represents the collective voice of many networks speaking for the young and old (Liederman & Ossofsky, 1987).

1987: Budget Reconciliation Act of 1987

This act authorized the increase of Title XX social services block grants by $50 million. Title XX of the Social Security Act is the major federal funding source to the states for a variety of social services for people of all ages.

1989–1990: United States Congress Passes Child-Care Legislation

Senate Bill S5, the Act for Better Child Care, produced by Senator Christopher Dodd and cosponsored by Senators Orrin Hatch, Ted Kennedy, Barbara Mikulski, Alan Cranston, and John Chafee, was passed by the Senate in June of 1989. The bill was designed to improve the quantity, quality, and affordability of child care, with a focus on low and moderate income families, and includes older persons as child-care providers to help sustain quality care. House Bill 3, the Early Childhood Education and Development Act of 1990, cosponsored by Gus Hawkins, Dale Kildee, and Thomas Downe, was passed by the House in March of 1990. The House bill focused on Head Start and child-care quality services, which include training, resource, and referral services, salary enhancement, and regulatory enforcement. The combined bills were integrated into the Child Care and Development Block Grant legislation in fall of 1990, with funding allocated in 1991.

1989: Family Friends Project

The Administration on Aging and the Robert Wood Johnson Foundation funded the Family Friends Project, which became a national model. The project, coordinated by the National Council on the Aging, is committed to the principle that senior volunteers over 55 can offer support, patience, and compassion to families with chronically ill or disabled children under 13, enabling these families to cope with issues related to these children. Currently, there are 35 Family Friends programs across the country.

1989: First Comprehensive Text
on Intergenerational Programs Is Published

Intergenerational Programs: Imperatives, Strategies, Impacts, Trends (Newman & Brummel, 1989) reported on the status of intergenerational programs from the perspective of aging, children, and youth, multicultural education, and public policy. It gave an historical and current accounting of intergenerational programs and raised questions about their future. Articles written by professionals in diverse fields presented ideas on program development, evaluation, research, and the role of foundations in the growth of these programs.

1989: Project Linking Lifetimes

This multiple-foundation and multiple-year mentoring, research, and demonstration initiative was funded by the Florence Burden, Edna McConnell Clark, Ittleson, and Charles Stewart Mott foundations. Project Linking Lifetimes utilizes mentoring strategies to address specific problems of at-risk youth in selected inner-city communities in Atlanta, Georgia; Hartford, Connecticut; St. Petersburg, Florida; Miami, Florida; Los Angeles, California; Detroit, Michigan; Memphis, Tennessee; Portland, Oregon; Springfield, Massachusetts; Birmingham, Alabama; and Syracuse, New York. The project was coordinated by Temple University's Center for Intergenerational Learning, with research conducted by Lodestar Management Research.

1990: National and Community Service Act

This act created the Commission on National and Community Service to provide funds, training, and technical assistance to states and communities to develop and expand service opportunities. A key component of the legislation was the creation of national and community service programs that would engage individuals 17 years of age and over in service to the community. The Learn and Serve and Americorps programs were created to provide these opportunities for high school and college-age youth.

1990: Generations United Initiates Public Awareness Campaign

The Administration on Aging awarded a grant to Generations United to initiate an intergenerational child-care public awareness and dissemination campaign and to identify, select, and disseminate information on intergenerational child care. The project funded the preparation of a compendium that focused on selected programs involving older adults as volunteers in child care. The compendium included an annotated bibliography, a list of experts, and other resources related to intergenerational child care (Helfgott, 1992).

1990: Training Initiatives

Annual statewide training initiatives in Illinois, Massachusetts, New York, South Carolina, and Texas improved community awareness, communication, and information sharing among practitioners in intergenerational programs.

1990: Pennsylvania Commission

Governor Casey established a commission to address issues concerning the state's children and their families. The commission included representatives from the Department of Aging and from the state's intergenerational leadership. Recommendations from the commission included intergenerational approaches to problems affecting children and their families.

1990–1993: Fund for the Improvement of Post Secondary Education

Intergenerational community service grants were awarded to several universities as part of the Fund's Community Service Initiative. Examples of these projects include the University of Pittsburgh's "Intergenerational Community Service to Elderly Residents in Pittsburgh's Housing Communities" and Temple University's "Our Elders, Our Roots."

Generations Together and the University Challenge for Excellence program of the University of Pittsburgh coordinated the intergenerational community service project, which included first-year African American college students and senior citizens as colearners in a credit-bearing course on community service and aging. In addition to weekly classroom experiences, teams of youths and older adults provided weekly service to other high-rise residents.

Temple University's "Our Elders, Our Roots" project was sponsored by the Center for Intergenerational Learning. The project involved university students in translation, advocacy, and educational services to refugee, immigrant, and Native American elders in their community. Latino, Asian, Caribbean, Eastern European, and Native American university student participants in the project received academic credit or work-study stipends for their participation.

1991: National Community Service Act

Passage of this act authorized $73 million to promote the ethic of volunteer community services that include the participation of all ages in community volunteer experiences. In this context, 11 RSVP grants were awarded across the country to establish partnerships with local youth organizations. The grants funded projects that provided unique opportunities to solve problems using the special abilities of both older and younger populations.

1992: Rasmussen Foundation in South Carolina

The foundation funded a multiyear project to develop seven intergenerational programs across the state. The project was designed to meet the needs of at-risk children and youth and created an administrative and programmatic partnership among the United Way, the state's Department of Education and Aging, the Strom Thurmond Institute of Clemson University, and Generations Together of the University of Pittsburgh.

1992: American Association of Homes for the Aging

The American Association of Homes for the Aging, a nonprofit national association of nonprofit nursing homes, retirement communities, senior housing facilities, and community service organizations serving the elderly, promoted the development of intergenerational programs involving nursing home collaboration with local schools and child-care centers.

1992: Brookdale Grandparent Project

The Brookdale Foundation established this project to support programming and research efforts for projects that focus on grandparents as caregivers. Several funded initiatives included the establishment of the Brookdale Grandparent Caregiver Information Project at the University of California in Berkley, support for selected grandparent groups across the country, the establishment of the AARP grandparent information center, the creation of the Harlem Hospital Center Grandparent Program, and the Mount Sinai Medical Center Pediatric School Health program.

1992: Development of the National Mentor Corps Act of 1993

Senator David Pryor, chair of the Senate special committee on aging, convened a roundtable of intergenerational specialists to advise on the development of a mentoring bill—the National Mentor Corps Act of 1993 (Senate Bill 1007). This bill would have systematically linked schools and the aging networks such as RSVP, AARP, and the FGP. The bill was introduced in May 1993 and was integrated in part as an amendment to the 1994 Education 2000 Bill.

1993: First Annual National Intergenerational Training Institute

Generations Together of the University of Pittsburgh convened this institute, which was designed to increase the skills of practitioners, administrators, students, and academics working in the intergenerational field. The institute was the first formal university effort to standardize a knowledge base and performance of professionals working in intergenerational settings. It represents a major effort of Generations Together in promoting the development of the intergenerational field as a recognized human service specialty.

1993: Administration on Aging
and U.S. Department of Health and Human Services Grant

A grant was awarded to develop nine new intergenerational projects across the country. Technical assistance for these projects was conducted by Generations United, the National Council on the Aging, and Temple University's Center for Intergenerational Learning, with evaluation conducted by the University of Pittsburgh's Generations Together program. Projects focused on providing intergenerational experiences for at-risk older adults, children, and youth. Projects are located in Massachusetts, New York, North Carolina, Texas, Michigan, and Pennsylvania.

1993: Corporation on National and Community Service

This organization was formed as the result of the National Commission on Community Service Act. The Corporation awarded a grant to Generations United to identify and highlight opportunities for intergenerational community service. Generations United, the National Advocacy Agency for Intergenerational Programs, has created a database of information on intergenerational community service programs across the country, developed a practical "how to" resource guide for programmers, and identified service programs and specialists to provide technical assistance for program directors.

1993: National Recreation and Parks Association
Develops Intergenerational Projects

The Charles Stewart Mott Foundation awarded a multiyear grant to the National Recreation and Parks Association to develop intergenerational projects throughout their network. The project involved training, technical assistance, and product generation. Training and training assistance were provided by AARP, the University of Pittsburgh's Generations Together program, and Temple University's Center for Intergenerational Learning.

1994: Ohio Intergenerational Coalition Formed

This coalition was formed with funding from the Corporation on National and Community Service. The coalition represents a partnership between the governor's office and the Departments of Aging, Education, and Human Service. The coalition convenes conferences, provides training to leaders who train local programmers, has created a program development manual, and has produced a statewide inventory of intergenerational programs.

1995: White House Conference on Aging

At this conference, a set of intergenerational resolutions was adopted as part of the national agenda for older adults for the next decade. The resolutions included the following: (a) to promote older people as mentors in the preschool, K–12, and higher education public and private educational systems; (b) to involve older persons in the promotion of high-quality child care and early childhood and youth development programs; (c) to engage the productive and humanitarian potential of the older population to meet the human, educational, social, environment, health, and cultural needs of children; (d) to support policies that promote intergenerational programs; (e) to encourage older persons to use their power and influence to advocate for all children; (f) to develop public education campaigns to combat ageist stereotypes; (g) to promote intergenerational programs to strengthen the family unit in grandparent-headed households; and (h) to develop and fund ongoing public education campaigns that highlight the diverse roles and activities of older adults.

1995: AARP National Survey

This survey was initiated to determine the status of shared site projects in the United States. These projects provide resources and services to people of more than one generation and schedule intergenerational activities as a regular part of their programming. Typically these sites provide daytime care to preschool-age children and older adults who are frail and still live in their own domiciles.

1995: National Academy for Teaching and Learning About Age

The University of North Texas created this academy in collaboration with the Center for Understanding Aging.

1991–1996: Manuals and Handbooks

Intergenerational instructional materials in the 1990s have expanded to include a variety of print materials on basic and new intergenerational programs. These materials describe procedures for developing diverse types of intergenerational programs and information on accessing program related resources. Selected materials are available for generic and specific intergenerational program models. They are referenced in *Intergenerational Readings/Resources 1980–1994: A Bibliography of Books, Book Chapters, Journal Articles, Manuals, Papers/Reports/Studies, Curricula, Bibliographies, Directories, Newsletters, Data Bases, and Videos* (Wilson, 1994).

Examples of generic intergenerational program models are *Friendship Across the Ages* (Camp Fire Boys and Girls, 1992); *SPICE: Intergenerational Programs* (Camper, 1992); *Young and Old Together* (Seefeldt & Warman, 1990); *How to Organize and Manage Intergenerational Partnership Programs* (McDonald, 1990); *Getting Started Now: A Concise Guide to Developing Effective Intergenerational Programs* (Angelis, 1990); *Link Ages: Planning an Intergenerational Program for Preschool* (Griff et al., 1996); *Life Spectrum Programming Bringing Generations Together: A Library Guide to Supporting Community-Wide Intergenerational Programming* (Wood, 1992); *Let's Link Ages in Northern Virginia* (Northern Virginia Planning District, 1992); *Creating Intergenerational Coalitions* (Angelis, 1992a); and *Connecting the Generations* (AARP, 1994).

Examples of specific intergenerational program models are intergenerational community service (see Couch, 1993; Melcher, 1990), older workers in child care (see Everline & Schmitz, 1990; Ward, 1993), children and youth serving older adults (see Hegeman & Linsider, 1992; Stout, Boyd, & Volanty, 1993), school-based programs (see "Becoming a school partner," 1992; Kramer & Newman, 1986), mentoring (see Henkin, Perez-Randall, & Rogers, 1993; Tice, 1993), intergenerational service learning (see Laterza, 1995; Hammack, 1993), grandparenting (see Minkler & Roe, 1993), and child care in long-term settings (see Griff et al., 1996; Vujovich, 1987).

CONCLUSION

This chapter is divided into two sections; the first provides an historical overview of the individual components that are integral to the evolution of intergenerational programs, and the second provides a chronology of events that have influenced and that reflect the status of intergenerational programming since its inception in the late 1960s.

The first section highlights overall patterns of development and change in intergenerational programs, publications, networking, professionalism, and funding and gives the reader an awareness of each component's role in the history of this work. The second section shows the chronological relationship between the components and enables the reader to see how program development and its products may relate to funding, networking, and public policy and how the systematic and consistent expansion of intergenerational initiatives prepares for a new human service field.

The chapter chronicles the change in the focus of intergenerational programs from generational to societal. With this change came a significant increase in funding and legislative support. The relevance of intergenerational initiatives to compelling social problems has resulted in proposed legislation and more diverse large-scale funding commitments. Linked to this increase in support is the expansion of networks that promote and advocate for intergenerational initiatives. The history of local, state, and national networks is integrally connected to the funding and legislative history. As a critical mass of supporters and advocates is reached, there is often response from both the public policy and funding arenas. Illustrative of the effect of a critical mass is the passage of the Act for Better Child Care (ABC) legislation and subsequent funding opportunities for intergenerational child care. In advocating for this legislation, support groups at the local, state, and national levels spoke passionately on behalf of young children, families, and older adults.

The growth in types and numbers of intergenerational programs is concomitant with a need for the professionals charged with their implementation to be competent and successful. A call for competence and standards of performance has prompted discussions on alternatives for professionalizing an emerging intergenerational human service field. The next step in the evolution of the intergenerational field, therefore, will be the creation of intergenerational specialists who can assume a variety of roles and participate in all components integral to the field. A competent and diverse cadre of professionals are essential for the growth and evolution of the intergenerational field as it continues to address the needs of young and old in American society.

The overall impact of intergenerational programs nationally can be realized as public policy and funding are united in support of local, state, regional, and national program initiatives. These combined efforts will help to sustain the momentum of new programs and ensure the replication of established programs and will begin to address issues of institutionalizing an intergenerational approach to social problems directly affecting children, youth, and older adults. The information provided in this chapter can be used to motivate program development, increase program visibility, and promote public policy initiatives that support intergenerational program efforts.

The chronology of events and initiatives in intergenerational programs reveals a consistent overall growth in interest from local and national constituencies. This growth reinforces the need to maintain connections between the generations as Americans strive to reconnect their communities. These initiatives and their varied origins reflect the broad-based effort that has the potential for fostering major change in American society in order to contribute to the well-being of our most vulnerable populations, the young and the old.

5

Types and Models
of Intergenerational Programs

James M. McCrea, MPW, and Thomas B. Smith, MLS

Never doubt that a small group of thoughtful citizens can change the world. Indeed, it is the only thing that ever has.

—Margaret Mead

No overview of the contemporary intergenerational field would be complete without a discussion of the programs that operate within it. Perhaps uniquely in this field, programmatic initiatives have often outpaced the theoretical and policy groundwork for such programming, which is only beginning to catch up in the effort to explain and promote intergenerational benefits.

As noted elsewhere in this book, intergenerational programs have been started and operated by a wide variety of human-service agencies, and the programs address a wide variety of social concerns. Faced with the need to examine these programs in a systematic manner, professionals in the field largely agree that the most useful way to categorize them for purposes of discussion is to divide them into categories that represent the population being served. This chapter, then, discusses intergenerational programs as belonging to one of three major program types:

- older adults serving children or youth;
- children or youth serving older adults;
- children or youth and older adults serving others.

This useful organizational scheme does contain one possible area of confusion, which may require some clarification. Sorting programs according to the population served might appear to contradict one of the basic assumptions of the intergenerational field, which is that both older and younger age groups derive mutual benefits from their participation in such programs. Even accepting this basic defining characteristic, however, it is usually possible to examine an intergenerational program and determine a basic direction of service. Typically in such programs, members of one age group provide a service, and members of the other age group are recipients of that service. The positive intergenerational outcomes realized by the members of the providing age group might be seen as secondary, but to program designers they are no less important than those that accrue to the recipients.

Of course, as with any broad categorization scheme, there are intergenerational programs that do not fit easily into any of these three program types. These programs are best described as hybrids; that is, they combine elements of the main program types and offer equal levels of service to and from both participating age groups. Shared-site care facilities, for example, offer a service to both young children and older adults by providing an intergenerational caregiving environment for both age groups. Similar characteristics are shared by programs such as those that provide shared housing situations for youth and older adults. In these programs, designed and managed by a third-party individual or agency, each age group receives equal benefits and the program is designed to serve both.

The vast majority of intergenerational programs, however, fall more or less easily into one of the three basic types. In the sections that follow, an overview of each type is provided, with descriptions and details. At the end of each program type section, a summary of the information is presented in chart form to enable quick comparisons within and between program types.

OLDER ADULTS SERVING CHILDREN AND YOUTH

When older adults share their time, skills, and experiences with children and youth, they become a valuable resource to the school, teacher, parent, student, and community. Programs that utilize older adults as resources are typically found in communities and school classrooms from kindergarten through college. The role that an older adult may play includes mentor, tutor, caregiver or nurturer, mature friend, or coach; in all cases they serve as positive role models. The following sections illustrate some of the most common models (see Table 1).

Mentors

Professor Uri Bronfenbrenner of Cornell University, after consulting with Japanese scholars about similar relationships in their culture, described mentoring as a one-to-one relationship, developmental in nature, between a pair of unrelated individuals, usually of different ages. "A mentor is an older, more experienced person who seeks to further the development of character and competence in a younger person" (Freedman, 1993, p. 31). Interactions may take many forms, including demonstration, instruction, challenge, and encouragement "on a more or less regular basis over an extended period of time" (Freedman, 1993, p. 31). Furthermore, this relationship is distinguished by "a special bond of mutual commitment" and "an emotional character of respect, loyalty, and identification" (Freedman, 1993, p. 31).

Programs in which older adults serve as mentors to children and youth are characterized by the type of relationship developed between the mentor and mentee. In mentoring programs, older adults may become tutors, counselors, and support persons for youth. In addition, they become their friend, advocate, and motivator. Participants include older adults who may or may not be retired. Often they share a common interest with the young person such as a specific academic subject or a hobby. The youth can be of any age, up to and including college students. Intergenerational mentoring programs may be school based or community based, depending on the agency that is conducting the program.

Table 1 Older adults serving children or youth

Model	Amount of training required	Level of formal education required	Duration of interaction	Type of contact	Paid or volunteer	Level of interpersonal commitment required
Mentors	High	Medium	1–2 hr per week	1 on 1	Both	Very high
Tutors	Medium	Medium	1–2 hr per week	1 on 1 or group	Both	High
Caregivers or nurturers	Medium	Low to medium	1–2 hr per week to full-time	1 on 1 or group	Both	High
Mature friends	Medium	Low to medium	1–4 hr per week	1 on 1	Both	Low to high
Coaches	High	High	5–10 hr per week	1 on 1 or group	Both	High

Mentoring programs are often jointly operated by a school and a community agency and conduct activities at both locations. Program activities are varied and often have a major focus such as improving academic skills or enhancing the self-esteem of a particular group of young people. For example, mentoring programs for fourth- or fifth-grade students may focus on improving math or reading skills as a vehicle to help students improve their self-image and feelings of being successful. High school mentoring programs may focus on helping students succeed in academic, vocational, or problem-solving courses that enable them to recognize their readiness for the workplace. Mentoring programs typically include social experiences that bond the young person with the older mentor, resulting in the building of confidence and trust. Other activities may include tutoring, field trips, after-school recreation, sporting events, or dining out.

Mentoring programs require, as a minimum, a coordinator from either the school or community agency, who performs necessary functions such as recruitment of mentors and training, evaluation, and support of participants. Outcomes for youth include improved academic achievement, increased motivation to learn, enhanced self-esteem and self-image, broadened career awareness, and exposure to the knowledge, skills, life experiences, and culture of older persons. For the older adults, outcomes include improved life satisfaction, the creation of new, useful, and respected roles, and the opportunity to share life experiences with and transfer skills to the younger generation.

Tutors

Unlike mentoring models, tutoring programs involve older adults in roles specifically designed to improve the learning of young people in one or more academic areas. This academic focus, however, does not necessitate the type of bonding and personal commitment that is characteristic of mentoring programs. Older adults who participate in intergenerational tutoring programs often have an interest or experience in the academic subject. Youth participants can be of any age from preschoolers to college students. Tutoring activities may take place at the school or in a community agency. Some intergenerational tutoring programs involve one-on-one instruction in the young person's home.

Tutoring activities vary widely and are determined by the subject area. For example, a literacy tutoring program may include reading aloud, practicing pronunciation, using or creating word games, or helping with homework, whereas a math tutoring program may involve using flash cards, practicing long division, or memorizing algebraic formulas. The common denominator among activities is that tutoring programs usually involve individual or small-group interaction and focus on learning content. Some programs include social or recreational activities to help foster relationships between the participants.

The same staffing needs required in mentoring programs apply to tutoring programs. At a minimum, a coordinator is required to operate and maintain the program. The outcomes of tutoring programs for youth are the same as in mentoring programs, with an emphasis on academic enhancement. For older adults, the outcomes are also similar to those of mentoring programs: improved life satisfaction, increased feelings of usefulness, and the opportunity to share life experiences with youth, to transfer their skills, and to acquire new skills.

Caregivers and Nurturers

Many intergenerational programs are designed to provide care of one sort or another for children whose needs are not being satisfactorily met by existing social mechanisms. Most of these programs take advantage of existing child-care systems, which offer a clearly defined nurturing role at a specific location. To implement such a program, a child-care center may develop a plan for recruiting and training older adult classroom volunteers. In other cases, the recruiting and training is performed by an outside agency, which places volunteers at convenient child-care sites. This volunteer model has also been adapted to provide job training and placement for older adults within the early childhood field.

Non-child-care models also exist, although they are less common. Premature infants and "crack babies" in hospital maternity wards, for example, benefit from the presence of older adult nurturers. Also, children with special needs may benefit from the regular home visits of an older adult who has been trained to provide short-term care or simply some extra attention. Older adult nurturing, in fact, can be of value to children in almost any setting.

Child-care models usually accommodate children from birth through about 12 years of age, and older adults provide care throughout this age span. Caregiving or nurturing intergenerational programs typically involve healthy, mobile older adults, although many programs do involve less high-functioning caregivers in nurturing roles.

The wide variety of caregiving intergenerational programs is reflected in the diversity of the settings in which such activities may take place. Child-care centers and schools are typical sites for older adult nurturers to deliver their service, but such caregivers can also be found in hospitals, clinics, family support centers, libraries, and sometimes the children's homes.

Older adult caregivers in early childhood programs often function as auxiliary staff members (or as paid employees), providing the kind of basic daily care that children in such settings require. Volunteers with special talents may lead activities that reflect their particular interests or skills (e.g., cooking, art projects, games). Older adults may also be assigned to provide special attention to specific children, whose needs for extra nurturing are difficult to meet under normal child-care staffing conditions. Caregiving for older children is often combined with other functions described elsewhere, such as mentoring and telephone reassurance, and takes place in schools or at extended-day-care sites.

Intergenerational caregiving programs may be initiated by schools, child-care organizations, religious groups, or senior-care agencies of any sort. An intergenerational caregiving or nurturing project is usually tailored to the needs of a particular sponsoring agency (e.g., a volunteer recruitment and training program operated by a child-care center for its own classrooms), although a successful program may grow to include other, similar agencies. Many such programs, regardless of the agency with which they originate, involve close collaboration between two very different organizations (e.g., a library and a senior center or a child-care agency and a senior employment program).

In such cases, both partner agencies may contribute staff time to the intergenerational effort. The staffing needs vary from program to program, but all types of intergenerational caregiving programs require at least the presence of an administrator or coordinator. These programs also require a training component, especially for the older adult participants. If the project leader is not also skilled in designing and implementing appropriate training for the participants, a trainer will be necessary for at least part of the program.

Intergenerational caregiving programs yield a variety of positive outcomes to all of their participants. Older adult volunteers benefit from a sense of being needed and appreciated, by both the children they nurture and the staff they support. They acquire a new role, vital to their community and helpful in meeting their own developmental needs. Older adult employees benefit additionally from the economic support provided by a steady job. The staff members of participating agencies—librarians, child-care providers, hospital nurses, waiting room receptionists—benefit from the presence of an extra set of hands and from the special skills and perspective that many older adults possess. The children in these programs profit as well from these factors, of course. They also learn about aging, becoming better prepared to cope with the aging of their grandparents and their parents and with their own eventual aging.

Mature Friends

Programs that utilize older adults as support persons for nonrelated young people fall under the broad definition of mature friends. Examples may include telephone reassurance programs, latchkey programs, or family or child support programs. Participants are most often young children up to high school age and older adults. These types of programs are typically home-based programs, although the systems representing the young people are often schools. In telephone reassurance and latchkey programs, there may not be any physical contact between the participants. Older adults may phone the children on a regular basis such as daily or weekly to provide academic or social support. In some programs, the child initiates the call to the elder when assistance is needed or when he or she just wants someone to talk to. Sometimes the participants may meet each other at an end-of-the-year recognition event.

In family or child support programs, the participants meet on a regular basis, usually in the young person's home. The older adult provides support and companionship to children or their parents. They may read stories, play games, or share hobbies or household tasks. They may also provide information or other assistance, such as accompanying a parent to a medical appointment. In addition to schools, the systems involved may include a child-care center, hospital, or community agency. Staffing needs are determined by the scope and size of the program. In all programs, a coordinator is required who can recruit older adults, provide training, match participants, and provide ongoing training and support.

Outcomes for mature friends programs include decreased feelings of isolation and heightened feelings of security for youth at home alone; increased support for children, youth, and their families; and the establishment of connections with older adults. For the elders, outcomes include improved life satisfaction, increased feelings of usefulness and self-worth, and the establishment of connections with youth.

Coaches

Some intergenerational programs are designed to provide children with coaching by older adults. Although the coaching function contains elements of both mentoring and tutoring, it has certain characteristics that make it a unique activity. This model focuses on the development of a particular skill or talent, possessed by the older adult and being learned by the child. Coaches support learning and skill development in sports and games such as swimming, soccer, tennis, and chess. They are also found in visual and performing arts such as dance, drama, painting, music, and photography.

The coaching relationship involves one-to-one interaction and extends over time as the pupil moves to higher levels of skill and performance. This involvement extends beyond the school setting to a sports field, artist's studio, theater, concert hall, or community center.

The participants in coaching programs, then, include accomplished older adults who are capable of teaching their skills to members of younger generations. The pupils are interested in developing these skills and talented enough to benefit from an intensive coaching relationship. Such coaching programs may be sponsored by schools; they may also originate with the older adult coaches themselves. Coaches in organized programs may volunteer their time; individuals are likely to be in the business of coaching and expect a fee for their services. Young participants may take advantage of school-based facilities (e.g., athletic equipment, musical instruments, or art materials), visit the older adult in his or her studio, or be visited themselves in their own homes.

The activities involved in coaching depend heavily on the coach's personal instructional style, although the term does imply the coach's use of observation and feedback as an instructional method. Students typically learn, practice, demonstrate, receive a critique and more instruction, and the cycle begins again. Most coaches develop a unique mixture of instruction, support, and criticism that matches their own personalities and styles. Students may work with many coaches, in fact, before finding someone whose teaching methodology matches their own learning style.

Intergenerational coaching programs with only a few participants may require no staffing beyond the coaches themselves. There are large programs, however, that utilize an administrative staff to recruit participants, match coaches and students, and possibly collect fees.

Older adults usually become coaches because of the opportunity it offers to continue an activity that is extremely meaningful to them but in which they can no longer participate at a competition or performance level. Coaching also provides an opportunity for older adults to share their achievements and their passion for their life's work with equally passionate young people. The pupils benefit from that passion, which is transmitted along with the skills they are developing.

CHILDREN AND YOUTH SERVING OLDER ADULTS

Programs in which children and youth serve as resources to older adults often focus on elders who are frail and in need of some level of assistance or support with daily living. These include programs in which children and youth visit older adults in their homes or institutions. However, some programs that are traditionally defined as "youth serving elders" programs involve children and youth interacting with well elders. These programs are often focused on learning, either young people learning from older adults or older adults learning from young people. The following sections illustrate some of the most common programs in which youth serve older adults (see Table 2).

Visitors

Programs in which young people visit with frail older adults can take many forms. They may be friendly visiting programs in which children and youth visit frail elderly and engage in social activities. Visiting programs may also involve visiting activities

Table 2 Children or youth serving older adults

Model	Amount of training required	Level of formal education required	Duration of interaction	Type of contact	Paid or volunteer	Level of interpersonal commitment required
Visitors	Low	Low	1–2 hr per week	1 on 1 or group	Volunteer	Moderate to high
Companions or helpers	Medium to high	Medium to high	1–4 hr per week	1 on 1, pairs, or group	Volunteer	Moderate to high
Teachers	Medium to high	Medium to high	1–2 hr per week	1 on 1 or group	Volunteer	Moderate to high

that are not face to face but rather involve telephone contact such as telephone reassurance programs, contact through the mail such as pen-pal programs, or over the Internet through E-mail programs. Visiting programs typically involve children and youth of all ages from preschoolers to college students, visiting for one or more hours. Sites include individual homes and institutions, such as nursing homes, personal care homes, and adult day-care centers.

In institutionalized settings, participants may engage in structured group activities or visit one-on-one with residents. Group activities may consist of games, exercise programs, reading aloud, discussions, arts and crafts, music, taking walks, dining out, attending shows or sporting events, or watching videos. One-on-one activities may include talking, reading or writing letters, games, or watching television.

In home visiting, young people may visit alone or in pairs. Activities may include all of the above, and because the elders are not as frail as those in institutions, the duration of the activities is often extended. Telephone visiting, pen-pal, and E-mail programs typically involve young people calling or writing to elderly persons on a regular (daily or weekly) basis to see how they are doing, to talk, and to share experiences. Participants may or may not meet each other face to face, depending on the structure and intent of the program.

The systems involved in a visiting program include an agency representing the young people, such as a school or youth group, and an agency representing the older people, such as a long-term care facility. Other systems may include senior centers or senior citizen high-rise apartments or housing agencies for pen-pal programs, governmental aging agencies or other nonprofit aging agencies for telephone visiting, or referral agencies such as a visiting nurse association for home visiting programs. Staffing is required in all visiting programs. A coordinator is needed to recruit volunteers, conduct training and orientation, and match volunteers with the elderly. This role is often assumed by a teacher or an activities coordinator at an aging facility.

Visiting programs result in positive outcomes for youth and older adults. Outcomes for youth include increased self-esteem, development of a commitment to community service, friendship with an older person, feelings of being needed and of empowerment, better community connections, and knowledge about culture, history, aging, and survival. For older adults, outcomes include increased self-esteem, less fear and isolation, friendship and companionship with a young person, opportunities to share life experiences and culture, and improved life satisfaction.

Companions or Helpers

Related to visiting programs but having a different focus, programs in which young people serve as companions or helpers are geared toward providing care for older adults or assisting them with activities of daily living. Examples of this type of model include hospice and respite care programs, chore service programs, escort programs, and physical activity or rehabilitation programs. Because the level of sophistication or skill required of a volunteer in these programs is high, the young participants will often be middle school, high school, or college students. Sitting with a dying older adult or one who suffers from dementia, driving an older adult to the doctor's office, cleaning a frail elderly person's house, or repairing a broken screen for a home-bound elder all require a more mature young person.

When intergenerational service is combined with academic classroom experiences, referred to as *service learning*, the added educational component results in increased meaning for the young person. Service learning is integrated into the academic curriculum and extends learning beyond the classroom and into the community. It provides young people with opportunities to use newly acquired academic skills and knowledge in real-life situations and provides structured reflection time for students to think, talk, and write about what they did and saw in the community. One example is an oral history program in which students interview older adults about local or national historical events and then produce a report, booklet, film, or audiotape to be shared with others. Another example is a college field placement in which a student of gerontology, physical therapy, social work, nursing, or other discipline learns through directly serving older adults. Service learning requires careful planning on the part of the teacher and partnering agency, training and preparation for students and older adults, reflection, and celebration.

Companion and helping programs can take place in institutions or individual homes. For example, young people who serve as companions to terminally ill older adults will often visit them at a hospice. Respite care programs, in which a young person gives a needed break to family members who are caring for someone with Alzheimer's disease, will involve visits in the home. Escort and chore programs are conducted to and from or at an individual's home. A student studying physical therapy may assist a therapist at a nursing or rehabilitation center or on a home visit.

Activities in these programs are determined by the specific type of program. Some of the social activities listed above in the friendly visiting programs apply naturally to hospice or respite care programs. Chore service activities may include cleaning, washing and ironing clothes, cooking, light repairs, and errands. Escort activities include trips to the doctor, dentist, pharmacy, food store, or to friends' houses to visit. The systems involved are similar to those in visiting programs. Schools, universities, aging facilities or agencies, referral agencies, and governmental agencies may be involved. The staffing needs are also identical.

Outcomes for companion or helper programs are also similar to visiting programs. For young people, there are learning outcomes if the program has an academic component. For example, if a vocational-technical class did home repairs for community elders, the students' classroom learning would be enhanced by the community service. The same holds true for physical and occupational therapy students who practice techniques through service to older adults. For older adults, tangible benefits to home, life, and health are apparent, as well as the intangible benefits identified above for the visiting programs.

Teachers

In some intergenerational programs, the role that the young person assumes is that of a teacher or presenter of information or skills. Examples include intergenerational computer projects in which youth teach older adults how to operate a computer, literacy programs in which youth teach or tutor older adults on how to read,

English classes in which youth teach immigrants how to speak English, or income tax programs in which youth teach elders how to file their income tax returns. Youth participants are usually middle school through college age, and older adult participants may be anyone with an interest in learning. Although learning activities may take place at a school setting, the typical site for these programs are places where older adults congregate, such as senior centers, community agencies, retirement communities, or senior apartment complexes. Activities are always hands-on and interactive. For example, a young person and an older person may sit side by side at a computer terminal learning the keyboard, youth and elders may practice English by reading to each other, or an accounting major may guide an older adult through a computer program for taxes. Participating systems include schools, colleges (including community colleges), senior centers, housing agencies, and community agencies. Intergenerational teaching programs will often involve a classroom teacher as a coordinator; however, in community-based projects a community representative may assume coordination responsibilities. Outcomes for youth include improved learning, appreciation of the value of lifelong learning, increased self-esteem, and improvement in teaching and presentation skills. For older adults, outcomes include increased learning, contact with youth, improved life satisfaction, and cognitive stimulation.

CHILDREN, YOUTH, AND OLDER ADULTS SERVING TOGETHER

Programs in which children, youth, and older adults join together to serve others significantly broaden the scope and type of programs that can be defined as intergenerational and expose the participants to the traditional benefits derived from intergenerational programs. Any nonintergenerational program can be made intergenerational by teaming elders and youth together as the service providers. For example, when a group of high school students volunteer at a homeless shelter for young women, it is not an intergenerational program and therefore the benefits, such as those of forming interpersonal relationships with an older person, and of exposure to the life experiences, skills, and culture of older adults, cannot be realized. However, if a group of older adults join with the high school students to provide the service, then all of the benefits of intergenerational programs can be attained. In addition to the benefits realized when one age group serves another, there are unique benefits that result from the act of older and younger generations volunteering together. Often a special relationship will develop between team members that is not unlike a mentoring relationship. This relationship adds to and enhances the service being performed. The result is an intergenerational partnership that not only affects the youths and the older adults but also extends beyond the team to the community at large. "Together, young and old participants serve as change agents to build a better community; participate in opportunities that focus on their strengths, and that identify them as community assets; serve as both learners and teachers; gain awareness of the value of service and the need to take responsibility for their problems; and, increase their skills, confidence, knowledge, and contributions" (Scannell & Roberts, 1994, p. 5).

Certain types of projects lend themselves particularly to models in which elders

Table 3 Children or youth and older adults serving others

Model	Level of training required	Level of formal education required	Duration of interaction	Type of contact	Paid or volunteer	Level of interpersonal commitment required
Civic beautification	Low	Low	1–2 hr per week	Group	Both	Low
Community planning	Medium	Medium	2–4 hr per week	Group	Volunteer	High
Visitors	Low	Low	1–2 hr per week	Pairs or groups	Volunteer	Moderate to high
Advocacy	Medium	Medium	1–2 hr per week	Group	Volunteer	High

and youth serve together. The following sections illustrate some of the more common models (see Table 3).

Civic Beautification

This type of intergenerational program model focuses on teams of youths and older adults participating in projects that are hands-on, usually conducted outdoors, and result in physical improvements to a community. Examples include intergenerational gardening projects in which the teams plant flowers, shrubs, vegetables, or trees; recycling programs in which teams collect bottles, paper, cans, and so forth from throughout the community; trash pick-up projects in which teams clean vacant lots or highways; and outdoor conservation projects in which teams reclaim forests, build playgrounds, and convert unused railways to jogging and hiking trails. All ages of individuals can participate, usually on a volunteer basis. However, many states have structured conservation corps in which the youths and adults are paid, full-time employees.

As noted above, this type of intergenerational project usually takes place outside. In some projects, however, teams of older adults and youth may collaborate on a gardening project, for example, that takes place in the atrium of a long-term care or other facility serving frail elderly or children. The systems involved may include schools, colleges, senior centers, housing and community agencies, corporations, conservancy organizations, and nurseries, as well as governmental agencies.

The staffing needs of intergenerational civic beautification programs vary according to the nature of the project. For example, a state-sponsored conservation corps project requires several levels of staff from crew leaders to people skilled in trades, whereas a small gardening project may only require a coordinator to recruit, orient, and match team members and purchase plants and supplies. The resulting outcomes of these programs for youth and older adults, in addition to those listed above, include the development of a sense of community responsibility and citizenship. The community at large, as well as individual community members who enjoy or utilize the results of these programs, also benefit from a more beautiful, cleaner, and resource-friendly environment.

Community Planning

A common model for older adults and young people working together involves tasks related to community planning and improvement. In such programs, older adults and young people typically form committees and task forces to identify neighborhood and community problems, collect data, develop potential solutions, and advocate for the implementation of their recommendations. The power of these projects grows out of the collaboration between the age groups, who, in the process of reaching a consensus, become familiar with issues specific to each age group as well as with larger issues facing the entire community.

The older adults who participate in community planning projects are often retired from careers in civil service, politics, and fields requiring expertise in public service. They are joined by other older adults, recruited from senior centers and residences, whose stake in the life of their community is more personal. The interests of the younger participants also usually reflect a concern with civil engineering or human service; in fact, they are often enrolled in service learning courses in these areas.

The community task forces of older adults and young people meet regularly at a convenient location, perhaps a room at a school or a sponsoring agency. Much of the activity, however, takes place in areas where the necessary resources are available: libraries, government buildings, computer centers. Activities include the gathering of information related to the status of the community, which may involve interviewing residents and experts as well as library research. This data is shared with other members of the planning team, which uses it to identify the needs of the community and propose solutions. Through further research, the solutions are rethought and refined, until a concrete proposal is developed on which all participants can agree.

Such programs require very little external support, although the involvement of sponsoring systems such as schools or government agencies may be helpful in locating meeting space, accessing resources, and establishing contact with other community members. Likewise, community planning programs may require no staffing beyond the efforts of the participants themselves, although coordinators and advocates within supporting systems can be quite valuable.

The primary outcomes of community planning programs may be the actual adoption and implementation of recommendations made by the intergenerational task force. As noted, such recommendations are particularly forceful, coming as they do from a united team of community members representing the entire age span. Other outcomes relate to the benefits received by the individual participants. Older adults may learn research skills; young people learn the value of communication and consensus building. Members of both age groups are empowered by the experience of tackling and solving important real-world problems.

Visitors

Programs in which teams of young people and older adults visit with frail elderly are somewhat similar to those described above involving young people by themselves visiting frail elderly. The difference is that there is a special synergy that develops between the team members when they are serving someone together. A relationship may develop between the youth and the older team member that realizes some of the same benefits and outcomes apparent in some mentoring programs. The frail elder with whom the team visits benefits from this synergy and enjoys the attention of two individuals instead of only one. Visiting in teams also has advantages inherent in the approach, such as the ease of conversation with three instead of two people, more ideas for activities, the ability to support each other (thereby reducing the fear or hesitation possible if one were visiting alone), and the opportunity to process the experience together.

Team visiting programs need not be limited to visiting frail elderly. Other examples include visits to hospitals, homeless shelters, AIDS patients, and institutions serving children with special needs.

Advocacy

Intergenerational advocacy programs are closely related in structure to the community planning programs described elsewhere. They involve teams of older adults and young people who identify worthwhile causes and engage in activities designed to promote desirable outcomes. Such projects focus on a particular local or national issue that is related to the needs of one or both of the participating age groups. Examples of local issues include support for recreation facilities or senior services; national issues include policies related to education or health care.

The older and younger participants in intergenerational advocacy projects are usually individuals who are highly committed to a particular cause. Program sites may range from participants' homes to community centers, political headquarters, or agency offices. The activities include data collection, preparation and distribution of publicity materials, media contacts, lobbying, and testifying at governmental hearings. These activities are usually coordinated by a director or administrator, who may be on the staff of a local politician, an advocacy group, or some other public or private organization. As with community planning, the outcomes of these projects reach beyond the issues being advocated, empowering the participants and helping them learn to work with members of other generations.

CONCLUSION

The program examples presented in this chapter offer a glimpse of the creativity and diversity that has characterized the development of intergenerational programs. Although an effort was made to describe models that are clear examples of the four categories, it may be true that there is really no such thing. As it exists in the 1990s, *intergenerational* is a word that does not describe pure models. Rather, it represents a concept, or an approach, that can be woven into almost any human service initiative. The concept gains much of its power and value, in fact, from this particular characteristic; by transforming traditional human service models into intergenerational programs, practitioners can increase the benefits for all of their participants.

6

Program Profiles

James M. McCrea, MPW, and Thomas B. Smith, MLS

*When you retire you are cut off from every thing you did: The children
brought me back to a new vitality.*

—Henry Anderson

Even within the organizational scheme presented and used in chapter 5, intergenerational programs retain a uniqueness and diversity that makes generalizations difficult. In this chapter, individual intergenerational program models are examined in greater detail. These case studies reveal the variety of origins, participating agencies, and methods by which such programs achieve similar human service goals.

The chapter is organized according to the categories introduced in chapter 5:

- older adults serving children and youth;
- children and youth serving older adults; and
- children, youth, and older adults serving together.

At the end of the chapter, an example of a hybrid program is presented. As noted in chapter 5, this is not really a separate category; rather, it contains those programs that cannot be precisely defined in terms of the age group they are designed to primarily serve. As can be seen in the example that was selected, such models provide opportunities for members of both participating age groups to serve and receive service, combining characteristics of the three most common program types.

From the many excellent intergenerational program models that represent each of the three primary categories, two were selected and profiled. The criteria applied when making the selections were somewhat arbitrary, although an attempt was made to identify program models that typify each category of program types as well as to illustrate the variations that exist within the categories. An additional attempt was made to select program models from locations across the United States, helping to make the point that intergenerational programming is possible to implement in almost any culture or geographic area.

To present as realistic a picture as possible of the current state of intergenerational programming, the case studies contain information about each program's struggles as well as its successes, the stumbling blocks as well as the positive outcomes. To further ensure that the program models selected will be of practical use to readers of this chapter, selection criteria included the existence of additional documentation, usually prepared by the leaders of each model, that is easily available to intergenerational programmers who wish to develop similar models. This documentation, as well as appropriate contact information, can be located through the lists of resources in the appendix to this book.

OLDER ADULTS SERVING CHILDREN AND YOUTH

The Senior Citizen School Volunteer Program

Since the early 1960s, the introduction of volunteers in schools has been accepted for kindergarten through the 12th grade within the United States. Traditionally, these volunteers have represented the parent generation. Rarely were older persons a part of these programs, although, historically, the role of the elderly was an integral part of the structure of the family. The Senior Citizen School Volunteer Program (SCSVP) is a modern extension of this historic role (Kramer & Newman, 1986, p. 1).

SCSVP was created by Generations Together at the University of Pittsburgh in 1978. Since then the program has been established in over 100 schools, primarily in western Pennsylvania. SCSVP has been recognized by the Pennsylvania Department of Education as an exemplary program and has received national awards from the National School Volunteer Program for recognition of its quality work in developing intergenerational school volunteer programs.

The goals of SCSVP reflect the values generally inherent in intergenerational programs. They are

- to expand opportunities for intergenerational exchange;
- to provide opportunities for older persons to become directly involved in promoting aging awareness among students;
- to utilize the experiences and skills of older persons;
- to involve senior citizens in the education of students;
- to enhance the growth and learning of students;
- to stimulate mutual interest and support among the school, students, and people from the community; and
- to strengthen the link between the school and the community (Kramer & Newman, 1986, p. 4).

The senior citizens who volunteer in the program are over the age of 55 and come from diverse socioeconomic and racial backgrounds. As volunteers, they give half a day per week to work with a variety of kindergarten through 12th graders, including special needs students. They serve as tutors, teacher's helpers, listeners, career models, oral historians, resource people, artists, and crafts people. Volunteers reinforce students' basic skills, share lifelong skills and experiences, and help students achieve academically and socially by providing support and enrichment.

Implementation of the SCSVP program involves a team effort. Team members typically include school administrators, teachers, parents, the Generations Together coordinator, and a school liaison. The sequence of activities required to ensure success are gaining school approval, recruitment of teachers and volunteers, orientation, training, placement, program maintenance, and evaluation.

Gaining school approval. Although approval to implement a program varies from school district to school district, SCSVP recommends that endorsement by the super-intendent and board be sought. This endorsement helps coordinators by providing additional support, funding, recruitment assistance, and problem solving. At a mini-mum, however, the support and endorsement of the school principal is essential.

Recruitment of teachers and volunteers. The success of this program is directly related to the level of support and commitment given it by the involved teachers. After expressing an interest, teachers participate in planning and implementation. They also provide continual support and guidance to the volunteers.

The challenging task of recruiting volunteers consists of developing community awareness of the program; producing and distributing publicity documents such as brochures, flyers, and news releases; contacting the media; making presentations to community groups; and contacting and inviting prospective volunteers to an infor-mational open house at the school.

Orientation. The open house serves as the initial orientation to the program for potential volunteers. It is designed to present all of the information necessary for the person to be motivated to sign up as a volunteer. It includes basic program informa-tion, describes the volunteer's role, presents the benefits of participation, and con-cludes with a tour of the school. Finally, it gives volunteers an opportunity to get answers to any questions or concerns that they may have.

Training. Training is conducted at the school and consists of four 2-hr work-shops. The first session is for teachers. It includes program information on the goals and the roles and responsibilities of teachers. In addition, the workshop explores past experiences that teachers may have had in working with volunteers, their per-ceptions of older people, and the role of the senior citizen volunteer.

The second 2-hr workshop is for volunteers. This workshop provides volunteers with information on the program, reviews school procedures for volunteers, dis-cusses their role, presents guidelines for them to follow in their interactions with the students, and presents an overview of the developmental needs and characteristics of children in grades K–12.

The third and fourth workshops involve the teachers and volunteers together. At the third workshop, teachers and volunteers become acquainted by interview-ing each other about their backgrounds, interests, hobbies, travels, and skills. This process facilitates matching between a teacher and a volunteer based on common interests and skills and encourages the teachers to prepare classroom activities that utilize the volunteer's background. Finally, volunteers are instructed on the develop-mental and behavioral procedures for observing a classroom and are scheduled for an observation.

The fourth workshop is scheduled after the volunteers have completed their class-room observations. Volunteers have an opportunity to report on their experience and discuss questions or concerns. This is followed by an exploration of the curricular materials and a discussion on effective ways to work with students.

Placement. The fourth workshop ends with the completion of forms by teachers and volunteers that result in the matching and scheduling of teacher–volunteer teams. The forms ask about availability of volunteers (i.e., day and time) and whether either the teacher or volunteer has a preference regarding a particular partner or, in the case of the volunteer, a subject area or grade level. The project coordinator and principal review the forms, identify the teacher–volunteer teams, and determine the schedules.

Program maintenance. Maintaining the SCSVP program involves conducting follow-up meetings for teachers and volunteers, providing opportunities for continuation workshops, and recognizing the volunteers for their dedication and service.

Follow-up meetings are typically held separately for teachers and volunteers. This promotes free discussion among peers and facilitates problem solving. Two-hour continuation workshops are held at least once per year. They include teachers and volunteers and may focus on specific classroom activities, ways to expand the volunteer's role, concerns or problems, skill development for volunteers, or special events that utilize the volunteers' background, such as an ethnic fair or hobby day. The workshop is a collaborative effort between the coordinator, principal, and school liaison.

Recognition of volunteers is provided by administrators, teachers, students, and parents on a continual basis and at special events. The recognition of volunteers in the SCSVP program helps to reinforce the volunteers' interest in continuing their participation in the program.

Evaluation. SCSVP conducts a yearly evaluation as a regular, ongoing component of the program. The evaluation objectives are

- to assess the degree to which the program's goals and objectives are being realized;
- to identify the strengths and weaknesses of the program;
- to measure the effectiveness of the program;
- to assess the impact of the program;
- to gain school and community support for the program;
- to help plan future program activities and direction;
- to develop credibility for the program;
- to secure funding for the program;
- to develop a profile of the participants in the program;
- to generate recommendations for improving the program; and
- to acquire program information for dissemination (Kramer & Newman, 1986, p. 65).

SCSVP has collected data on the impact of the program since its inception. The following are outcomes of the program (Newman & Larimer, 1995, pp. 1–2).

- The three most common roles performed by older volunteers in the classroom were tutoring, assisting students with special projects, and providing enrichment.
- More than 99% of teachers reported that their students reacted positively to the volunteers.
- Teachers reported that volunteers had a positive impact on students' growth in reading, mathematics, spelling, handwriting, communication skills, grammar or English and language, and creative writing.
- Teachers reported that the volunteers had a positive impact on students' self-esteem, attitude toward older persons, understanding of aging, behavior toward others, and social growth.

- Seventy-three percent of the volunteers reported positive changes in their attitudes toward public schools.
- Fifty-six percent of the volunteers reported improved attitudes toward youth.
- Volunteers reported a positive impact on their well-being, including their interest in children's education, feelings of being needed, and satisfaction with life.
- Forty-seven percent of the teachers reported improved attitudes toward older persons.
- Fifty-two percent of the teachers reported improved attitudes toward their own aging.

Care Castle

Throughout the 1980s, families in Colorado Springs, Colorado, were no different from other families across the country. They experienced unprecedented economic and social pressure, the number of working parents expanded, and the need for quality child care was rapidly increasing. In 1988, Pikes Peak Seniors, Inc., in search of a worthy community service project, identified this growing need and recognized a match with their organizational mission to promote the value of older adults as important, contributing members of the community. After carefully researching the possibilities, the group created Care Castle, a not-for-profit intergenerational child-care program.

The rationale for this group's participation in the business of running a child-care program is contained in the introduction to Care Castle's senior volunteer manual, *The Grand Connection* (Care Castle, in press). It speaks to the critical needs of young, growing children, the valuable contributions that older adults can make in the lives of these children, and the responsibility for leadership borne by the oldest generation. The center is funded through tuition, although its income is supplemented by grants, fund raisers, and other contributions. These supplemental income sources enable Care Castle to offer a sliding fee scale according to family income, providing affordable quality child-care that is unique to the Colorado Springs area. Forty-five percent of the center's families receive some degree of tuition assistance. Minority families make up about 20% of the Care Castle clientele, a reasonable reflection of the larger community's composition.

The program consists of two linked components: a professionally operated child-care center and a senior volunteer training and placement program. The child-care center provides developmentally appropriate care for 72 children, from infancy through age 5. Each classroom at Care Castle is staffed by a lead teacher and an early childhood assistant, who strive to provide activities that promote the children's social, emotional, and cognitive growth and development. These caregiving staff members are also carefully oriented to the center's intergenerational philosophy and must demonstrate a commitment to the value and presence of older adults in their program. The older adult presence is primarily in the form of 50–75 senior volunteers, whose participation enables the center to maintain the high adult–child ratios that are known to be indicators of high-quality service. The senior volunteer program at Care Castle represents a highly organized approach to the problem of recruiting, training, and placing volunteers in a child-care program.

Recruiting. Aided greatly by the connections with Pikes Peak Seniors, Inc., Care

Castle conducts ongoing recruitment activities among older adult groups through-out the Colorado Springs area. The very location of the center also serves as a recruiting tool. It occupies a storefront in a local shopping center that also contains a number of senior-related shops and offices as well as the Colorado Springs Senior Center. The visibility of the center and the recruiting efforts of its staff and board members provide a steady flow of older adults who are interested in working with young children. The flexibility of the program also helps encourage the older adults to participate; schedules are negotiated on an individual basis, and the volunteers are encouraged to work in age groups with which they are most comfortable.

Training. Perhaps the most important component of the senior volunteer pro-gram is the preservice training sessions conducted by Care Castle staff members. Once recruited, the older adult volunteers participate in 12 hr of classroom instruc-tion. The training contains a basic orientation to the center itself: the building, the center philosophy, and routine procedures. In addition, the volunteers are intro-duced to fundamental child development concepts. Through lecture, discussion, role play, and other hands-on instructional methods, the trainees develop an understand-ing of the demands and rewards of child-care work and of the professionalism they will be expected to maintain when they begin their volunteering.

Care Castle offers three of these training cycles per year, and the classes usually consist of 5–10 older adults. Recently, additional group sessions have been imple-mented as needed to facilitate the timely preparation of interested volunteers. As part of the training program, senior volunteers are helped to prepare the paperwork and obtain the clearances that are required by licensing and law enforcement agen-cies. All of these costs, as well as the cost of the training itself, are figured into Care Castle's annual budget.

Placement. As the training course proceeds, the instructor and other staff mem-bers begin the process of matching particular volunteers with appropriate center activities. Senior volunteers at Care Castle perform many services besides direct care for the children: office duties, janitorial tasks, clerical support. Occasionally, during the training period, an older adult is identified who is unable to perform the class-room tasks required of professional child-care providers. Such an individual is en-couraged to participate in the program by performing some of these non-care-related duties, providing an intergenerational experience without compromising the quality of the center's classroom care.

Most of the trainees are interested in, and capable of, appropriate performance in a classroom setting. These settings vary widely, though, even at a relatively small center such as Care Castle, and each trainee's strengths and preferences are evalu-ated carefully before a volunteer placement is made. Some active, healthy older adults may enjoy the challenge of playing with the 2-year-olds in the toddler group. Others may prefer a quieter experience, such as reading a story to preschoolers or rocking an infant. Additional factors that may be considered in making this match include

- availability (hours per week),
- the needs of each classroom, and
- the personalities of the volunteer and the classroom teachers.

Care Castle staff members have learned to take the matchmaking process very seriously. They have also learned the value of flexibility and will move volunteers and work with staff members to ensure a good fit in their classrooms. The flexibility also extends to the role of volunteers, who may grow into new abilities and take on additional responsibilities as their self-confidence and child-care skills develop.

The intergenerational experience provided by the senior volunteers is enhanced and supported in various ways. The Care Castle children read books with older adult characters and discuss the differences between themselves and their older adult friends from the time they are able to talk. Special curriculum activities are also used, especially with the older children, to help them understand the nature of aging and of the life cycle. All of the classrooms visit the nearby Colorado Springs Senior Center on a regular basis, meeting and getting to know a wide range of older adults, experiencing their casual presence as a routine part of their everyday lives.

The Care Castle senior volunteer program is evaluated on an ongoing, informal basis. The observations and experiences of the classroom staff serve as indicators of training effectiveness and are used to help plan appropriate training lessons. The behavior of the children, and feedback from the center's parents, are also rich sources of evaluative information. Finally, Pikes Peak Seniors, Inc., retains a high level of interest in its project and its effectiveness in meeting the needs of Colorado Springs families.

The positive outcomes of the Care Castle senior volunteer program are many and varied. They include

- meaningful roles for older adults,
- the benefits of intergenerational contact for young children,
- increased community awareness of child-care-related issues,
- increased community awareness of intergenerational benefits, and
- improved support for working parents at all income levels.

The most concrete outcome of the program, perhaps, is demonstrated by a calculation that is performed each year: Older adults log over 6,000 volunteer hours annually at the Care Castle center, a minimum-wage value of about $25,500. In the child-care field, that figure represents a cost that can not be covered by any other means. In a labor-intensive field such as child care, the figure translates directly into higher quality programming for center children and their families.

CHILDREN AND YOUTH SERVING OLDER ADULTS

Self-Esteem Through Service

A very active intergenerational organization located in Kensington, Maryland, Interages is a nonprofit agency that has been implementing a wide variety of inter-generational programs since the mid-1980s. One of these programs, Self-Esteem Through Service (SETS), is an excellent example of the ways in which young people can be engaged in providing service to older adults. Because of the benefits the SETS program provides to its younger participants, it also illustrates the mutuality inherent in all intergenerational efforts.

SETS is a service-learning program; that is, it is based in schools that provide a classroom component to enhance the students' intergenerational experiences. Beginning in 1992, at-risk middle school students have participated in a series of visits to nearby older adult apartment complexes, performing joint activities, learning about the needs and lives of their community's older adults, and reflecting on the meaning of their experience. The goals of the program reflect an intent to provide benefits to both participating age groups, aspiring to

- provide opportunities for at-risk students and isolated senior adults to interact together and build relationships,
- assist these youth and seniors in developing a positive self-image and increase their self-esteem, and
- enable senior adults to be active listeners for young people who want to share their experiences (Hammack, 1993).

The rationale for the program design is based partly on the intergenerational benefits described elsewhere in this book. The frail older adult participants in particular are expected to profit from regular contact with the students. Additional support comes from literature documenting the value of community service as a way to provide positive, esteem-building experiences for at-risk adolescents (Maryland State Board of Education Technical Team, 1992). The fact that the project addresses the needs of two difficult populations also adds to the strength of its rationale.

Interages designed the program when the agency was contacted almost simultaneously by a middle school teacher of at-risk children and an activity coordinator working with frail elders at a local senior residence. Through a series of meetings and planning sessions, the basic components of the program were established with input from all sides. These include the selection of participants, orientation and training, activity planning and implementation, and project evaluation.

Selecting the participants. The younger participants are drawn from a pool of middle school students who are confirmed by school administrators as being at risk of dropping out of school. In the first year, the pool was a small group of eighth graders who were already enrolled in a special intervention project designed to provide individual support and build self-esteem. The intergenerational program was viewed as a highly appropriate add-on to this project, and the students were required to participate in an initial activity. After the first session, they were given the option of continuing in the program (and typically, all do).

The older adult participants are volunteers, recruited from a group identified by the housing site counselor as both needy and capable of benefiting from the intergenerational program. Recruitment begins with an orientation meeting, at which the program is presented. Written materials are provided, and personal individual follow-up conversations are initiated by the counselor. Typically, about two thirds of those attending the orientation meeting commit to program participation.

Orientation and training. Much of the student orientation and preservice training takes place in the school, under the direction of the middle school teacher. A series of classroom sessions was designed to describe the program and the nature of work with older adults. In other sessions, students are given the opportunity to discuss their expectations, examine any stereotypical attitudes, and share their anxieties about this new experience.

Following the classroom sessions, the students participate in a standard volunteer orientation session. These sessions, conducted at the senior residence and led by the resident counselor, help the students to understand their role as volunteers and some of the duties for which they will be responsible. Communication with the teacher enables the counselor to address specific concerns identified in the classroom sessions. This volunteer training workshop is the final step in preparing the students, and the program coordinators begin the program with a minimum of delay by scheduling an immediate opportunity to meet the participating seniors, tour the facility, and implement the first activities.

Activity planning and implementation. Intergenerational programmers generally agree that visiting programs need to involve much more than simply bringing the age groups together. The visits need structure and focus and ways to spark interaction and communication. The SETS program activities are carefully planned with input from the teachers, the older adult staff, and eventually the participants themselves. Some of these activities involve an exchange between the age groups, for example, sharing mementos (participants display and describe favorite objects), a game exchange (participants teach each other their favorite board games, card games, etc.), and sessions wherein members of each age group share their favorite music and demonstrate various dance styles. Other activities are joint projects in which the participants work together to create a product or provide a service. These include gardening activities and several community service projects, in which students and older adults help to meet the needs of other community members.

The service-learning component of the project also contributes activities; for example, students hone their writing and speaking skills by designing, performing, and evaluating a personal interview session with a selected senior.

Several times during the program cycle, the participants are brought together for special group reflection sessions. Led by skilled facilitators, these meetings provide an opportunity for both the students and the older adults to sort out, analyze, and express their feelings about the program. In addition to critiquing the activities and logistics, the participants talk about the impact of the program on their lives and the changes it has produced.

In service-learning models, the end of the school year usually means the end of the intergenerational activity as well. SETS program coordinators take this ending as an opportunity to schedule a formal, culminating activity: a concluding luncheon to honor the participants and celebrate the successes of the project. In addition to participants and program staff, special guests—family members, school officials, politicians, and so forth—are invited to the luncheon. Participants and staff agree that the luncheon, held at a local restaurant, is a genuine highlight of the program. The event provides both celebration and closure, as well as an opportunity for the participants to express their appreciation of one another.

Program evaluation. SETS programmers conduct several types of formal and informal program evaluations, eliciting input from program managers as well as the older and younger participants. Through the largely informal reflections of coordinators and other staffers, several key issues that require ongoing coping strategies have been identified:

- *Staffing the program*—Someone from either the school or the older adult facility must be identified as an overall program leader.

- *Transportation*—Visiting programs by definition involve physical movement between sites, requiring either specific funding for transportation or the development of a reliable network of volunteer drivers and vehicles.
- *Scheduling*—The necessity of working within the school calendar and daily schedules, as well as the routines of the older adult facility, can mean a large reduction in program flexibility.

Formalized input from the participants is obtained through the use of standard questionnaires. Data was gathered after the first year through a questionnaire that was distributed at the end of the project. In subsequent years, attempts have been made to measure attitude changes through an instrument administered at both the beginning and the end of the program year. Anecdotal information gathered through the reflection sessions as well as other, more informal discussions also provides an important source of guidance and feedback to SETS staffers.

The anecdotal information reflects a consistently high degree of satisfaction, even excitement, on the part of the participants. The comments thus collected contain numerous references to positive changes in attitudes toward members of the other age group and frequently articulate the value of the nonjudgmental acceptance most participants feel. The data collected through the questionnaires also reflects important changes in the perceptions and attitudes of each age group; in addition, this formal evaluation indicates a statistically significant positive change in the participants' self-esteem.

A final indicator of the program's success has come through sustained and increased funding. In 1995, the Maryland Governor's Commission on Service named SETS as a model program and announced financial support that would enable the program to expand to a total of four sites by the end of the 3-year grant ("Maryland names," 1995).

The Community Intergenerational Program

Established in 1988 in Phoenix, Arizona, the Community Intergenerational Program promotes regular visits of school children to nursing homes, where they engage in recreational and educational activities. The program has the following goals (Mersereau & Glover, 1990, p. 2):

- to facilitate the formation and maintenance of long-term friendships between young people in classrooms or youth groups or individual children and nursing home residents;
- to improve the quality of life of nursing home residents, both through direct interaction with young people from the community and through the advocacy of families, friends, and community groups engendered by the interaction;
- to facilitate positive attitudes of young people toward the elderly and to enhance their learning and development regarding issues of aging; and
- to involve community agencies and schools in this process of increasing community interaction with nursing homes through direct participation, facilitation of interactions, or financial support of projects. Feedback to supporting groups will serve to increase community understanding of issues of aging.

The young people in this program range in age from preschoolers to secondary school students. They visit in groups on a regular basis, usually weekly or biweekly. Typically a teacher or other youth leader goes with them, but coordination of the overall project requires a collaborative effort between the nursing facility staff, such as an activity director or social service director, and the youth leader. Parents, adult volunteers, school administrators, or nursing home administrators are often involved as well. Preparation for the project includes selling the idea to the nursing home or school (or both), planning meetings, orientation for the young people and residents, and planning the evaluation.

Selling the idea. The Community Intergenerational Program requires the support of the several departments and individuals in the nursing home. The administration helps with staff time, resources, budgetary needs, and conflict resolution; the nursing staff prepares the residents for the visits; the social service director assists in orientation, links with residents' families, and often facilitates activities; dietary often provides refreshments; and of course, the residents' needs and ideas are incorporated into the program plans.

Planning meetings. Prior to implementation, the program team meets to discuss roles and responsibilities of the partners. In addition, they deal with issues such as transportation, scheduling, orientation, needs of the residents, pairing of youth and residents, activities, materials, training, supervision, and communication. The team may also meet periodically as the need arises.

Orientation for the young people. The Community Intergenerational Program divides youth orientation into four phases: teacher-initiated classroom activities, an introduction to the nursing facility, information about the nursing home experience, and information on issues related to the illness and death of residents.

Teacher-initiated classroom activities. These activities are designed to introduce the young people to the project. They deal with attitudes about the elderly, nursing homes, and aging. They include writing stories, attitude surveys, reading, discussions, and family interviews. The Community Intergenerational Program has produced a videotape of this introduction.

Introduction to the nursing home. In this phase, youth are introduced to the facility by a nursing home staff person, who comes to the school to speak to the students. The goal of the session is to provide a comforting and welcoming introduction to the facility. The nursing home staff person will talk about the residents, often including a biography of one or more of the residents, possibly show a slide show of the facility, talk about resident needs, and answer questions. Parents are usually invited to participate in this 45-min session.

The nursing home experience. This session is designed to sensitize the young people to the needs and limitations of the residents. It includes activities and hands-on experiences for students that deal with illnesses such as diabetes and Alzheimer's disease; sounds, smells, and sights of the facility; diminished senses of older adults; and wheelchairs, geri-chairs, walkers, and restraints. The program has produced a videotape of this training.

Illness and death. The Community Intergenerational Program deals with illness and death in two ways: first by providing the young people with information on the subjects and second by having a plan of action in case one of the young people's friends dies. Information is provided by reading literature that introduces these topics and then discussing them or by planning a unit of study on death and dying. Developing a plan of action is done in collaboration with nursing home staff and involves notifying the school of a death prior to their visiting. Sometimes, a nursing home staff person visits the school to inform the students and to initiate discussion.

Orientation for the Residents. Orientation for the residents consists of informing them about the program, such as the ages of the young people, types of activities, and length and frequency of the visits. In addition, the residents will also want to know what they can expect from the young people and what the young people will expect from them. The Community Intergenerational Program Coordinator put it this way:

> *The question they ask me is "What can we give these children? Our hands are crippled, our minds don't always work the way we want them to, some of us can't even walk." I tell them "You can give them the past, a part of America that no longer exists. It's a history that the children will only know if you tell it to them. When you're gone, it's gone too."*
>
> *Once one of my residents asked, "What are they going to do for us?" I told him, "You're going to give them history. They're going to give you the future. It's the only way that you're going to get ahold of the future. When these children are your age, they will probably remember you." (Mersereau & Glover, 1990, p. 30)*

Activities. Participants in the Community Intergenerational Program engage in a wide variety of activities, depending on the age of the young persons and the capability of the residents. The activities include arts and crafts; drama, music, and dance; games and toys; literacy; cooking; holiday projects; sharing; special events; and sensory and mental stimulation activities. In addition, there are classroom activities, such as weekly processing of the visits, and related content studies, such as reading, writing, the human body, diseases, political issues of aging, and economic and social issues, to name a few.

Evaluation. Evaluation in the Community Intergenerational Program takes two forms: ongoing evaluation and beginning or end evaluation (or both).

Ongoing evaluation. The purpose of the ongoing evaluation is to assess how the program is going, whether the participants are happy, and whether the program should continue. Informal techniques such as conversations with residents, staff, teachers, and students are used to collect relevant information. Some of the program activities themselves have an evaluative aspect to them. For example, students are encouraged to keep weekly logs, and these are useful in documenting their feelings and thoughts and serve as a record over time of how thinking and attitudes have changed. Other ongoing evaluation techniques include video or audio recordings of processing sessions, observation, short surveys, and parent feedback.

Beginning and end evaluation. Beginning and end, or pre–post, evaluations are more formal and targeted than ongoing evaluations. For example, some intergenerational programs assess attitudes about aging and the elderly through a survey given at the beginning of the project and the same survey given again at the end. This method enables changes in attitudes or perceptions to be measured. The Community Intergenerational Program, however, chooses to do an informal ongoing assessment combined with a more formal end-of-program evaluation. Children, parents, nursing home staff, and residents and their families often participate in the end-of-year evaluation, which consists of a different one-page questionnaire for each group. Items common to all of the surveys include positive and negative experiences, suggestions for improvements, most and least liked activities, and an overall rating of the project. For example, residents are asked to circle a word ranging from *great* to *poor,* whereas young children are asked to circle faces ranging from a smiley face to an unhappy face.

Outcomes. Outcomes for the pilot year of the Community Intergenerational Program were many (Mersereau & Glover, 1990, p. 3). Residents

- retained an involved role in society;
- channeled their need to nurture and enhance the growth of children;
- developed new friends;
- got individual attention from a caring person;
- gained an eager listener about life experiences and wisdom;
- gained an audience for therapeutic life review;
- who were confused or almost never spoke began talking, remembering, and anticipating the visits;
- had play legitimized and encouraged;
- recognized that their life has meaning and importance for others;
- gained a greater sense of self-worth and esteem; and
- got their lives infused with youthful energy and a zest for life.

Children

- developed new friends;
- developed compassion and looked for the inner beauty of other people;
- developed tolerance and patience;
- learned awareness and understanding of aging-related issues;
- understood the cyclical nature of life;
- gained an opportunity to talk about childhood issues;
- dealt with death and dying in a supportive environment;
- gained a link with the past; and
- developed a sense of responsibility for self and others.

CHILDREN, YOUTH, AND OLDER ADULTS SERVING TOGETHER

The Full Circle Theater Group

Arts-related programs provide some of the best examples of intergenerational programming that joins older and younger participants in the creation of a product or service to be shared with the larger community. Such programs have been built around a wide variety of creative media, including music, visual arts, poetry and writing, and crafts of all kinds. The process of creating something intergenerationally encourages self-expression while providing instruction and guidance for all of the participants; each age group can learn from the other. Such programs offer the affirmation of an older adult's continuing value to succeeding generations while facilitating the development of young talent. The participants take pride in their products or achievements, and the element of sharing, with each other and with the public, encourages their personal and artistic growth and development.

Some of the most powerful intergenerational arts programs involve the dramatic arts, in which older adults and young people join together to create or perform theatrical productions. One of the oldest of these groups is the Full Circle Intergenerational Theater Troupe, which was founded in 1982 by Temple University's Center for Intergenerational Learning (CIL) in Philadelphia, Pennsylvania.

As described in the information packet available from CIL, the Full Circle Theater is one of the most successful and long-standing programs created at the center. It began as a small group of teens and elders who were taught a variety of improvisational theater techniques. They then used these techniques to engage audiences in learning about age-related concerns and in breaking down myths and stereotypes about the aging process. Since then, Full Circle has become an ensemble of over 60 actors offering workshops and performances to more than 200 organizations each year. Full Circle is funded by the Philadelphia Corporation for Aging, the Carpenter Foundation, and a variety of short- and long-term contracts. It is now one of the most diverse theater troupes in the country, with actors ranging in age from 15 to 88 and representing a broad spectrum of racial, ethnic, cultural, and socioeconomic backgrounds. Full Circle uses improvisation, psychodrama, and interactive theater techniques to help audiences gain a deeper grasp of social issues and practice healthier, more effective strategies for resolving conflicts. A typical Full Circle performance begins by engaging audiences in experiential improvisational exercises and games. Next, a series of brief skits are performed in which Full Circle actors dramatize conflicts pertaining to specific social concerns of interest to audience members. A skilled facilitator encourages audience members to interact with the characters in the skits. Audience members are literally brought into the action to actively resolve the conflicts. Full Circle has performed for a wide variety of organizations on topics such as diversity, AIDS, domestic violence, parenting, drugs, violence prevention, death and dying, interpersonal communication, and aging. The last stage of each performance consists of a discussion, led by the facilitator, in which both audience and actors alike share what they learned about themselves personally and about the issue the performance explored.

The performers are recruited through open casting calls and auditioned by Full Circle staff and volunteers. Trained theatrical professionals work with the actors as they develop their skills through improvisation and discussion. Performances are booked by management staff, who promote the program to schools, senior agencies, religious groups, and other community organizations. The group also presents its unique theatrical performance for corporations, health care institutions, and other organizations whose employees can benefit from the sensitizing impact of the experience. In addition to the typical 1-hr performances, a new 10-session violence prevention package is currently being marketed to schools. Data collected through informal feedback and survey questionnaires indicates a high degree of satisfaction among the group's audiences, who confirm the effectiveness of this educational and sensitizing experience.

There are many challenges to the successful implementation of a program such as

Full Circle. The ongoing marketing, recruitment, and casting efforts require a great deal of time and energy. Certainly, the task of training and managing a large troupe of actors—scheduling rehearsals, booking performances, dealing with diverse personalities, and cast turnover—is a barrier in any context. Full Circle's staff and actors must also cope with the additional pressure of performing for continuously changing populations on a variety of complex topics. In addition, staff must engage in ongoing fundraising efforts. In short, the program demands a high level of dedication and commitment from everyone involved, but participants and audiences agree that the rewards are worth the effort.

Neighborhoods 2000

Recognizing that youth and older adults are rarely in a position to effect change in their communities, Neighborhoods 2000 was developed "to help youth and senior adults have input into what their neighborhoods will look like in the future" (Kaplan, 1994, p. 3). The structure of today's society separates people according to age. The result of this is that despite sharing neighborhoods, youths and older adults live in different worlds and opportunities for contact are limited. Neighborhoods 2000 seeks to increase opportunities for youth and older adults to join together to improve the quality of their neighborhoods, which has a profound impact on the quality of their lives. Through planned activities and an educational curriculum, Neighborhoods 2000 captures the interest of young people, enabling them to learn about their neighbors and community as well as a number of skills and disciplines.

Neighborhoods 2000 was established in 1987 in Mount Vernon, New York, and has since expanded to Long Island City and East Harlem in New York, and to Honolulu, Ala Wai, Ewa, and Waikiki in Hawaii.

As its goal, the program helps young and old participants to

- learn about each other and from each other;
- develop a greater understanding of their neighborhood and its users;
- develop analytical, interpersonal, and presentation skills;
- attain new knowledge in a wide range of academic disciplines; and
- achieve awareness of community planning dynamics and the value of individual participation in the community planning process (Kaplan, 1994, p. 4).

Neighborhoods 2000 involves 3–7 seniors paired with a fourth-, fifth-, or sixth-grade class. Activities take place in small, intergenerational groups, where the teams discuss, evaluate, and present their ideas on their communities to those responsible for making local development decisions. Activity sites may be the classroom or neighborhood sites. The program consists of nine units, each containing several activities. The units are Introductions, Model Building, Reminiscence Interviews, Land-Use Mapping, Walking Tours, Community Interviews, Improving the Neighborhood, Display Day, and Concluding Meeting. Each unit has its own objectives and support materials and introduces new concepts to the participants. For example, the Land-Use Mapping unit has the following objectives:

- to familiarize participants with the distribution of land-use functions in their neighborhoods;

- to stimulate critical thought about what is missing or what should be changed in local neighborhoods;
- to provide a meaningful experience with maps for participants, through the use of aerial photographs and the mapping of places relevant to their lives; and
- to stimulate the exchange of information and the discovery of unknown places and features in the local environment (Kaplan, 1994, p. 50).

New concepts in this unit include that of neighborhood and environment, use of maps, and the use of spatial arrangements. Support materials include copies of neighborhood maps, aerial photos, compasses, and rulers.

Team approach. Neighborhoods 2000 utilizes a team approach to management, which consists of teachers and program leaders; administrators from participating schools and agencies; interns from local universities; community representatives such as historians, members of senior groups, or government employees; parents and grandparents of participants; a liaison from the group representing senior participants; and a youth representative.

Recruiting. Older adult participants are recruited from local senior citizen groups, senior volunteer programs, and youth participants' relatives. In addition, the program uses local newspapers, open houses, flyers, and word of mouth to generate recruits.

Training. Training is a collaborative effort that includes school teachers, government planning officials, and the project coordinators. Information is presented on the program, school, community resources, planning, zoning, citizen participation, and intergenerational programs.

Evaluation. Evaluation is a critical component of Neighborhoods 2000. Some of the criteria used to assess the program include awareness of age-related stereotypes, enhancement of understanding and cooperation between youth and older adults, improvement of understanding and appreciation of the local environment, greater understanding of human relatedness to the environment, and development of values and ethics that suggest an enhanced sense of citizen responsibility. Tools used in the evaluation include journals, questionnaires, and log sheets completed by the coordinator detailing observed behaviors, and informal feedback.

Outcomes. Neighborhoods 2000 is designed to support school-based learning. As a local studies initiative, it promotes a view of citizenship in which the individual is an active participant in local issues. Participants learn that their neighborhoods are greatly affected by human action, that they have a responsibility toward their neighborhoods, and that they have the potential to improve their neighborhoods beyond the program (Kaplan, 1994, p. 4).

A HYBRID PROGRAM: CHILDREN, YOUTH, AND OLDER ADULTS SERVING EACH OTHER

Generations

Generations is a collaborative, intergenerational partnership of Heritage Day Health Centers, an adult day program, and the YWCA of Columbus, a child-care center, which share the first and second floors, respectively, of a building in Columbus, Ohio. The cooperative intergenerational program spans the entire facility. The Generations intergenerational program was developed in the context of an increasing need for both child-care and adult day services. Working single parents and families with two working parents lack sufficient child-care options, particularly for newborns or infants under 2 years of age. For mothers in transitional housing programs, lack of affordable child care is one of the greatest barriers to family stabilization and self-sufficiency. Likewise, working persons with parents or other relatives in need of care during the day often have difficulty finding that care. Caregiving responsibilities weigh heavily on these persons' work lives, sometimes causing them to turn down promotions or transfers. Moreover, the responsibilities related to caregiving for older adults are not yet as recognized in the workplace as are those related to caring for children. Caring for older adults also carries an uncertainty about length of time one will spend in caregiving, a concern not generally associated with caring for children.

The Generations partnership was built not only on the history of individual and agency partnering but also on a shared vision of what an intergenerational partnership would look like. Heritage and the YWCA shared a philosophy of taking their respective adult day care and child-care expertise and linking them in a facility so that each group could do what it did best. Thus, the partnership did not intend to build a new, independent organization with its own expertise in intergenerational care but to link two independent organizations under one roof with joint programming.

Goals. The stated goals of the Generations program are as follows (Ward & Streetman, 1995, p. 6):

- to provide affordable child and adult day-care services to the community by sharing financial and program resources between two agencies;
- to create a day-care environment that is stimulating, educational, and supportive by broadening opportunities for personal development and social interaction for each adult and child;
- to create a model of intergenerational day care so that others may learn of the benefits of shared interactions and life experiences;
- to create a model of collaboration that will inspire other meaningful partnerships by businesses and service organizations throughout the community; and
- to provide needed health services to children and adults and to provide a clinical educational site for medical, nursing, and teaching educational programs.

Secondary goals include the provision of service to downtown and inner-city Columbus; building a service that is on the forefront of human services and is new in Columbus and Ohio; serving any client in need of services; and developing a commitment to quality service.

Heritage Day Health Centers. The adult day services portion of the program serves two populations. One group is older adults with an average age of 75. They are physically or cognitively impaired persons who need care and supervision during the day while their caregivers work or take care of other responsibilities. Approximately 60% have Alzheimer's disease or a related dementia. Generations also serves younger adults who range in age from 25 to 55 years of age and need services, care, and supervision during the day similar to those needed by the older adults. These young adults have suffered brain injury, a major stroke, a heart attack, or have diseases such as multiple sclerosis or severe arthritis. This group adds a third generation to the intergenerational center and their acute physical needs present new care and program challenges to the staff.

YWCA Child Day Care. The Generations child-care program is operated by the YWCA of Columbus. Its purpose is to serve at-risk, low-income children. About 90% of the 62 children (6 weeks to 6 years of age) come from families below the poverty line. Some have been in foster care, and some were born addicted to drugs or alcohol. The children who have been in foster care may have been there while their mothers were in treatment programs. They do not always know their mothers very well. Stress and behavior problems are quite common, although they are not characteristic of all the children. In late 1996, 80% of the children came to the center from homeless shelters.

Activities and programming. The Generations program efforts are shaped by a number of ideas, including

- the importance of program collaboration between the adult day and child-care programs;
- the value of a shared philosophy among staff members about programming;
- openness to experimentation;
- an approach that starts adults and children separately on activities and then brings them together for an intergenerational activity; and
- activities that emerge from observing what participants' interests are (Ward & Streetman, 1995, p. 10).

A guiding principal in the organization of the intergenerational program has been that it have a very specific, visible structure. The calendar of intergenerational activities is a planning document for the two staffs. However, the structure and visibility of activities has enough flexibility so that children and older adults can interact spontaneously.

Generations conducts three kinds of joint programming: planned calendar events, spontaneous interaction, and planned one-to-one pairing. The planned intergenerational calendar provides scheduled activities each day for at least some of the children. Many of these activities are developed from those already listed on the adult day services calendar. For example, in preparation for the adults' Chinese New Year celebration, the preschoolers engage in an intergenerational lantern-making activity. Then, on the day of the celebration, the children participate with the older adults in their Chinese New Year activities.

A second important set of intergenerational activities are spontaneous. These group activities occur when staff take advantage of unplanned opportunities for interaction between children and adults. For example, someone may notice that the weather is nice outside and say to the older adults, "It's warm out today. The babies are going out. Do you want to go for a walk with them?" Adults may also come in at any time to pick up and rock infants in the nursery on the first floor.

A third kind of intergenerational activity is one-to-one pairing, in which individual relationships between a child who is having difficulties and an older adult deemed appropriate for that child are fostered by staff. Teachers approach the intergenerational coordinator when they have identified a child who needs more attention or who is restless during nap time. The coordinator then finds an older adult with whom to pair the child for an indefinite period of time.

Administration and management. Each organization is responsible for its own program and its own staff. Administrators indicate that they like the coupling of two agencies, each with its own responsibilities, rather than the creation of one new agency. Their rationale is that each group brings experience and expertise in its own domain. They can learn and cooperate on the intergenerational program, but they do not have to take on the burden of running a program with which they are not familiar.

The working relationship is marked by collegiality and discussion. Although the responsibilities for various portions of the building, such as the elevator, and the formal relationship between the two organizations was set down in writing, there seems to be little reference in day-to-day practice to these formal links. Rather, the important links are personal, established within the center through cooperation and negotiation around the intergenerational program.

Staffing. Heritage and the YWCA each employ their own staff for the Generations center. The intergenerational coordinator is an employee of Heritage. Her relationship to the child-care staff is collegial, not supervisory. The two programs share a receptionist, who is an employee of Heritage, with reimbursement from the YWCA. Staffing levels and requirements, training (other than intergenerational), and supervision are the responsibility of each organization.

The philosophy of senior management in both organizations is that they administer broadly. They visualize, plan, collaborate, and raise funds—and let the other professionals do their day-to-day work with a relatively free hand.

Training. Generations prepares staff with both initial and ongoing training.

Initial training. Prior to opening in 1994, the intergenerational coordinator conducted three sessions of joint training for the adult day care and child-care staffs. The first session included icebreakers to introduce staff members to one another, an introduction to the intergenerational program, and a discussion of the program's philosophy.

In the second session, the emphasis turned to building sensitivity to the two age groups. A representative from the Area Agency on Aging did training on aging, and a child development expert talked about high-risk children's behaviors and how parents' drug and alcohol abuse might affect that behavior.

The final session brought both staffs together in small groups to discuss calendar planning, issues such as the positive and negative aspects of working together, and possible conflicts the staff members would encounter. As a large group the staff members discussed specific issues that they would soon face, such as what term they should use to refer to the older adults.

Ongoing training. Generations' ongoing training occurs at the monthly meeting of the child-care teachers and the adult day activities staff. At these meetings, they discuss the monthly calendar, problem solve, discuss children that might benefit from special help, and go over activities for the next month. In addition, the intergenerational coordinator sometimes makes presentations at the child-care staff meeting.

Outcomes. Program outcomes for Generations include the following (Ward & Streetman, 1995, pp. 16–18):

- Older adults in the Generations program are slightly less agitated on afternoons following their participation in intergenerational activities than they are on afternoons when they have not participated in intergenerational activities.
- The Generations program is having a very positive effect on the 3- to 5-year-old children, as measured by increases in their social competencies over a 4-month period. The positive effects hold true for both girls and boys.
- The positive behaviors of older adults and children at Generations demonstrates that both groups enjoy their intergenerational activities together.
- The program helps to teach children about tolerance and understanding about older adult disabilities and each other.
- The opportunity for interaction with the older adults, which often has a calming influence over the children, helps child-care staff deal with children who are acting out, experiencing separation anxiety, or who just need an older adult to smile, give a pat on the head, or a kiss on the cheek.

CONCLUSION

As noted earlier, the specific programmatic information contained in these case studies may be of great value to practitioners who are interested in establishing their own programs. Certainly, the materials produced by each of these enterprises, as well as direct contact with their current staff members, will greatly assist such an effort.

However, the chapter serves another purpose as well. Taken together, the program models, chosen almost at random, present a telling illustration of the current state of intergenerational programming. Even within the organizational categories, significant differences can be seen in the descriptions. Vital components such as funding, goals, specific objectives, location, and sponsoring agencies show tremendous diversity and creativity. However, the overriding theme of intergenerational connectedness, its power and value, can also be clearly seen, especially in each project's projected impact on the lives of its participants. It is this unifying theme that defines intergenerational programming, and it has driven practitioners from a wide variety of program initiatives to begin thinking of themselves as "intergenerational professionals."

III

RESEARCH AND EVALUATION OF INTERGENERATIONAL PROGRAMS

7

Evaluation of Intergenerational Programs

Christopher R. Ward, PhD

The best age is the age you are.

—*Louis Armstrong*

The intergenerational movement has focused on developing programs that promote and support relationships between young and old. In pursuit of this goal, the movement and its practitioners have tried to understand the impact of programs on participants and to learn more about the processes by which the programs are implemented. Thus, evaluation has been an important aspect of the intergenerational field from its beginnings.

This chapter includes explanations of common evaluation strategies and methods and a discussion of the importance of planning evaluation as part of the program development process. The chapter concludes with examples of intergenerational program evaluations and resources. The following chapter discusses research related to the intergenerational field.

EVALUATION AND RESEARCH: NOT ALWAYS DISTINCT

In the intergenerational field, as in many other applied human service fields, the distinction between evaluation and research is not clear cut. In general, an evaluation focuses on a specific program and gathers information for practical purposes such as program revision or the justification of continued funding. Evaluation outcomes tend to be summarized in reports circulated to program staff, the community served, and funding agencies. Some evaluations may be reported very informally, with findings and recommendations communicated in person or via letter or memo to key program personnel or members of the community.

Research, on the other hand, focuses on broad concepts, often collects information about multiple programs, and uses this information to increase a field's knowledge about basic questions. Intergenerational research findings are published not only in reports to funding agencies but also in scholarly books and in journals such as *Activities, Adaptation, & Aging; Childhood Education; Educational Gerontology; The Gerontologist;* and *Journal of Children in Contemporary Society.* Research outcomes are discussed at academic or professional conferences and in university courses to increase the knowledge base of professionals. Intergenerational research has also been the topic of a growing number of doctoral dissertations.

As a very young and emerging discipline, the intergenerational field has not developed the rigid distinctions that characterize many fields. Thus, intergenerational studies make no absolute distinction between research and evaluation. Intergenerational evaluation results are often published as applied research, and many of the same questions, approaches, and instruments are used in both research and evaluation. For most practitioners, whether a study is labeled evaluation or research is not important. They assess the study's contribution to what is known about the relationships between elders and youngsters or about the workings and outcomes of intergenerational programs. Moreover, because many of the concepts and theories in the intergenerational field are at early stages of development, evaluation findings can contribute to shaping the field's basic concepts to a degree usually not possible in more developed fields.

Further reflecting the overlap between intergenerational evaluation and research are the challenges they share based on the nature of intergenerational programs (Bocian & Newman, 1989). Carrying out studies with two different populations means that in most cases evaluators and researchers must first grapple with two fields, each with its own theories, instruments, and programming traditions. For example, in evaluating a colocated child day care and adult day care site, practitioners must understand child development and the strategies and instruments for gathering data on teachers' assessments of children's development; aging and aging-related dementia such as Alzheimer's disease and means of measuring older adults' levels of agitation; and the assessments of intergenerational components such as the interaction between older adults and children.

CHALLENGES OF EVALUATION AND RESEARCH

Intergenerational programs often address the needs of two of the most at-risk populations in society. This focus on the vulnerable creates challenges for intergenerational evaluators and researchers. Sometimes they find special difficulties in accessing information from young children who don't read or from older adults who are demented or who have trouble seeing or hearing. In some cases, one or both of the populations will be in an institution (including schools) where researchers need to get special permission to collect data or clearance to enter. In the colocated program example cited above, the design might include groups of infants and demented elderly, each presenting its own challenges to data collection and requiring creative approaches to assessing interaction.

In addition, intergenerational evaluation and research often involve two or more partner agencies or systems, each with its own traditions, professional standards, and levels of resources. Developing strategies for understanding the views of staff, of parents or caregivers, and of other agencies in each partner's system requires knowledge of professionals in all the systems.

This introduction closes with a note on the term *intergenerational*. This book uses the term to refer to the programs that bring young and old together for mutual benefit and to related activities such as evaluation, research, policy formation, and the like. However, several other disciplines use the term *intergenerational* but give it different meanings. For example, the term is often used in economics to refer to the transfer of money or goods from parent to child. The term is used in studies of families to refer to the relationship between generations within the family, such as the relationship between parents and their adult children. Although the context generally makes a specific usage clear, the multiple meanings of the term may be confusing when doing literature searches or when initially encountering a title to a book or article. Thus, those who engage in intergenerational research and evaluation need to keep the existence of these multiple meanings in mind as they utilize the relevant literature.

EVALUATION

Interest in intergenerational program evaluation has grown in the last decade. Many foundations and government agencies have increased their emphasis on evaluation. For example, a major intergenerational initiative conducted by the Administration on Aging from 1993 to 1995 required and supported evaluation for all its funded projects. In a few cases, foundations have even been willing to fund the evaluation of intergenerational programs through independent grants.

At the same time, individual programs and their staffs have become more aware of the benefits of evaluation. Interest in evaluation by the field's professionals has grown, as evidenced by attendance at training sessions at national conferences such as those sponsored by Generations United and at Generations Together's annual National Intergenerational Training Institute. Many "how to" manuals now include sections on evaluation. For example, the National Council on the Aging and Save the Children Federations' project manual *Rural Family Friends Replication Manual: A Project of the National Council on the Aging and Save the Children Federation* (National Council on the Aging, 1992b) has a chapter on evaluating the program's impact and includes extensive examples of evaluation questionnaires. Bi-Folkal Productions' *A Guide to Community: An Intergenerational Friendship Program Between Young People and Nursing Home Residents* (Mersereau & Glover, 1990) offers suggestions for qualitative, user-friendly evaluation.

The rising interest in evaluation comes from several sources. First, intergenerational programs have been increasingly put forward as a means to address society's problems, adding to intergenerational programs' more traditional functions, such as changing attitudes, increasing self-esteem, and providing fulfilling roles for older adults. The growing emphasis on programs as solutions to social problems has meant that funding agencies and other stakeholders are more interested in outcomes that are not directly related to the elder–youngster relationship. Other funding agencies intent on solving a particular social problem may focus on only one of the two age-group constituencies. For example, state and federal education agencies who fund intergenerational programs typically want to know the impact of a program on students but usually have little interest in the program's impact on older adults.

A second and more recent development important to evaluation of intergenerational programs has been the reshaping of the American political landscape. Funding for many programs that address the social problems listed above has been reduced. At the same time, discussion of entitlements has given new opportunity to the proponents of intergenerational conflict to picture Americans as divided by age and age-related economic issues. In this context of leaner times and more scrutiny, intergenerational programs need to describe what they do with passion and accuracy and demonstrate their positive impacts to a degree they have not had to in earlier eras. Overall, quality evaluation has become much more important to the well-being and future of the intergenerational movement.

STRATEGIES

The planning and development of an intergenerational program evaluation parallels and interacts with the planning and development of the program activities. To develop effective evaluation strategies, teams responsible for developing program evaluations step through a series of questions similar to the following:

What does the project team want to know about its program? Project team members list what they need to know to improve the program, to make it more effective, and to better understand its processes or impact. They assume that the evaluation's purpose is to provide information that is useful to them. They do not concern themselves at this initial point with what they should do or what others have done in other programs.

Who are the audiences for the evaluation? How will they use the information provided to them? Most evaluations have an audience beyond the immediate program staff. Among possible audiences are funding agencies, boards of directors, supervisors, other groups interested in implementing intergenerational programs, the public, and program participants. Funding agencies and other decision makers may use the evaluation to judge whether or not the program continues, to recommend changes, or to increase or decrease funding. Before the program starts, the project team determines the primary audience for the evaluation and estimates how the audience will use the evaluation and what information they most value.

How do the requirements of the audience modify what the project team wants to know? In some cases the audience for the evaluation may have the same interests as the staff. In other cases, their interests may differ. For example, staff may want a great deal of information on a program's processes to modify what they do. A board or funder may be more interested in the impact of the program on one or more constituencies. A crucial—although sometimes difficult—function of the planning process is to prioritize what various groups wish to learn and to adequately and appropriately address the needed areas in the evaluation.

What specific kinds of information does the project team need? Evaluations can gather a wide variety of information, in many forms. For some audiences, anecdotal or case history information best summarizes the program. In other cases, the audience will wish to know information related to its own mission or concerns. For a public agency mandated to reduce teenage drug abuse, for example, the information needed would likely be statistics on the change in the level of drug usage. In some intergenerational programs, youth-serving or elder-serving agencies may be most interested in changes in attitudes about their own constituencies.

How will the project team gather the information? It is at this point in the planning process that the team responsible for the evaluation decides how to gather the information it needs. All too often, however, persons developing program evaluations begin to select instruments before considering what they want to learn, what their audience wants, and what kind of information is most important.

Among the options for gathering information are questionnaires, interviews, observations, and existing institutional data (standardized test scores or school grades, for example). There are many existing instruments that can be used for evaluations. Some measure phenomena such as life satisfaction, self-esteem, knowledge of aging, and attitudes on aging, and can be used across a wide range of intergenerational programs for diverse populations. They can also include those measuring outcomes related to the particular social problem an intergenerational program is designed to address. Such instruments can range from scales measuring parental stress to surveys on alcohol and tobacco use to questionnaires on knowledge about a particular disease.

How will the team report information? During the planning process, attention is given to how the results of the evaluation will be conveyed to the audience and when the evaluation must be complete. Some audiences prefer a simple oral presentation that gives a few highlights of the evaluation findings. In other cases, the information will be reported in summary form but with many graphs, tables, and other illustrative material to help busy people understand the richness of the evaluation's findings. For a limited number of audiences, an evaluation may be reported in great detail with a lengthy narrative and appendixes with extensive data tables.

What must the project team do with the information it gathered so it can be reported clearly? The information gathered in questionnaires, observations, interviews, existing records, and so forth must next be converted into a meaningful form. In some cases, special expertise is required for statistical analysis and to review the data to determine an appropriate format for presentation. However, most audiences will prefer a clear, brief presentation to one that is highly complex or technical. Thus, the most important task for the team is to summarize the evaluation findings so that they convey the most important information in ways that are easy for the audience to understand and—if needed—to act on.

What are the resources and constraints on the evaluation? As the team plans, they consider what the program and its budget can devote to the evaluation. For example, the team may ask how much staff time can be given over to the evaluation and what human resources are available—does someone on the program or agency staff have experience in setting up a database to track participants? Does the agency or a partnering agency have someone skilled in interviewing who can help gather data?

Several constraints relate to the participants in intergenerational programs. For example, if the program includes very small children or very frail elderly, will they be able to complete certain kinds of instruments? If they will not be able to complete the instruments, what other options are available to gather needed data? Answers to these questions modify the types of information gathered or the way in which information is gathered. In addition, institutions that serve the elderly and youth have constraints on evaluation (and research) to protect the privacy of their clients. Evaluation of a school-based program may require very specific clearances and permission from parents.

Who is responsible for what? Finally, the team planning the evaluation must be as precise about roles and responsibilities for the evaluation as the staff is about program roles and responsibilities. Before the intergenerational program begins, planners determine who is responsible for overall planning and management; for selection or construction of instruments; for data gathering; for data coding, entry, and analysis; and for writing the evaluation report.

For some programs, a critical decision will be whether to do the evaluation internally or to contract with an outside evaluator. An outside evaluator can bring special expertise, will not be influenced so greatly by existing agency views of the project, and will lend credibility. At the same time, an outsider may have certain drawbacks. For example, an outside evaluator may not work on the project long enough to understand the views of its people and the nuances of its politics. Likewise, an agency may have difficulty in finding an outside evaluator with sufficient experience in the subject matter of the project. Finally, for many smaller programs, the scale of an evaluation is such that an agency's own staff may be able to do the project more cost effectively.

COMPONENTS OF EVALUATION

The specific methods used in an evaluation are best determined by a careful planning process. Among the components included in most intergenerational evaluations will be some of the following.

Demographic Information

Most programs will collect participants' (both older and younger) ages, gender, race or ethnicity, income level, education, family situation, and other characteristics that can be used to understand who does (and does not participate) and to present a picture of the program for others. Categories should be drawn from standard sources such as census data. Programs should collect only the very minimum amount needed. Moreover, participants may not always wish to share all information. Some intergenerational programs have found, for example, that older adults are reluctant to respond to questions about income.

Program Information

To track both the progress of the program implementation and to help determine the level of impact a given program may have on participants, the staff should gather information on the number and type of activities, the number of participants in each activity, and the dates participants reached key points (recruited, screened, trained, etc). In evaluations that seek to understand the process by which a program is implemented, the staff can also keep journals or notes on significant events. Some professionals find that such notes can be kept most easily on audiotape and transcribed or reviewed as needed, depending on program resources.

Both the demographic and program information are usually gathered by program staff in collaboration with the fiscal staff, who need the information for billing and for preparing financial reports. This information also constitutes a major portion of program documentation. Although documentation is primarily a descriptive process, it is important to intergenerational programs not only for writing reports and "telling one's story" to funding agencies and the public but also for preparing program model descriptions that can be used for program replication.

Outcome Information

Most groups and individuals connected with a project will be interested in outcomes. They wish to know what changed or became better as a result of the project. In many cases, the particular outcomes that the evaluation focuses on will be those related to the project's objectives. However, many evaluations will focus on a few key outcomes, particularly if there are financial or other constraints on the evaluation. Among the methods for gathering outcome information are the following:

Open-ended questions. In many evaluations, it is important to ask participants about their views and opinions on particular aspects of the program and to have them reply in their own words and to the extent they wish. Open-ended questions are often included on evaluation questionnaires and are a mainstay of interviews (individual or group) that can establish what a program means to people. Examples of open-ended questions include: "How did this project change your views about older adults?" or "How have you benefited from participation in this project?"

Open-ended questions can be adapted for many uses. For example, they can be used before and after with staff and other stakeholders to determine expectations prior to the program and perceptions during or after the program. The changes in responses can then be compared and discussed to help understand how the project has impacted staff, the community, and others.

Observations. For evaluations, observations can range from informal site visits to assess progress toward achieving objectives to carefully coded observations done by one or more trained observers. Site visits can include discussions of project goals and objectives, consideration of problems and how they are being addressed, and conversations with a variety of participants. They should not be done at the time of special programs or events. More formal observations require a protocol or check list and some degree of regularity in the scheduling of visits. An important concern may be that of the effect of the observer's presence. To lessen such an effect, the observer may spend a period of time on site prior to the formal observations.

Standardized questionnaires. Intergenerational evaluators have used several kinds of standardized instruments. Some, such as the Children's Views on Aging (Marks, 1980; Marks, Newman, & Faux, 1993), are designed specifically for use in intergenerational programs. A second group includes those that measure variables often associated with intergenerational programs: The Life Satisfaction Index (Neugarten, Havighurst, & Tobin, 1961) is one such instrument. Finally, there are standardized instruments that measure variables related to social problems. One such instrument is the Piers–Harris Children's Self-Concept Scale (Piers & Harris, 1969), a tool that has been used in the evaluation of intergenerational mentoring programs. As the number, variety, and scope of intergenerational programs grows, the range of the instruments that could be included in this last category increases. In some cases, the best sources of information are experts in content area—for example, drug prevention—who are familiar with appropriate measures.

Existing data. Some intergenerational programs—especially those working with schools or other institutions—utilize information on participants that is gathered by the institution for other purposes. For example, many intergenerational tutoring or mentoring programs utilize existing school grades or standardized test scores to evaluate progress. Data on older adults' ability to perform daily activities collected in some institutionalized settings may be useful in assessing the effects of intergenerational programs. As with other sources of data, issues of permission from parents or caregivers are increasingly important and require extra efforts. Care should be taken to get all necessary paperwork prepared ahead of time.

CASES AND EXAMPLES

Many intergenerational evaluations have examined short-term, limited programs. These have sometimes been reported in journal articles as outcomes for intergenerational programs. In addition, descriptions of more complex evaluations are beginning to appear in a variety of journals or as reports available from the projects that were evaluated. Some examples follow.

A University-Based Intergenerational Community Service Project

Ward and McCrea (1996) reported on the evaluation that Generations Together conducted on an intergenerational community service and service-learning project funded by the U.S. Department of Education's Fund for the Improvement of Post-Secondary Education at the University of Pittsburgh. The project brought first-year students in the University's program for entering at-risk students to serve and learn with older adults from public housing communities. The planning of the evaluation included a number of common issues facing intergenerational program evaluators: the use of multiple methods reflecting the project's diverse partners; recognition of the complexities of collaboration by multiple systems, populations, and funding agencies; and planning for long-term assessment of the students' grades and retention. The evaluation found that compared with the grade point average of a control group, participants' grade point average increased during the semester of participation and that participants tended to show greater change over the semester of participation in responses to questions about community service, education and career plans, and perceived level of knowledge about older adults than did the control group.

National Multisite Intergenerational Mentoring Project

Linking Lifetimes, a multisite, 5-year initiative coordinated by Temple University's Center for Intergenerational Learning, was designed to demonstrate the effectiveness of utilizing elder mentors to help at-risk middle school students and young offenders become more productive and self-reliant. The project evaluation, conducted by Lodestar Management/Research, represents the rare outside evaluation done in the intergenerational field. The evaluation used a variety of approaches, including on-site and telephone interviews with participants and staff, program observations, and focus groups with mentors. Coordinators and mentors filled out forms on activities and progress toward outcomes. Data on youth came from existing information, including school records and courts. The results of the evaluation were published in four reports on outcomes for mentors and youth, site profiles, organizational issues, and a summary and description of the evaluation process (Henkin, Rogers, Lyons, & Charner, 1994).

A Community-Based Elderly–Youth Exchange Program

Chapman and Neal (1990) evaluated the Elderly–Youth Exchange program in Portland, Oregon. In the program, youths helped older persons with yard and house care, and older adults tutored and led recreational programs for youth. This report represents a comprehensive, highly structured evaluation that focused on outcomes important to the project and to answering basic questions (about attitude change, for example) of interest to the intergenerational field in general. The evaluation examined intergenerational contact prior to participation and attitudes toward the other group. The evaluation found attitude change only in youths who helped older adults. These youths enjoyed being with older adults more, showed decreased social distance from older adults, and had a more positive perception of older adults' attitudes toward young people.

RESOURCES

There is a wide variety of resources for evaluation, many of which are written from the perspective of a particular discipline or profession. For intergenerational practitioners who are beginning to do evaluation, one useful resource is the *Program Evaluation Kit*, a series of books developed by the Center for the Study of Evaluation at the University of California, Los Angeles (Herman, 1987).

Other resources include "how to" program manuals and evaluation manuals designed for programs closely related to the intergenerational field. For example, the National Dropout Prevention Center has produced an *Evaluation Guide for Tutoring Programs* (Weatherford & Seoane, 1992). The interest in drug and alcohol prevention led to the publication of a number of user-friendly evaluation guides, such as *Measurement in Prevention: A Manual on Selecting and Using Instruments to Evaluate Prevention Programs* (Kumpfer et al., 1993), which reviews many instruments useful in intergenerational programs.

Many resources can be obtained by contacting successful intergenerational programs and professionals or through libraries. An emerging area that should be explored is the Internet through the World Wide Web and Gopher sites. Generations Together's home page on the World Wide Web (http://www.pitt.edu/~gti) can provide links to other programs. Search engines such as Yahoo and Lycos can be used to find evaluation resources. The home page of the ERIC Clearinghouse on Assessment and Evaluation at the Catholic University of America (http://www.cua.edu/www/eric__ae) provides access to searchable databases for reviews and information on various standardized instruments. These resources should provide practitioners with the tools needed to conduct the kinds of quality evaluations that the intergenerational field has found so important over the last several decades.

8

Research on Intergenerational Programs

Christopher R. Ward, PhD

The best way to predict your future is to create it.
—Unknown

Intergenerational research begins with theories upon which intergenerational programs are based (Cohon, 1989). Various historical, political, economic, and intellectual factors have also shaped the development of intergenerational research over the last three decades.

The use of theory as the basis for research is one of the important elements that distinguishes research from evaluation. However, as was discussed in the introduction to chapter 7, research in the intergenerational field is not distinct and separate from evaluation. Much of the intergenerational research is applied research grounded in programs as well as theory. The field has yet to undertake a significant amount of fundamental research on basic questions that have little direct relation to programs.

Among the ideas that have contributed to the research agenda in intergenerational studies are

- the concern for guiding the next generation (Erikson, 1959, 1963),
- the push by each generation to transmit cultural traditions (Mannheim & Stewart, 1962),
- a desire by the old to leave a legacy and to share with the young (Butler & Lewis, 1977), and
- the developmental growth and needs of both older and younger persons.

Theories of aging are among the important concepts that have shaped the intergenerational field. These theories have changed over the past several decades. Aging is now pictured as less uniform, less deterministic, and more focused on people's environments. From these concepts have evolved intergenerational research variables such as life satisfaction, self-concept, attitudes toward aging, meaningful relationships, cognitive functioning, physical health, self-esteem, and other measures of the quality of life, including economic factors (Cohon, 1989).

Recent child development theories have also contributed to the development of intergenerational research. Many experts have described the disintegration of the nuclear family and breakdown of the cultural and social supports for families and children in modern, industrial society. These changes, when added to the need for children to have consistent nurturing and adult role models, have resulted in an emphasis in research on how children and youth view older adults, how stereotypes about older adults can be eliminated, and how attitudes can be changed by increasing contact between older adults and children (Cohon, 1989).

Political and ideological issues have also shaped the intergenerational research agenda. The emphasis on youth and generational differences in the 1960s came at a time when stereotyping and restricting the elderly was first conceptualized as ageism. Calls for intergenerational equity and the responding calls for intergenerational interdependence have raised interest in intergenerational research and related policy. The Gerontological Society of America presented research findings related to these issues in a report titled *Ties That Bind: The Interdependence of Generations* (Kingson, Hirshorn, & Cornman, 1986). The intergenerational research agenda has also been shaped by the availability of funds, which reflects the interests and commitment of government and foundations to particular lines of programming and inquiry.

At the same time, the outcomes from several decades of intergenerational research have had an impact on the development of programs and policy. Examples from the many areas of this research follow.

AREAS OF RESEARCH

Attitudes

Development of intergenerational attitude research. The attitudes of children and youth about older persons have been a major focus of intergenerational research. In comparison, there is a much smaller body of research about older adults' attitudes toward younger persons. Originating in the 1950s in a broader inquiry about the general population's attitudes toward the elderly, the intergenerational attitude studies were fueled by an increasing awareness of ageism and by emerging positive images of aging.

The era of the "generation gap" in the 1960s and 1970s brought worries that the massive baby boomer generation would grow up with negative attitudes about the elderly and aging. As the question of whether or not children held negative attitudes about the elderly and aging grew in importance in the 1970s, studies of their attitudes began to appear. Some of these studies suggested that greater contact between the young and the old would change attitudes; subsequent studies investigated specific interventions and their effect on attitudes. Applied research on specific intergenerational programs followed.

Many of these studies drew on work on intergroup relations, particularly on race relations between African Americans and Whites in the United States. Studies about children's attitudes used methods developed for the study of attitudes about race.

Attitudes toward older adults and aging. The research on the general population's attitudes toward the elderly and aging established two important issues for intergenerational research. The first issue is whether or not older adults are viewed more negatively than are other age groups. The second issue is more technical and relates to methodology. Several review articles address these issues, summarize the research on attitudes toward the elderly and aging, and serve as useful guides to a complex field (Green, 1981; Lutsky, 1981; Kite & Johnson, 1988; McTavish, 1971).

Kite and Johnson (1988) examined a large number of studies to learn whether people's attitudes toward older individuals are more negative than are their attitudes toward younger people. They concluded that although the research shows somewhat more negativity to older persons, not all studies have found that people view older adults more negatively than they view youth. Among the reasons for these varied research outcomes, Kite and Johnson argued, are the research design, the questions that subjects are asked about older adults, and the setting of the questioning.

Kite and Johnson (1988) found that people judge older adults most negatively on their competence and on their physical appearance. People judge older adults more negatively when they do not have information about individual older adults, when they evaluate elders and youngsters together, and when the context is not work related. In contrast, older persons are judged less negatively in studies where the authors are older, the study is more recent, and evaluative measures have large numbers of items.

In another review of the research, Green (1981) attributed earlier studies' negative results to problems with methodology:

- They asked participants to categorize the elderly using other people's categories (a problem with standardized instruments).
- They depended on stereotypes—researchers usually asked participants to respond to questions based on what they believed about all older adults, not about what they believed about specific older adults.
- They contained bias because participants were frequently aware of the answers that researchers were looking for.

Green also noted that many studies had technical problems related to instruments' reliability and validity.

In contrast to the largely negative attitudes toward elders reported by these studies, studies that have asked about specific older adults have found more positive attitudes. The use of observations of actual behavior and the use of social distance scales also has produced more positive results (Green, 1981).

Children's attitudes toward older adults. The attitudes of children and youth toward the elderly and aging became a focus of research in the 1970s. These studies were based on several assumptions: that attitudes about a group are important because they influence policy and action that can help or hinder that group, that negative attitudes toward older adults in the form of ageism are widespread, and that increased contact with older persons can improve attitudes.

Researchers studied the attitudes of children and youth of all ages. Although these studies did not always find that contact with the elderly changed stereotypes or attitudes, some found enough of a relationship to recommend intergenerational programs as interventions for change. Others suggested the need to develop curricula on aging for young children, for college students, and for professional school students. Such curricula could counter the often negative attitudes about the elderly that studies had shown were frequently held by university students preparing for human service, medicine, education, and other fields (Bennett, 1976).

Although the evidence as to what degree children share negative stereotypes and attitudes about older people is ambiguous, children clearly recognize age and generational differences at an early age and become more sophisticated about these differences as they develop. A number of studies have found that children identify older adults with negative adjectives or describe them in negative, stereotyped ways. Miller, Blalock, and Ginsburg (1984) reported negative attitudes toward older adults among preschool children. However, they found no relationship between attitude and amount of contact with older adults (as reported by parents). Other research has shown that young people do not share negative stereotypes (Thomas & Yamamoto, 1975). Other studies have found that children's attitudes about older adults are positive but that their attitudes about their own aging is negative (Marks, Newman, & Onawola, 1985). Another study found that although older adults were overly optimistic about how positively children would perceive them, the children indicated generally positive attitudes toward them. The high degree of contact between children and grandparents in the community where the study was undertaken was suggested as a possible explanation for the positive attitudes toward the elderly (Nishi-Strattner & Myers, 1983).

Some studies have examined whether children manifest negative attitudes in their behavior toward older adults and have compared the development of ageist attitudes with the development of other prejudicial attitudes such as those based on race or gender (Isaacs & Bearison, 1986). Isaacs and Bearison used specific individuals— older and younger—with whom children interacted in a carefully defined task. They observed behaviors such as how close children voluntarily sat to an adult, how often they initiated eye contact with adults, and the initiation and content of speech by the younger to the adult during an assigned task. They found that prejudice could be seen in behavior and develops early.

An important study about children's attitudes toward the elderly explored the components of children's attitudes and suggested implications for intergenerational programs. The attitude components included children's knowledge of age, the interaction and behaviors they display toward older persons, and their feelings about aging and the elderly (Seefeldt, Jantz, Galper, & Serock, 1977). These components have been cited in later studies and are used frequently in the development of intergenerational programs. This study also found that the use of pictures plus interviews is an effective technique to learn about children's knowledge about age, affective feelings, and projected behaviors.

- Children understand the concept of age and can identify the oldest person from a set of pictures and arrange pictures of older adults in age-sequential order. By third or fourth grade children are able to correctly identify the ages of persons in the pictures.
- Children tend to relate negative feelings to the picture of the oldest person. Younger children were more negative than are older children.

Seefeldt et al. concluded that children's negative views show the need for age-graded aging curriculum, for realistic models in books and elsewhere, and for the presence of older adults as school volunteers. In particular, they recommend that because the physical aspects of aging appear to be what produce the most negative attitudes in children, children should have personal experience in school with active, healthy older people.

Children's and youths' attitudes in intergenerational programs. Intergenerational programs and program research have assumed that children and youth's attitudes about the elderly and aging can be changed through increased contact, discussion, and knowledge. To test what factors are most important in changing attitudes, intergenerational researchers have used experimental models, setting up limited interventions to test hypotheses. One experimental study held short workshops to test which method produced the most positive attitude change and found that direct contact with an older person was most useful (Murphy-Russell, Die, & Walker, 1986). Another experimental study found that a period of beneficial contact with older adults in an intergenerational program can change children's attitudes. Carstensen, Mason, and Caldwell (1982) set up a reading program run by older adults to examine changes in children's perceptions of older adults. The intervention changed children's attitudes but did not change those of the older adults.

Intergenerational attitude research has studied existing intergenerational programs. Some of this research has shown clear changes in children's attitudes and knowledge about older adults. In one such study, children in two day-care centers were compared. One center had a staff that was made up of mostly older adults and also had many older volunteers. In the other center, the staff had no older adults. Children in the center with more older adults were better able to differentiate age groups and evaluated the elderly more favorably (Caspi, 1984).

Another program-based research project found that intergenerational programming over a 9-month school year significantly affected how elementary children perceive the elderly. Aday, Sims, and Evans (1991) conducted research in an intergenerational partners project, which was preceded by discussions and education about older adults and aging and discussion of students' feelings about older persons and the program. Although both participants and a control group had generally positive attitudes toward older adults, the participants had significantly more positive scores. The study supports the notion that increased contact produces improved attitudes and suggests that a number of conditions must be present for members of one group to improve their attitudes about other groups (Amir, 1969): equal status between groups, intimate (not casual) contact, contact that is pleasant and rewarding for both groups, and the involvement of both groups in important activities and goal setting. Moreover, participant comments also indicated the importance of structured activities and activities that participants perceive as useful.

Research shows that intergenerational programs that do not prepare students with information about aging and the elderly and do not have opportunities for discussion of feelings (thus only have contact) may produce less positive change. For example, a study of an intergenerational oral history project for junior high school students investigated the attitudes and knowledge of adolescents toward the elderly and the aging process. Youth had negative attitudes and expectations about aging. Participation in the project did not significantly affect their knowledge and attitudes about the elderly and aging, although they did view the older persons with whom they worked in the project positively. The students were prepared with information about the history of the community and about oral history but not about aging and the elderly (Doka, 1985/1986).

Attitudes toward older adults across cultures. As researchers studied the attitudes of children and youth toward the elderly over several decades, they sought comparisons between attitudes in the United States and those in other cultures. Questions such as "Is ageism universal?" began to interest both researchers and practitioners in the intergenerational field. The limited studies to date have found that negative attitudes toward the elderly are neither universal among youth nor more common in the United States than in other societies. Children in the United States may actually hold more positive attitudes toward the elderly than do children and youth in some societies.

Seefeldt (1984) concluded that negative attitudes toward the elderly are not unique to the mainland United States. In fact, her results suggest that the United States may be less ageist than the other societies whose children she studied. She administered the semantic differential subscale of the Children's Attitudes Toward the Elderly (CATE) instrument to children in the Aleutian Islands, the mainland United States, Australia, and Paraguay. The children in the Aleutian Islands, Australia, and Paraguay rated young people more positively than they rated old people, whereas children in the mainland United States rated young people and older people similarly.

Using the CATE, Zandi, Mirle, and Jarvis (1990) found that children of Indian origin living in the United States generally differed from other American children only in the type and pattern of behavior they chose to be involved in with older people. Overall, both groups of children had largely positive attitudes toward older adults. Also using the CATE, Jantz (1981) found that the attitudes of Greek children and American children to older people to be quite similar, although complex. A study comparing the attitudes toward the elderly of nursing students in the United States and Norway found positive attitudes by both groups to the elderly but an unwillingness to work with them (McCracken, Fitzwater, Lockwood, & Bjork, 1995).

Attitude change for preprofessionals. Another important area of intergenerational attitude research is that of the attitudes of young persons preparing for careers in nursing and other fields that will serve the elderly population. Studies have examined both the attitudes of preprofessionals and the effects of various curricula and related programs on attitude change. These studies assume that the elderly population is growing and that it will be a large consumer of health care services, with a resulting increase in the need for professionals to work with older persons.

Research has shown that health care professionals give a low priority to work with older persons (MacNeil, 1991) and that the unwillingness of professionals such as nurses to work with older persons reflects the generally negative societal stereotypes about the elderly (Carmel, Cwikel, & Galinsky, 1992). However, researchers and educators have concluded that courses or other means to increase students' knowledge and contact with older persons will reduce stereotypes and increase interest in working with older adults. Aday and Campbell (1995) demonstrated that a nursing curriculum with significant content on aging and older adults could change preconceived notions about the elderly. Moreover, their research showed that attitudes toward the elderly were correlated with work preferences. This leads to a conclusion that the use of such a curriculum can help increase the number of health professionals interested in caring for older adults.

Older adults' attitudes toward children and youth. The research on older adults' attitudes toward children and youth is very limited. Several studies in the 1970s reported that just as children and youth sometimes were found to have stereotypes about the elderly, so too did older adults have stereotypes about the young. For example, Higgans and Faunce (1977) found that older adults held inaccurate ideas about the amount of time that fifth graders engaged in helping and in thinking and worrying.

To learn more about older adult attitudes toward children, Seefeldt, Jantz, Serock, and Bredekamp (1982) developed the Elderly Persons' Attitudes Toward Children (EPATC) instrument to measure the affective, cognitive, and behavioral components of older adult attitudes. Results from a national survey of older adults using the EPATC showed that older persons generally had positive feelings toward children under 12, including positive feelings about the rights of children. Negative feelings appeared in certain areas, such as some personality characteristics of children. The older adults appeared to have general knowledge about how children behave. About half the older adults had regular contact with children under 12. Seefeldt et al. concluded that the results supported the implementation of intergenerational programs.

The research on older adults' attitudes toward children and youth in intergenerational programs is also limited. Chapman and Neal (1990), in the evaluation cited earlier, found no significant change in the attitudes of older adult participants about youth. However, they noted that the older adults' attitudes toward youth were more positive at the beginning of the project than were those of the youths toward older adults. The lack of change may have been due to the relatively positive attitudes older adults already had toward children.

Attitudes and intergenerational communication theory. In summarizing the research on attitude change, Fox and Giles (1993) asked whether contact between young and old, including contact within families, through education, and through intergenerational programs, fostered favorable images of older adults. They found that naturally occurring contact (such as that with grandparents) showed inconclusive results for attitude change. Studies have shown, however, that the quality, not the quantity, of contact appears to be most important in producing positive outcomes.

- Adding an educational program about aging to the contact produced more positive attitude change than does depending solely on naturally occurring contact.
- Intergenerational programs, including educational programs, were useful in reducing stereotypes held about older adults if the older adults were healthy and if they were involved in community projects.
- The research to date had not produced strong, clear results. To improve the quality of the findings, Fox and Giles recommended that future research should be theory driven, longitudinal, concerned with both generations, and focused on behavioral and communicative aspects of contact.

In arguing the need for more theory-driven research and practice, Fox and Giles pointed out that although intergenerational programs bring two different groups into contact, few studies have used contact theory (such as that of Amir, 1969) to explain how contact between groups could lead to more positive attitudes toward one another. They suggested the need for the refinement of a theory of intergenerational contact and for better understanding of the communication that occurs between young and old in contact situations. For example, do younger persons typically engage frail elderly in a way that discounts the older adults' difficulties, thus lowering the older persons' self-esteem?

A growing body of research that focuses on communication between older and younger persons has begun to address the issues raised by Fox and Giles (1993). Although the research has generally not been associated with specific intergenerational programs, it has direct implications for the outcomes of such programs and for practical training of participants. For example, some research has examined the use by staff and volunteers of "baby talk" with frail elderly and found that, compared with more neutral speech situations, those who received it were less satisfied with the interaction and that the caregivers who used baby talk were rated as less respectful and competent (Ryan, Hamilton, & See, 1994).

Young People's Knowledge About Older Adults

A number of studies have explored young people's knowledge of aging and their knowledge of older adults. Palmore's Facts on Aging Quiz (Palmore, 1977, 1980, 1988) is frequently used in this research. The amount and quality of contact with older persons (generally a grandparent is cited by the youth) has been proposed as important to the degree of knowledge about older adults. However, the results of research on this topic have shown mixed results, with differences in knowledge on specific questions about the elderly and aging related to gender. For example, adolescents who report the most contact with older persons are more likely to overestimate the percentage of the population that is over 65 than are those who have less contact with an older adult (Steitz & Verner, 1987).

Intergenerational Program Effects on Older Adults

Intergenerational research has also examined the beneficial effects of program participation on older adults. Among the areas of study have been self-esteem, life satisfaction, and cognitive function. Among the earliest intergenerational research was Saltz's (1970, 1971) study, which found positive effects of participation in the Foster Grandparent Program on older adults' life adjustment. The effects, which included increased life satisfaction and positive effects on health, appeared to last beyond the period of employment. Interestingly, the study also examined several other questions that would appear in later intergenerational research, including the issue of the job performance of older adults in child care.

A later study of the life satisfaction of older adults who volunteered in an intergenerational program found no significant difference in the scores of new and experienced volunteers on a standardized life satisfaction index (Newman, Baum, & Vasudev, 1983). Newman et al. did, however, find very positive reports on the program participants' experience on open-ended questions in semistructured interviews. They concluded that because the volunteers were self-selected and came with high life satisfaction, the instrument was not sensitive enough to the level of changes described by the interviews.

School volunteering has been a mainstay of intergenerational programs over the last several decades, one in which tens of thousands of older adults have participated. Newman, Karip, and Faux (1995) found that both everyday memory performance and older adults' perception of their memory performance changed as a result of participating in a school volunteer program. The positive effects of the school volunteer experience echo those found over more than a decade of study of older adult volunteers in Generations Together's Senior Citizen School Volunteer Program (Newman & Larimer, 1995).

Research has also examined the effects of intergenerational programs on older adults who are served by such programs. Reinke, Holmes, and Denney (1981) found that compared with a control group, nursing home residents who were visited twice a week by undergraduate students had improved cognitive functioning and morale. McGowan (1994) reported on the generally positive and enjoyable outcomes for elderly persons who took part in a mentoring and reminiscence project in which they were visited by college students to discuss their life histories. The study is noteworthy both because it examined a unique kind of intergenerational program and because it used intensive, qualitative interviews to study the effects of program participation.

A growing number of intergenerational programs address the needs of older adults with dementia. Ward, Los Kamp, and Newman (1996) compared the effects of music activities with and without preschool children present. They found significant differences in several positive behaviors. Touching was more frequent and head nodding was less frequent when the children were present. They also found that participation in activities with small children somewhat lowered residents' agitation levels later in the day on which the activities took place. Their study builds off of earlier work by Newman and Ward (1993).

Intergenerational programs have also been studied to understand their outcomes on learning. Among the reported research outcomes are a significant increase—as compared with a control group—in reading improvement (Cooledge & Wurster, 1985) and greater average gains in student reading and mathematics achievement and attendance (Powell, Wisenbaker, & Connor, 1987).

Intergenerational Behaviors and Interactions

Kuehne (1989) observed an intergenerational program in an adult day center where 4- and 5-year-olds came each week for an hour of organized activities with the older adults. She categorized the observed interactions as positive and negative and found that the great majority of observed interactions were positive. The most frequent positive interactions were giving affection, complimenting, and playing. Positive interactions over 9 sessions totaled 462. In contrast, Kuehne observed only 14 negative interactions during the same period, mostly aggression.

Lambert, Dellman-Jenkins, and Fruit (1990) first described an intergenerational program for young children and then summarized the impact of that program on the behavior of children toward the elderly. They wished to know how participation in an intergenerational program affected children's sharing, helping, and cooperating with older adults. The most striking results of their research was that children who participated in the program had nearly a 25% increase in their willingness to share with older adults compared with a group of children who did not participate.

Intergenerational Child Care and Older Workers

With the growth of intergenerational programs has come an expansion of inter-generational research to new and somewhat specialized areas. For example, for more than a decade, Generations Together has trained older workers for intergenerational child care and developed curricula, guidelines, and materials related to the training. In conjunction with these program efforts, Generations Together also developed a research agenda that studied a number of questions related to the training and work of the older adults. For example, Ward, Newman, Engel, and Karip (1994a, 1994b) examined older worker retention and attrition and the relationship between their work experience and their life satisfaction and self-esteem. They also studied how satisfied child-care employers were with their older workers' performance and the effect that older workers had on the child-care environment. Among the most important find-ings for intergenerational programming was that observations of paired classrooms with similar programs but different staff showed no difference in quality between rooms where an older adult (over 55 years of age) filled one position and those rooms where a person under 55 years of age filled the same position. Other research on older adults in child care has suggested that participation by older adults in child care supports the notion of generativity and enhances productive aging (Newman & Riess, 1992) and has examined what factors contribute to successful training and placement programs (Ward & Smith, 1992).

Surveys of Intergenerational Programs

Intergenerational research has also sought to describe the programs and to help understand how programs function and how they can be improved. This research has not been limited to North America. Yamazaki (1994), for example, described inter-generational programs emerging in Japan. Angelis (1992b) studied the beginnings of six diverse intergenerational programs. She found that common to the creation of the programs were a need or problem, committed leaders, a source of encouragement and support, and a system for linking young and old.

Research has also included the description of programs. One such study sur-veyed 39 courses in which students were involved with service learning on aging (Firman, Gelfand, & Ventura, 1983) and on the status of intergenerational programs (Wilson & Simson, 1991). Among emerging efforts in this area is an ongoing study at Generations Together to survey the variety of intergenerational studies programs offered at colleges and universities in North America.

Grandparents

Intergenerational research has also included a wide range of research on relation-ships between generations, primarily within families. Among the relationships stud-ied have been those of grandparents and grandchildren, such as the influence of grandparents on college students (Franks, Hughes, Phelps, & Williams, 1993). A broader questions is whether students really do have little contact with older adults, as is often asserted in general statements about American society. Through inter-views with parents, Sheehan (1975) found that a significant number of children from

4 to 6 years of age had regular contact with older adults. Most of these older adults were grandparents and great grandparents. Rose-Colley and Eddy (1988) examined the interaction of college-age youth and elderly persons. They found that young women had significantly more interactions with older persons than did young men.

During the 1990s, grandparents raising their grandchildren has become a major intergenerational topic. Parents' drug addiction is one major reason for the increasing number of grandparents taking on this role. Researcher have attempted to understand this parenting process and how it affects grandparents who are suddenly thrust into a new, stressful role (Minkler & Roe, 1993).

Intergenerational Politics

The influence of issues related to intergenerational equity and the politics of young and old is discussed elsewhere in this volume. Intergenerational program research has not yet explored linkages to issues raised by these policy debates. Much of the research related to these questions comes from fields such as economics and demographics. Summaries or highlights sometimes appear in the popular press or in aging, child development, or related fields' publications. For example, Rosenbaum and Button (1993) summarized the public opinion studies about the relationship between generations. These types of studies have found that the American public demonstrates little of the conflict among generations that is sometimes attributed to it.

Dissertation Research

Doctoral dissertations and master's theses offer great potential for furthering intergenerational research and the field of intergenerational studies. The dissertation literature is not as easily accessed as the literature that appears in journals and other publications. However, intergenerational dissertations first appeared more than two decades ago and continue to be produced. For example, Weinsberg (1974) wrote an early dissertation on high school volunteers' attitudes about the elderly in nursing homes. Other dissertations have included research on children's perception of the elderly (Marks, 1980), children's extrafamilial intergenerational relationships (Kuehne, 1990), and an intergenerational approach to community education and action (Kaplan, 1991). A recent example of a master's thesis is that of Angersbach and Jones (1996), who described intergenerational interactions in a child-care center. Advances in CD-ROM technology now mean that the abstracts of the dissertations can be found and downloaded with relative ease.

MEASURES

Issues in Intergenerational Research Methodology

Many of the issues in intergenerational research methodology are similar to those for evaluation. The research often focuses on two vulnerable populations, each of which requires particular methods and instruments. Both populations may have limits on their ability to respond to particular kinds of data collection. Both populations may not always be accessible or may require that researchers fulfill institutional requirements to gain access to participants.

Techniques and Strategies for Data Collection

The number of specific techniques for gathering data is very large. They include story writing based on pictures, drawings, semantic differential scales, interviews (individual and group, semistructured and structured), content analysis of previously produced material, sentence completion, observations in person or with videotape, and self-constructed questionnaires of many types.

Many types of standardized instruments can be used to collect research data. These include instruments to collect data on attitudes about older adults and children, about aging, and about knowledge of aging and child development. The standardized research instruments important for intergenerational research also include those that measure factors such as self-esteem and life satisfaction. Many other standardized instruments may also be used, depending on the particular focus of the research. These could range from questionnaires about social distance to attitudes toward one's community.

FUTURE RESEARCH

As an emerging field, intergenerational studies has produced a limited amount of research. As an interdisciplinary field it has drawn on many other fields for concepts and direction, resulting in more development in some areas (children's attitudes toward older adults) than in others (the effects of intergenerational program participation on health). As an applied field, intergenerational studies responds to the questions raised by practitioners and programs. In this regard the future of intergenerational research needs to focus much more intensely on learning about the effects of intergenerational programs and experiences on social problems (drug abuse, lack of school success) that intergenerational programs are increasingly addressing.

In practical terms, the field's agenda will need to move beyond short-term attitude research:

- Long-term, large-scale studies could contribute perspectives not available to date from research that has often focused on short-term projects. For example, little is known about how long the effects of intergenerational experiences are sustained after participation ends.
- Studies should compare the effects of programs using age as the variable of interest. The field needs to understand, for example, if two mentoring programs differing only by the age of their volunteers produce different effects. Likewise, research needs to compare the outcomes for two groups of children when the child-care professionals who care for them differ only by age.
- Intergenerational research should be more closely tied to policy. The intergenerational studies field could both deepen understanding and ensure its own growth

and development through a research agenda that examines questions related to public policy. For example, researchers could look at what effects school volunteer programs have on community support for education.

- Much of the research to date has been carried out with standardized measures that produce quantifiable outcomes. Although these instruments have been very useful, they requires older adults and children to respond to complex issues using predetermined categories, possibly limiting what researchers might learn about the participants' perspectives. To provide these broader perspectives, the field should utilize more in-depth ethnographic and other qualitative studies of intergenerational programs such as colocated adult and child day-care sites.
- The intergenerational studies field needs to conduct study and research on the impact of intergenerational programs on the systems within which it works. Included in such studies are those that look at the development and needs of the intergenerational field, such as surveys of intergenerational studies in colleges and universities, and the assessing and categorizing of the competencies needed by intergenerational professionals.
- A fundamental long-term research question is the impact of intergenerational programs on families and on the community.

Implementation of these steps, as well as continuation of current research strategies, should produce a body of knowledge that contributes to the success of intergenerational programs and to better understanding of the basic concepts and theories that underlie these programs and the intergenerational movement.

IV

---

*PUBLIC POLICY
AND THE FUTURE
OF INTERGENERATIONAL
PROGRAMS*

9

Intergenerational Programs and Public Policy: A Context for Growth and Change

Gary Calhoun, MSW, Eric Kingson, PhD, and Sally Newman, PhD

The quality of a nation is reflected in the way it recognizes that its strength lies in its ability to integrate the wisdom of its elders with the spirit and vitality of its children and youth.

—Margaret Mead

Without question, there is a growing interest in intergenerational programs and related policy thrusts. During the past 30 years, foundations, nonprofit organizations, and other private efforts have actively promoted intergenerational program models, and public funds have facilitated the spread of various approaches to intergenerational service. The title of the 1995 White House Conference on Aging—America Now and into the 21st Century: Generations Aging Together with Independence, Opportunity, and Dignity—speaks to the growing influence of intergenerational programs and themes in policy discussions about both younger and older Americans.

Today, intergenerational programs are an important human service field, with many documented benefits for the recipients of services as well as for those who provide them. Interest in intergenerational programs has come from many professional sources, including social work, gerontology, child development, education, psychology, sociology, family studies, and social policy (Newman & Larkin, 1997, in press, p. 7).

Advocates and service providers for the young and old have also come together to support the growth of these programs. Along with the development of intergenerational programs, there has been a growing expression of an intergenerational voice in important public policy debates. Service providers, advocates for children and older people, academics, and those within government at all levels have begun to argue for approaches to social policy that are based on a belief in the interdependence between generations and the need to create policy that responds to the needs of different age groups. Finally, those concerned with intergenerational programs and policy have begun to argue that the types of intergenerational thinking and exchange described above can do much to reinforce an important form of citizenship and to foster a society in which the generations interact and contribute to their communities in rich and meaningful ways for the betterment of all.

In spite of this growing attention to intergenerational programs and approaches to policy, there remain unanswered questions about the future of intergenerational programs and efforts to inject greater appreciation of intergenerational concerns into policy dialogues. It is not certain whether intergenerational programs can break out of the stereotype of being viewed simply as nice services to promote. It is also unclear whether the intergenerational dialogue that is based on a recognition of the interdependence of generations will be drowned out by the voices of those who promote the rhetoric of generational conflict and crises.

Chapters 9 and 10 trace the growth of intergenerational programs and the emergence of intergenerational themes in public policy debates. They analyze the policy context in which these programs and themes have developed and the challenges that intergenerational advocates face as they attempt to further an intergenerational agenda.

The analysis shows that, to date, intergenerational programs have met with more success than have attempts to frame public policy and advocacy activities in intergenerational terms. In part, this is a result of the circumstances and forces surrounding the development of intergenerational programs. Intergenerational programming poses little political threat, and the economic stakes are relatively small. Moreover, these interventions are almost universally applauded. In contrast, intergenerational themes—although not entirely new to discussion of public policy—have in recent years been injected into social policy debates about the future of Social Security, Medicare, Medicaid, and a variety of other social programs, largely as a defensive antidote to those charging that public expenditures for today's and tomorrow's old are unfair to the young and a cause of conflict between generations. The economic stakes are significant in these policy arenas and the political competition vociferous.

Chapter 9 begins by exploring the development of programs and enabling policies that have supported the growth of intergenerational service and then discusses the challenges that need to be addressed to further institutionalize these models. Prior to discussing some of the challenges involved in moving intergenerational programs to the next stage of development, there are many factors to be examined that have created a positive policy environment in which they could develop and thrive.

AN ENVIRONMENT FOR GROWTH

Intergenerational programs have experienced rapid development over the last three decades because they have increasingly become viewed as a valuable means to an important end. In communities all across the United States and even internationally, these programs have provided a means for young and old to participate in forms of exchange that provide powerful benefits to both (Scannell & Roberts, 1994, p. 2).

Broad-based support for these programs has come from service providers, advocates for younger and older Americans, public policy makers (at the local, state, and national levels), academics, corporations, foundations, and volunteers of all ages. This has led to impressive growth in the numbers and types of programs developed and the involvement of many thousands of people who participate in intergenerational efforts. It has also led to the development of the public policies, private initiatives, and public–private partnerships that have supported this program growth.

Some of the key factors that led to the growth of programs and supportive policies are explored below. They are

- concern over the potential alienation that can result from the segregation of the generations;
- a renewed appeal to voluntary action by citizens of all ages to address a variety of escalating societal concerns;
- a growing body of experience and research indicating that intergenerational programs can make important contributions in addressing those concerns;
- the development of a unified voice to advocate for the growth and coordination of intergenerational programs by national, regional, state, and local networks and coalitions;
- the popular appeal of these programs based on their connection to strongly held traditional family and community values and traditions; and
- a movement by older citizens to increase the opportunities for active, productive, and meaningful engagement in their communities and in society.

Bridging the Gap

Chapter 2 described a number of dynamics that have contributed to an increasing segregation between generations in American society, especially between the youngest and the oldest, and an accompanying sense of alienation for many. Addressing this segregation and potential alienation between older and younger citizens was an early focus of intergenerational programs. It was the primary focus of many of the earliest programs, which had the goal of simply providing structured opportunities for old and young to interact together for their mutual benefit. Older people interacting with children in schools or day-care settings, school or civic youth groups providing friendly visits in nursing homes or senior centers, and day-care centers for children being colocated in senior centers or nursing homes are all examples of the types of programs that offered opportunities for young and old to interact in positive ways (Newman, 1994). Chapter 8 reviewed the convincing body of experience and research that began to document the important benefits of such programs.

Fulfilling a Public Purpose

As the benefits of these programs became more widely known, their focus began to broaden, and they became identified as an important response to a number of other troubling community needs. Intergenerational programs began to "fulfill a public purpose" (Scannell & Roberts, 1994, p. 3) as they focused their efforts on an array of broader social needs that concerned all generations of society. An overwhelmed public education system; an escalating need for quality child care; an increase in teenage pregnancy, single-parent families, and divorce rates; growing numbers of children living in families in poverty; increasing numbers of youths and adults who abuse alcohol and other drugs; growing numbers of families needing assistance in the long- and short-term care of frail elders; a health care system in which costs are rising and important protections are lacking for many; the AIDS epidemic; homelessness and hunger (Corman & Kingson, 1995, pp. 6-12; Costello, 1991, p. 41; Etzioni, 1993, p.

12; Freedman, 1994, pp. 9–12; Helfgott, 1992, p. 2; Kingson, 1989, p. 96; Romney, 1991, p. 35; Scannell & Roberts, 1994, p. 3) are all concerns that began to capture the public attention and become the focus of intergenerational programs. Although much of the earliest and most significant program and policy development was focused on the education and child-care arenas, intergenerational programs have developed to address each of these important social needs.

A Growing Body of Experience and Research

The growth of intergenerational programs was supported by the dissemination of the results of early efforts at intergenerational research and program evaluation. As described in chapter 8, research on child and adult development and on the rich value of intergenerational interaction provided theoretical underpinnings for the development of a variety of program models. As programs became more established and as funders began to demand evaluative data, more sophisticated evaluation components were developed and produced convincing evidence of the benefits of intergenerational programming to its participants. Early program evaluation focused on the mutual benefits of intergenerational interaction for older and younger participants. Over time, as programs began to shift from providing forums for positive intergenerational interaction to a more focused effort to address social needs, the focus of program evaluation also began to shift correspondingly to the impact that programs had on addressing those needs. Reported positive results regarding personal impact and social change helped to create the environment of support that stimulated program growth and development (see chapter 8).

It is fair to say that intergenerational research and program evaluation, although it has been limited, has played an important role in convincing program planners and funders of the potential benefits of formal programs of intergenerational exchange. As results of these efforts were disseminated, they provided a rationale for investment in these programs. Chapter 8 put forth an agenda for the type of research and evaluation that will be necessary to further program growth and development. Other challenges in the research arena are also addressed later in this chapter.

A Unified Voice

The recognition and growth of intergenerational program models has also been facilitated by the development of intergenerational coalitions and networks (see chapter 4). In addition to facilitating coordination and collaboration among agencies supporting intergenerational programs, these organizations provided an important vehicle to spread knowledge about intergenerational models to other potential program sites as well as to decision makers and potential funders. Through these coalitions and networks, individual intergenerational programs began to be seen more broadly as part of a larger service model.

A Popular Appeal

When it comes to intergenerational programs, there is little controversy and little not to like. Programs that provide opportunities for positive interaction between generations, that serve to channel large numbers of elders and youths into community service, and that have proven effective in responding to important social problems while tapping relatively small proportions of public budgets are popular for obvious reasons.

Contributing to this appeal is the programs' foundation in longstanding and deeply held societal traditions and ideals. Though intergenerational programs have developed over the last 30 years, the idea and practice of intergenerational exchange is not new. Throughout history, the different generations have been involved in vital reciprocal exchanges that have sustained all members of families throughout their life courses (Kingson, Hirshorn, & Harootyan, 1987, p. 8). Though modern Western society has created some barriers to formal exchange between generations (Stearns, 1989, pp. 21–31), it has always been and still remains a part of the fabric of American families and communities. As program advocates called for support for the development of these formalized vehicles for exchange, their call rang true with long-held traditional values.

At the public level, federal, state, and local programs have received consistent bipartisan support. Presidents from Kennedy to Clinton have supported them both verbally and through supportive policies. Whether in the context of the social activism of the 1960s, the New Federalism of the 1980s, or in the current context, appeals have been made to young and old to engage in service to their communities and their country, and federal programs to encourage that engagement have been supported.

Two important events illustrate the value that the Clinton administration has placed on intergenerational programs. First, the National and Community Service Trust Act of 1993 continued support of the senior community service programs that have strong intergenerational emphases (such as the Retired Senior Volunteer Program and the Foster Grandparent Program) and established the new AmeriCorps program, which encourages intergenerational community service for youth. Second, Clinton's active support for an intergenerational agenda at the 1995 White House Conference on Aging demonstrated his interest in intergenerational approaches to public policy (Blancato, 1996).

Chapter 4 described how federal agencies such as the U.S. Office of Education, the U.S. Administration on Aging, and the U.S. Department of Health and Human Services have also provided support for program development in a variety of areas such as public schools, child-care settings, families with disabled children, and at-risk children, youths, and older adults. The Office of Substance Abuse Prevention has provided demonstration grants for intergenerational approaches to substance abuse prevention for high-risk youth (Henkin, 1996). In fact, much of this federal support takes the form of demonstration grants rather than ongoing program funding. It has been important in the development of influential and replicable program models.

Support from members of Congress has been bipartisan. Democrats and Republicans, liberals and conservatives have seen the advantages of developing programs of intergenerational exchange and have been involved in sponsoring and supporting policies that have helped those programs grow. Although they may certainly frame the problems to which these programs respond in different ways, there has been some agreement that intergenerational programs can be an important part of the response.

Some may see the root cause of the United States' social problems as being related to declining moral and social structures (Romney, 1991, p. 35), whereas others may emphasize the lack of essential public investment in social development; nevertheless, from either ideological position there has been some agreement that intergenerational community service programs can play a meaningful role in addressing these important problems.

At times congressional support has led to tangible sources of funding, but at other times the support has been more symbolic. Evidence of tangible support can be found in Congress's consistent support of the federal senior service programs now housed within the Corporation for National Service and its initial support of the AmeriCorps programs. It can also be found in the previous support for the preparation of low-income older workers for employment in intergenerational settings such as child care and education. This support has been provided by the Title V programs of the Older Americans Act as well as the Job Training Partnership Act. The 1990 Child Care and Development Block Grant provided funding to states for the improvement of child-care services, including the greater utilization of older caregivers. The effect of this federal initiative, however, is limited by each governor's commitment to training older adults for work in the child-care system.

An example of a more symbolic type of support that does much less than some Congressional advocates desired ("Intergenerational mentoring," 1992), can be found in the inclusion of language in the recent reauthorization of the Elementary and Secondary Education Act, which supports the concept of intergenerational mentoring programs in public schools but provides no funding for generating such efforts (see chapter 4).

Calls to intergenerational service have been echoed in states and communities across the country. Governors, state legislatures, and local authorities have developed enabling policies that support the involvement of older citizens as tutors and mentors in public schools or as volunteers or employees in child-care settings. As examples, state offices of aging or other state agencies have provided support for the development of a variety of program types, directly as well as through the support of statewide program networks or public education. Local governments have also put a significant emphasis on making greater use of older citizens in intergenerational settings such as school or for providing service-learning opportunities for youth (see chapter 4).

At the private level, foundations, advocacy groups, corporations, nonprofit agencies, and other civic organizations have provided people and finances to support developing programs. Again, chapter 4 documents the contributions of the private funding sources and organizations who have helped to generate new programs and new program models.

In summary, intergenerational programs have a popular appeal, which has led to tangible as well as symbolic support from a variety of constituencies. Although clearly greater support is needed, intergenerational programs have developed to their current stature in large part because they have demonstrated this popular appeal.

A Renewed Appeal to Voluntary Action

Another trend that has positively affected the growth of intergenerational programs has been a renewed emphasis on the need for voluntary action in response to escalating social needs. Voluntary action has been a consistent part of the United States' history and identity (de Tocqueville, 1900; Ellis & Noyes, 1990). Currently, a sluggish economy and a disinvestment in important areas of social spending have increased social need while leaving communities and social agencies with fewer resources available to them (Wilson & Simson, 1993, p. 18). This has created a call for voluntary action to take a larger role in addressing those needs (Brudney, 1990, p. 8).

Although volunteer programs cannot by themselves "substitute for comprehensive programs to address pressing social needs" (Costello, 1991, p. 41), Cohen (1995, p. 5) noted that volunteerism "is a call for seemingly small gestures that, one by one, can help restore the fabric of American society and conquer some larger problems." Engaging citizens of all ages in voluntary action to address those social needs has been a major focus in both the public and private spheres. Intergenerational programs, the majority of which involve volunteers, have been seen as having a unique role in addressing some of the United States' needs.

Recognition of Seniors as a Resource

As programs have sought to engage citizens in service, they have increasingly become aware of a rich resource: older Americans (Ellis & Noyes, 1990, p. 273). Demographic changes, which have included the numerical and proportional growth of the older population, increased longevity, better health, improved financial well-being, and higher levels of educational attainment for many older Americans, have led to the recognition of what has been called this country's "only increasing natural resource" (Freedman, 1994, p. i).

One way in which that rich resource has been tapped has been through intergenerational volunteer service. Although intergenerational programs involve many forms of reciprocal exchange between older and younger citizens, much of the person power behind these programs has come from seniors. Senior involvement in intergenerational programs and other forms of community service has been one arm of a larger effort to provide seniors with opportunities to remain actively, productively, and meaningfully engaged with their families, communities, and society in later life through a movement focused on productive aging. Health promotion, work beyond retirement, lifelong learning, economic security, and the development of opportunities for contribution have all been important emphases of this movement nationally and internationally (Butler & Gleason, 1985; Dychtwald & Flower, 1989).

The importance of providing opportunities for active engagement and productive involvement for older Americans has been strongly emphasized by gerontologists, health professionals, policy planners, advocates, and older Americans themselves. The Older Americans Act, with its emphasis on active engagement and opportunities for community service, represents an early expression of this thinking in federal policy. Organizations for older Americans such as the Gray Panthers and the American Association of Retired Persons have spearheaded efforts to educate, advocate, and create opportunities for active and productive societal engagement.

One important expression of this movement has been the involvement of millions of older citizens in volunteer community service of all kinds. In 1965, when the Foster Grandparent Program was initiated, seniors in volunteer service was seen as a novel idea (Costello, 1991, p. 42). Today, millions of older people, even many in their 80s and 90s, serve as volunteers in a wide variety of settings. According to the Marriott's Senior Volunteerism Study (1991), 15.5 million people age 60 and over volunteered in some type of organization during 1990. Because of the vital role that seniors in service can play in addressing social problems, Nee (1989, pp. 88–89) suggested that a good test of any social policy would be to assess the degree to which it encourages the contributions of seniors to solve social problems.

Increasingly, discussions of providing opportunities for productive aging have become more intergenerational in nature. For example, providing seniors with opportunities for intergenerational exchange has been an important theme in each of the three White House Conferences on Aging. The 1971 conference was an important stimulus to the expansion of the federal senior volunteer programs that became part of the ACTION network (Freedman, 1994, p. 26). The 1981 conference again put a major emphasis on creating opportunities for seniors to become involved in their communities, with a strong emphasis on intergenerational involvement (White House Conference on Aging, 1981b). The 1995 conference, Generations Aging Together With Independence, Opportunity, and Dignity, reaffirmed the importance of intergenerational themes, including the need to expand opportunities to allow older Americans to make vital contributions to pressing social problems for children and youth (White House Conference on Aging, 1995).

Seniors provide vast numbers of hours of service in intergenerational settings. It is suggested that in the schools alone throughout the United States, over one million older citizens volunteer their time in intergenerational service on a regular basis (Newman, 1989b, p. 4). Although many seniors are involved through formal intergenerational programs, others become involved in informal ways as they respond to natural family and community connections. The involvement of seniors in intergenerational service provides them with rich opportunities to contribute to the well-being of their communities and has been an important corrective to traditional stereotypes that portray seniors as being on the receiving end of benefits and services.

Although an emphasis on involving seniors in community service has been one thrust of this broader productive aging movement, so too has been the goal of providing seniors with greater access to employment opportunities and for expanded opportunities for lifelong learning. Intergenerational employment opportunities for seniors have been evident through programs funded by the Job Training Partnership Act and Title V of the Older Americans Act. These initiatives provide job training and placement opportunities for low-income older adults, often in intergenerational settings. A primary example of this opportunity is the child-care field, in which part-time employment is available to trained, skilled older workers (American Association of Retired Persons, 1993).

Other work opportunities are the school mentoring programs that employ older adults as part-time support staff specifically in programs for at-risk children and youth. These initiatives are evident in low-income communities where there is often a profound need for service to children and youth and for employment for older adults.

A final example of noteworthy opportunities for productive aging is the growing number of lifelong learning experiences that are available to older adults. Formal and informal programs for continued learning in higher education and in human service systems are offered throughout the United States. Academic or leisure learning courses may be options for older adults interested in credit or noncredit learning experiences. These opportunities help the older population keep current, intellectually challenged, and socially engaged. The community service, training for work, and lifelong learning opportunities contribute significantly to the productive aging of the United States' growing population of older adults.

CHALLENGES FOR INTERGENERATIONAL PROGRAMS WITHIN THE CURRENT POLICY ENVIRONMENT

The development and expansion of intergenerational programs has been dramatic, but their full potential has not been realized. Whereas some programs have grown and thrived, others have remained small and struggled to sustain themselves over time ("Intergenerational mentoring," 1992). Although they have played an important role in addressing a number of important social problems, there is potential to have a much greater impact. Although they are popular programs that have received public and private support, the support remains too modest relative to the important role that these programs can play in helping to address the United States' serious social needs. A fundamental challenge must be addressed as advocates for intergenerational approaches strive to institutionalize these approaches that deal with social problems. The challenge is to create structures and supports that lead to the sustainability of these approaches.

Harry R. Moody and Robert Disch (1989, p. 102) described public support for intergenerational programming as "a mile wide and an inch deep." Stating that public funding for intergenerational programs is "part of everyone's agenda and no one's budget," they argued that stronger efforts must be made to convince the public and public officials "of the crucial importance of intergenerational programming for essential public purposes" if support for these programs is to be "strong, consistent and enduring" (p. 102).

Experts also agree on the importance of expanding the base of support for intergenerational programs within the private sector (T. Scannell, personal communication, February 13, 1996; J. Leavitt, personal communication, 1996; B. Friedman, personal communication, March 8, 1996). Although federal support remains vitally important, private forms of support and public–private partnerships have provided much of the impetus behind program growth, especially at the local level. Although a number of private foundations have been involved in funding intergenerational programs, many are not fully aware of the important role of intergenerational programs and do not include them under their funding categories (B. Friedman, personal communication, March 8, 1996). Corporations as well as foundations are important targets for increased support. Tess Scannell (personal communication, February 13, 1996) of the Corporation for National Service noted the need to continue to reach out to "untapped markets," including corporations, not only for funding but also as important vehicles to reach more senior workers and retirees to become engaged in intergenerational service.

This section addresses a number of important challenges that intergenerational programs face as they seek to gain greater public and private support that will enable them to move to the important next stage of development. First, they must continue to demonstrate the significant role that they can play in effectively addressing some of the key social problems that so concern American society. They must show that they can make a serious impact. Second, they must find ways to garner support in a conservative policy environment in which the trends toward public disinvestment in social resources creates both greater need and less public support for those who would seek to address that need. Third, they must find ways to engage greater numbers of program participants of all ages.

Demonstrating Significance

Intergenerational programs have been limited by a commonly held stereotype that tends to view them as nice things but not as critical things. Barbara Friedman (personal communication, March, 8, 1996), chairperson of the Massachusetts Intergenerational Network, suggested that intergenerational programs need to continue a process of moving from being viewed as "a cute thing" to being more broadly recognized as an important form of service delivery that can have a significant impact on important social problems. Marc Freedman ("Intergenerational mentoring," 1992) argued that to increase recognition of these programs, not only is there a need to increase the numbers of programs and the numbers of people in service but also a need to "increase the voltage" of the programs that do exist by maximizing their three important areas of impact: "(1) benefits to those served; (2) benefits to those rendering service; and (3) benefits to the larger community." Two things are important in this process. First, these programs must continue to show an ability to effectively address the significant social problems that trouble American society. Second, they must focus on program approaches that make the greatest impact.

Identifying Areas to Address

One reason for the growth of intergenerational programs is that they have successfully targeted important problem areas and have then been able to demonstrate effectiveness in addressing them. Education, child care, and aging have been among the most important arenas for program growth. These are arenas in which the need has been great, public concern has been high, and intergenerational approaches have demonstrated a unique ability to make a positive contribution. It is vitally important that planners carefully scan the current policy environment to look for key areas where intergenerational programs can continue to make an important and unique difference. Reflecting this importance is the fact that in the last reauthorization of the Foster Grandparent Program and the Retired Senior Volunteer Program, language was added that directed these programs to focus their efforts on issues of national significance ("Intergenerational mentoring," 1992). There are a number of areas of national significance that may well provide important opportunities for future program growth.

Given the continuing need in the areas just mentioned (education, child care, and aging), as well as the positive outcomes and the high visibility of intergenerational efforts in those settings, it can be expected that they will remain fertile ground for program growth. As described earlier, intergenerational programs have also effectively responded to a number of other pressing social problems, suggesting that a number of other policy issues may present important windows (Kingdon, 1994) or opportunities for program expansion. Welfare reform initiatives will certainly contribute to the need for even greater child-care resources. The growing numbers of grandparents providing temporary or permanent care for their grandchildren will likely create a growing need for support as grandparents make this vital contribution to other generations of their families. Health care, public safety, the expanding numbers of seniors who will need home care, and environmental needs are among a number of social concerns to which intergenerational programs can make unique and important contributions.

Developing a larger place for intergenerational programs in these areas will take a concerted effort. Policymakers and service providers often do not naturally think of intergenerational programs when planning to address these problem areas. Advocates for intergenerational programs must continue to educate the public about the importance of these programs and the unique contributions that they can make (J. Leavitt, personal communication, February 13, 1996). In many ways, policymakers continue to think about problems and potential solutions categorically, that is, by age cohorts or by special issues. If thinking about program responses is to become less categorical and more intergenerational, the impetus for that change must come from specialists who recognize the value of an intergenerational approach to social problems.

Although categorical thinking can be seen as an impediment to intergenerational programming, it can also be seen as a potential opportunity. Rather than having a limited category of programs that are seen as intergenerational, advocates for intergenerational approaches to community service can actively educate policymakers and funders about the important role that intergenerational approaches to service delivery can have in a wide variety of need areas. In this way, the idea of intergenerational approaches to community needs can be expanded and a broader range of funding sources can be tapped (Henkin, 1996).

The Need to Demonstrate a Greater Impact

As planners identify important issues to address, they must also focus on ways to increase the level of demonstrated impact on those issues. This can be accomplished in a number of ways. First, program efforts can focus on ways to make a greater systems-level impact by developing more intensive and focused approaches consistent with the mission of the involved systems. Second, they must demonstrate that these approaches, which may involve significant cost, can also be cost-effective. Third, infrastructure strategies must be developed at the public and private levels that support the development and maintenance of these programs.

A method for convincing policy planners to make larger investments in intergenerational programs is to demonstrate that these programs have a system-level impact. Although outcome research done to date on intergenerational programs has demonstrated a number of important benefits, it has not focused enough on how intergenerational programs could have an impact on a broader systems level.

The Corporation for National Service (1995), in collaboration with Public/Private Ventures and the Johns Hopkins School of Medicine, is attempting to address the system approach through a new initiative. This initiative provides demonstration grants to the Foster Grandparent Program and the Retired Senior Volunteer Program in four sites across the country with the aim of evaluating these programs' abilities to more intensively address problems within a community system. Although some of the programs would involve seniors serving seniors, a major emphasis is on programs in which seniors provide service to children in schools and community youth centers. The demonstration calls for "corps" of seniors to provide service in public elementary schools and community youth organizations concentrated in targeted neighborhoods. The research component will examine the impact of this concentrated service on "the young people, schools, youth organizations, and seniors involved" (Corporation for National Service, 1995, p. 1).

Because senior service programs historically tend to be deployed in scattered fashion with a limited ability to document more of a systems-level impact, the demonstrations will focus on building a critical mass within specific neighborhoods and institutions. The corps of seniors will provide 15 hr of volunteer service weekly over an extended period. Through this concentrated involvement, the impact of the programs can be maximized (Corporation for National Service, 1995). This project is representative of the type of program and research development that will be necessary for developing greater public and private support of intergenerational programs. The development of local, state, and regional program network impact will also address issues of system levels.

Henkin and Sweeney (1989) described a number of networks across the country that have focused their efforts on larger systems within communities by bringing a number of agencies and organizations concerned with the needs of the young and the old together for joint planning and resource management:

Whether the system being addressed is a group of organizations with related goals in a geographic area, a special population within the community or the linking of age related organizations, the emphasis is on assessing the needs of community members and finding intergenerational solutions to gaps in services. . . . The systems approach allows organizations to address issues related to an organizational mission while ensuring a long-range commitment to solving the problems of multiple organizations and the generations they serve. (p. 166)

The Need to Demonstrate Effectiveness and Cost-Effectiveness

Along with demonstrating the positive effects of intergenerational programs, research must continue to demonstrate that they are cost-effective. Although part of the appeal of intergenerational programs might be an assumption that programs serving old and young together, often through the use of volunteers, may be an inexpensive way to meet needs, these programs are not necessarily inexpensive and they are certainly not free.

More relevant to issue of cost is the consideration that the limited funding available to systems serving either the young or the old can be used to provide service simultaneously to both populations. Although many intergenerational programs are dependent on some volunteer resources (both older or younger persons), the primary cost of these programs is related to professional aspects of project management, direct service provision, and services provided. Intergenerational programs can be cost-effective because they often involve the collaboration of personnel from partnering agencies, shared facilities and resources, and combined preparation of participants, volunteers, and staff.

The Need for Infrastructure

Marc Freedman ("Intergenerational mentoring," 1992, p. 21) argued that as advocates seek to expand intergenerational approaches, important infrastructure consideration will be needed. He saw an important role for government in providing that infrastructure:

> *It's not really so much we're saying that we need these programs to be government programs or public programs, but there is a need for government to play an enabling role with respect to programs, whether they be government programs or programs in the community, so that there is a way of sustaining efforts over time. ("Intergenerational mentoring," 1992, p. 30)*

Freedman suggested that it is vitally important to build on important structures that are currently in place. Along with government, private efforts and public–private partnerships can provide this important function.

At the federal level, the Corporation for National Service is a good example of this kind of infrastructure. This important umbrella organization is an example of a valuable organizing point for expanded efforts to develop more time-intensive intergenerational models as well as other creative efforts. It is one of those important structures that must be supported.

As described in chapter 4, federal agencies such as the Administration on Aging and the Office of Human Development Services have also provided consistent support, which has had the effect of sustaining ongoing program development. Support by government agencies at the state and local levels for efforts such as developing programs in public schools also provides infrastructure within a system that must be further developed and maintained. An example of where a public–private effort can contribute to this kind of infrastructure is the Public/Private National Intergenerational Initiative (Reville & Adams, 1988), in which the Elvirita Lewis Foundation provided the coordination for an important public–private partnership. In that important initiative, the Administration on Aging cooperated with nine private foundations that created a management system, Grantsmakers in Aging, to fund the development of nine programs. The goals of this initiative were as follows:

- to see whether replicable intergenerational programming could be a vehicle for solving many serious social problems involving both senior citizens and youth;
- to see whether intergenerational programs could prepare senior citizens for second careers; and
- to see whether an effort involving multiple funding from private sources (foundations) and public sources (the Administration on Aging) could produce quality programs in a cost-efficient manner.

This successful initiative proved effective in helping programs address key social problems and in demonstrating a model by which public–private partnership could provide an important form of infrastructure to support program development in more intensive, coordinated, and cost-effective ways. Although this was a time-limited 2-year initiative, it provides an important model for future partnerships.

Growth in a Conservative Policy Environment

A major challenge facing intergenerational programs involves the great risks posed by the conservative political and economic climate that is dominating the current policy environment in the United States. The types of cuts in social spending that are currently being proposed and implemented will increase levels of social need while decreasing the ability of programs to address those needs.

Greater need. Over the last decade and a half, cuts to social programs have increased the level of social need for millions of Americans. Proposed cuts to safety net programs such as Medicaid, Medicare, Social Security, and Aid to Families With Dependent Children (AFDC), as well as to housing and nutrition programs (just to name a few) would most certainly serve to create much greater social need. This increase would likely overwhelm all types of resource and service systems, including intergenerational programs.

Richard Wallace (1995) identified a number of proposed cuts in key social programs that were passed either by the House of Representatives or the Senate during the 1995 congressional sessions. If these cuts were all to become law, they would have the following effects. Federal aid to public schools would be cut by 17% or about $1 billion. A large percentage of those cuts would be absorbed by schools serving primarily low-income families. The Head Start program would be cut by approximately $130 million over 7 years. Federal summer employment programs for youth, which were projected to create 600,000 jobs in the summer of 1996, would be eliminated. Federal funds allotted to job training programs would be reduced by over 30%. Federal assistance to poor families to pay heating and cooling bills would be abolished. Programs to provide low-income public housing would be cut by about 20%. The Food Stamp program would be reduced by approximately $2 million. States would no longer be required to use federal money provided through the Clinton Crime Bill to hire more police officers. Nor would they be required to develop and implement the crime prevention programs designed in the original bill.

These cuts are in addition to proposed cuts of $270 billion in Medicare and Medicaid over 7 years (*Medicare: What's at Stake*, 1996; *Medicaid: What's at Stake*, 1996) as well as the proposals to convert federal funding to state AFDC programs into block grants that are the centerpieces of proposals to trim the federal budget deficit by lowering spending on entitlements. All of these would dramatically increase levels of social need for many vulnerable citizens. A system of social resources that is currently under great stress will be even more overwhelmed. Resources like intergenerational programs will be stretched even further in an effort to meet these greater levels of social need. These proposed cuts could have a long-range impact on the United States, creating a climate in the next decade of greater need for programs that serve multiple ages.

Less support. These same cuts in social spending not only increase levels of social need but also cut into the programmatic infrastructure of organizations that strive to address that need. Along with public programs, the nonprofit sector has been hit hard by cuts in social spending. Continued cuts to nonprofits while asking them to respond to increased social need can weaken their ability to develop and maintain programs of all kinds (Costello, 1991, p. 53), including intergenerational programs.

Costello (1991, p. 53) noted that an "unfortunate assumption has emerged" in the current political arena that the nonprofit sector will step forward to cover the gaps left by withdrawn public investment. She argued that the opposite is true. "Since community-based service organizations often administer government programs, reduced government funding for social programs has a negative effect on the infra-structure and staffing of these organizations" (Costello, 1991, p. 53). Managing inter-generational programs has significant costs. Recruitment, training, supervision, and recognition of staff and volunteers are important components of successful inter-generational programs. These are activities that must be financially supported (Morris & Caro, 1995, pp. 34–37).

Wilson and Simson (1993, pp. 16–18) described the impact of the current eco-nomic and political climate on human service agencies. They specifically addressed how those conditions affected voluntary action centers (VACs), currently referred to as volunteer centers, around the country between 1988 and 1993. The 400 local centers across the country, coordinated through the Points of Light Foundation, serve as the "the nation's most extensive network of volunteer assistance and infor-mation" ("Volunteer centers," 1995, p. 6). In doing so, they promote opportunities for volunteers of all ages to become involved in service that is increasingly intergen-erational. According to this study, those organizations are "being asked to manage with fewer resources despite greater needs. They have less financial support, in-creased client loads, a heightened demand for services and increased costs for insurance and salaries" (Wilson & Simson, 1993, p. 16). Funding had decreased for 38.75% of VACs included in Wilson and Simson's (1993) study. The number of senior citizens providing service had increased 58.75%, the numbers of clients served had increased 71.25%, and the number of units of volunteer service had increased 50.62%. Investment in programs such as the volunteer centers and intergenerational programs by both the public and private sectors is vitally important in creating and supporting an infrastructure that can support program growth.

The Need to Engage Greater Numbers
of Program Participants of All Ages

As noted above, both public policy and private support has been important in bringing large numbers of seniors and youth into intergenerational programs. At the public level, the senior service programs have played a valuable role in developing and expanding programs and program models through which great numbers of se-niors have become involved in intergenerational service. Currently, these programs engage over 500,000 seniors in service to their communities, providing an estimated 111.3 million hours of service ("National Senior Corps Programs," 1995, p. 4). Tess Scannell (personal communication, February 13, 1996) of the Corporation for National Service noted that the federal senior programs have always received broad and bipartisan support and that support continues even in the current conservative fiscal environment. During a time when other programs have received large cuts in federal support, the traditional senior programs (the Foster Grandparent Program, the Retired Senior Volunteer Program, and the Senior Companions Program) have received relatively smaller ones. Scannell noted that the policy environment remains positive for these programs and that much bipartisan support remains from the Clinton Administration and the Congress.

Though these federal programs that bring seniors into intergenerational service seem reasonably secure, the federal program that has been more responsible for bringing youth and seniors into intensive community service is at risk. Although AmeriCorps, which involves youth in service, has survived in a highly political environment, it is a program that has been so linked with the agenda of President Clinton that it has come under attack from the political opposition and may continue to be at risk (T. Scannell, personal communication, February 13, 1996). Its program initiatives, such as Summer of Safety and Learn and Serve America, have provided important avenues for youths and seniors to engage in more intensive community service (The National and Community Service Trust Act, 1994).

Earlier in this discussion, the importance of seniors in providing much of the person power for intergenerational programs was described. Although large numbers of seniors are involved in intergenerational and other forms of community service, many gerontologists and policy analysts argue that the potential contribution of older Americans remains underutilized (Fischer, 1993, p. 17). There is convincing evidence that the number of seniors serving in intergenerational settings could be expanded. Marriott's Senior Volunteerism Survey (1991) indicated that along with the 15.5 million people age 60 and over who did volunteer in 1990, an additional 14 million would have been willing to volunteer if they had been asked. Forty percent of seniors included in that study also reported that they felt federal, state, and local governments were "doing less than they should to promote opportunities for volunteerism" (*Marriott's Senior Volunteerism Study*, 1991, p. 2). A study conducted by the American Association of Retired Persons reported that 40% of older volunteers participated less than 10 hr a month and that 35% participated between 10 and 20 hr a month (Costello, 1991, p. 43).

Although the ability to volunteer and to have access to volunteer settings (including in intergenerational settings) has become an important and meaningful activity for millions of older Americans, it has remained somewhat inaccessible to many others. Low-income seniors are one group who are underrepresented among volunteers. Romero (1986, pp. 34–35) noted that "volunteering is primarily a middle and upper class phenomenon." Further efforts must be made to make volunteering more accessible to low-income seniors, especially within the communities of greatest need. Modest enabling stipends and reimbursements for expenses incurred in volunteer work can help some seniors become involved who might not otherwise be able. The experience of the Foster Grandparent and Senior Companion programs have shown that a modest level of financial support can make meaningful volunteer work available for many low-income seniors who otherwise might not be reached.

Volunteering options have also been less accessible to older and disabled seniors. Although some seniors in these groups will not choose or be able to volunteer, others would benefit from volunteer work and could make important contributions.

Accessing these groups will require serious effort and flexibility from intergenerational programs. Intergenerational options for this populations are varied and include opportunities to serve younger disabled and needy youth from the domicile of older or disabled seniors. Addressing issues such as flexible work schedules, transportation, and specialized job assignments that are geared to the particular skills of the older people involved can all be important ways that more members of this group may be helped to enter the intergenerational volunteer force (Cook, 1993/1994, p. 28).

While being very involved in providing informal support and assistance within their families and communities, ethnic minorities are underrepresented as volunteers within formal organizations. Both Blacks and Hispanics volunteer at lower rates than Whites. Susan Chambre (1987, p. 87) acknowledged that although the relationship between ethnic membership and volunteering has not been adequately studied, the fact that rates of volunteering go up and differences in volunteer rates between Whites and minorities tend to disappear as income rises suggests that differences in rates of volunteering due to ethnic membership may be most related to socioeconomic status. The same type of efforts to reach out to low-income seniors, in general, may be very helpful in reaching out to low-income ethnic minority seniors. Certainly, issues of cultural competence within the intergenerational programs and the organizations that support them must also be addressed.

THE STATUS OF INTERGENERATIONAL PROGRAMS

In this chapter, the many positive elements involved in the growth and development of intergenerational programs have been described, as have the important challenges that must be addressed if these programs are to achieve more of their potential for meeting important needs in U.S. society. Although there has been a generally receptive environment for intergenerational programs that have enabled this important model to grow and develop, many important challenges remain if intergenerational programs are to reach their full potential.

10

Intergenerational Approaches to Public Policy: Trends and Challenges

**Gary Calhoun, MSW, Eric Kingson, PhD,
and Sally Newman, PhD**

National service is about rebuilding the American community. It is about providing a useful meaningful role for our children, youth, and older adults.

—Bill Clinton

This chapter examines the emerging intergenerational voice in broader social policy issues and the potential of this intergenerational thinking to have broader influence on the development of social policy. It concludes by highlighting the importance of a vision that guides and advances efforts to further develop intergenerational programs and approaches to policy. This vision, it is suggested, is an essential ingredient to a future that values and supports the contributions of all generations.

Although the growth of intergenerational programs faces little opposition, the development of a positive intergenerational voice in public policy debates meets greater resistance. Advocates for intergenerational programs have been largely proactive, whereas advocates for intergenerational approaches in broader public policy arenas have generally expressed their voices reactively. Advocates for intergenerational approaches to broader public policy seek to express a positive intergenerational message within a very difficult policy environment.

The interest on the part of advocates for children and elderly persons in developing and advancing an intergenerational approach in the broader public policy arena is seen as a potentially effective way to advocate for the development of social policy beneficial to all generations. This approach has also been a reaction to the efforts of individuals and neoconservative organizations to limit the scope of government through a strategy that frames public policy discussions in terms of competition and conflict between age groups. For example, as discussed by John Wasik (1996) in a recent *Consumer's Digest* article, deficit cutting groups such as the Concord Coalition and the Third Millennium and conservative think tanks such as the Cato Institute create a generational conflict rhetoric to justify and cut and radically change Social Security, Medicare, and related programs. Their primary goal is to reduce the federal deficit by shrinking the government's role in responding to social needs, not to promote fairness between generations (Kingson & Williamson, 1993; see also Quadagno, 1996).

In terms of positive developments, Generations United (see chapter 4), cosponsored by the American Association of Retired Persons, the National Council on the Aging, the Child Welfare League of America, and the Children's Defense Fund, has been the largest and most influential of the intergenerational advocacy groups seeking to advance an agenda based on a belief that the generations are interdependent, not in conflict. By uniting the voices of these important advocacy groups for older Americans and children with over 100 other advocacy, health, and social service agencies around the country, Generations United seeks to present a united front in advocacy around policy issues that affect all generations (Scannell & Roberts, 1994, p. 111). As noted earlier in chapter 4, several state, regional, and local networks and coalitions that bring together advocates and service providers from the aging and child–youth networks are other intergenerational voices in the policy debates at the state and local levels.

Advocating for the development of intergenerational programs and approaches to public policy has the primary value of more effectively meeting the social needs of all generations. A united front by advocates for children and elderly persons is also very important in the current political climate, in which there are strong themes of "intergenerational warfare" (Nathanson, 1989, p. 111). A portion of the impetus and support behind intergenerational advocacy comes from those wishing to blunt charges of "greedy-geezerism" and "generational inequities" as well as from the advocates for children who see such charges as an important opportunity to leverage the political power and good intentions of elderly persons and their advocates on behalf of the young.

Certainly, there is nothing new about the idea that generations (in families and in society) depend on one another or in the idea that policy development should reflect the needs of all members of the community. The recognition of this interdependence of generations can be found in the biblical injunction to honor thy father and mother, to care for thy neighbor. From the American colonial period through today, care giving and financial support of dependent family members have always been considered—by norm and by law—an integral part of family life; mutual aid and volunteerism have always been considered an important aspect of community life. The Social Security Act of 1935 (and other social policies) formalized this interdependence of generations with provisions directed at responding to a variety of needs across life—what President Franklin Roosevelt referred to as "the vicissitudes of life" (Roosevelt, 1934). Writing about the philosophy of Social Security, J. Douglas Brown observed that there is an implied covenant in Social Security, arising from a deeply embedded sense of mutual responsibility in civilization, that underlies the "fundamental obligation of the government and citizens of one time and the government and citizens of another time to maintain a contributory social insurance system (Brown, 1977, pp. 31–32).

Those advocating an intergenerational voice in public policy draw on an understanding of human development as a lifelong process, with outcomes at various stages—in childhood, young adulthood, middle age, and old age—reflecting what has happened to individuals and cohorts earlier in their lives. Their positions build on a recognition that the reciprocity that characterizes relationships between generations is given expression through the various exchanges that flow among generations in families and in society (see chapter 1). Such views provide a rationale for why advocates of the old need be concerned with the well-being of children, the next generation of workers and elders of the future. They also provide a rationale for an approach to policy that recognizes the cross-generational and longitudinal implications of various policy options.

Kingson, Hirshorn, and Cornman (1986) suggested that recognition of the interdependence of generations over the course of life leads to a broader understanding of transfers. Transfers should be understood as public and private; as cash and in-kind; and as occurring to varying degrees and in varying ways throughout life. Early on, individuals and cohorts are primarily recipients of private transfers in the form of family care, housing, and basic expenses and of public transfers in the form of education. In youth and middle age, individuals and cohorts both typically transfer more than they receive in the form of caregiving to the young and sometimes to functionally disabled family members and in tax payments to support the various functions of government. In old age, especially advanced old age, the flow of transfers generally reverses, with the receipt of Social Security and Medicare and often family care, when disabled, though many among the old also transfer care and other resources as well (Kingson et al., 1986).

There is a narrow perspective related to transfers that suggests it is children and the old who receive transfers and the young adults and middle aged who give. This perspective, which primarily considers the flow of resources at one point in time, often results in claims of inequities between cohorts and between age groups with respect to the costs and benefits of Social Security and Medicare. This perspective suggests that it is only the old who benefit from Social Security and only the young who pay. (No recognition is given to the benefits that the young can expect to receive as they age, nor is there acknowledgment of the many indirect and social benefits that flow from programs for the old.)

A longitudinal transfer perspective does more to highlight generational reciprocity over time. From this perspective, the prior contribution of older family members to the young and to society can be seen as justifying the claims of the older population to a reasonable return in the form of retirement and health benefits (National Academy on Aging, 1994) and caregiving. The longitudinal perspective highlights the cross-generational benefits that flow from policies supporting programs such as Social Security, public education, and biomedical research on aging. It does more to highlight the reality that in protecting the economic security of the old, Social Security frees up the middle-aged generations to devote more resources to their children. And it clarifies that Social Security provides many direct benefits to the young, being the principal source of life and disability insurance for most working Americans and their families and providing regular cash benefits to over 3.8 million children—mostly the dependents of deceased or disabled workers. It also clarifies that investment in the education (and future productivity) of the young will reap benefits for many of today's and tomorrow's elders. And it points out that it is today's young adults and children—not today's old—who are most likely to benefit from government investment in research into such age-related afflictions as Alzheimer's disease and osteoporosis (Kingson et al., 1986).

The discussion now turns to how the intergenerational themes—and counter themes—have insinuated themselves into public policy discussions. It also addresses the challenges and opportunities before those seeking to inject a larger intergenerational agenda and policy voice.

THE REEMERGENCE OF INTERGENERATIONAL VOICES
IN THE POLICY ARENA

The intergenerational voice—as described here—is most clearly exemplified by the themes highlighted by the 1995 White House Conference on Aging, the activities of Generations United, and the growing interest of some elder advocates in developing coalitions around concerns such as the future of Medicaid, caregiving to persons with disabilities, and productive living.

The 1995 White House Conference on Aging

In May 1995, 2,200 delegates from around the nation heard President Clinton, Vice President Gore, and others call for a shift in the nation's approach to aging policy and issues from a largely exclusive concern with today's old to one that is inclusive of all age groups and cohorts. A clear message was sent that Social Security, Medicare, and Medicaid should not be cut to fund tax reductions for the well off. But along with this, the President issued a new challenge to the aging community to think broadly about how the generations can work together; to recognize the diverse circumstances of today's and tomorrow's old; and to think about how the gift of added years of life should be used to the benefit of all.

This enunciation of intergenerational themes permeated the conference and was reflected in a significant portion of the resolutions that were adopted. Not surprisingly, of course, the strongest support was found for the basic income, health, and service structures that have done so much to transform old age during the later part of the 20th century. But this does not diminish the importance of the steps that were taken to redefine aging from a largely exclusive concern with today's old to one that embraces all who are aging. The new vision of aging provides a rationale and opportunity to promote a broader role for the advocacy efforts of the old and strengthens the argument of those calling for more investment in intergenerational programs.

The 1995 White House Conference on Aging was the first national aging conference to adopt a resolution calling for elders and their advocates to seek a common ground and advocate on behalf of the young. Along with encouraging older Americans to use their talents, skills, and time on behalf of children and youth in volunteer service, this resolution called on older Americans to "form and/or join existing coalitions of older persons and use their power and influence to be advocates to benefit all children" (White House Conference on Aging, 1995, p. 60). Although much of this falls into the realm of symbolic activity, the fact remains that the need to link the fortunes of the young to that of the old has pierced the consciousness of elder advocates.

Generations United and Other Coalitions

Generations United and the growing numbers of state and local organizations are giving voice to two types of intergenerational concerns. Nearly all advocate the expansion of intergenerational program models, and some also seek to develop an agenda of advocacy for policy concerns that cuts across age groups and cohorts.

Although much work remains to be done, these coalitions can point to successes in bringing attention to the need for the development and support for intergenerational program models among both public and private decision makers. As previously discussed, foundations have invested in the development of such activities, as have several university-based centers (e.g., Generations Together at the University of Pittsburgh and the Center for Intergenerational Learning at Temple University) that develop, assess, and disseminate intergenerational program concepts. Similarly, these coalitions bolster support on the federal level for intergenerational programs and related volunteer efforts. Consequently, although many National Service Corps programs were seriously threatened by the 1995 and 1996 federal budget negotiations, at no time were the Foster Grandparent Program, the Retired Senior Volunteer Program, and related senior initiatives threatened with extinction.

The search for common cause in the advocacy of an intergenerational agenda is more complicated to pursue. Many social policies and publicly funded programs direct benefits to specific groups. There are a growing number of examples of senior citizen leaders such as Lovola Burgess, Immediate Past President of the American Association of Retired Persons, and Elsie Frank, the President of the Massachusetts Association of Older Americans, speaking out for the needs of low-income children and other nonelderly groups.

Interest group politics present formidable barriers, not the least of which are the perceptions by some advocates—and sometimes the reality—that the short-term local, state, and federal budgetary interests of children, elderly, and disabled may conflict. There are citizen groups, however, like supporters of Generations United, that are concerned with both the young and the old and especially with those who are economically disadvantaged.

Generations United, with networks across the nation, has pulled together modest support from within its coalition for intergenerational advocacy. The types of issues that Generations United and other intergenerational advocacy groups have focused on include the following:

1. The organization took an active role in supporting legislation advocating for the successful restoration of funds to the Title XX Social Service Block Grant, which has been a major source of federal support for a variety of essential social services for children and older adults.
2. It has consistently been an advocate for health care reform as it has argued for the need for accessible and affordable health care for all age groups and for continued support for the Medicaid and Medicare programs.
3. It was a strong supporter of the Claude Pepper Young Americans Act of 1990, which established the Administration of Children, Youth, and Families and provided funding to states to support a range of health and social services on behalf of children and families.
4. It has focused on providing support and services that would prevent abuse of children and elders and that provide support to entire families.
5. It has advocated for policy and services that would provide support to grandparents who are providing care for their own grandchildren. Because of issues such as drugs, AIDS, unemployment, and teenage pregnancy, an increasingly large number of grandparents have been assuming the physical, financial, and

emotional care of their grandchildren. Those grandparents often experience a number of problems. Gaining custody in order to make important decisions, having difficulty applying for and receiving Medicaid coverage, or having difficulty in receiving Aid to Families With Dependent Children or foster care payments have presented barriers to grandparents as they seek to make this important contribution to their families. Generations United has joined others in advocating for legislation and policies that will address these problems.

6. Supplementary Security Income (SSI) is a truly intergenerational program that addresses the needs of persons with disabilities of all ages. Generations United has supported efforts to protect and improve this program for the large number of people of all ages who receive essential support through this important program.

7. Generations United has been an active member of the coalition supporting the reauthorization of the Older Americans Act, which has been so essential to the well-being of millions of older Americans and their families.

8. It was a major supporter of the National and Community Service Act of 1993, which has served as a vehicle for thousands of older and younger Americans to become involved in community service to all age groups.

9. It has most recently taken a very active role in fighting against major elements of the Republican Contract With America. Block grants for nutrition and other important social programs, which would weaken federal investment and responsibility for meeting important areas of social need, and threatened cuts in Social Security, Medicaid, Medicare, and other important social programs have been the target of intergenerational advocacy (Generations United, 1993, 1994, 1995).

10. It has been an advocate of maintaining strong Social Security and Medicare programs.

A Radically Different Intergenerational Voice

Ironically, the loudest generational themes have been sounded by individuals and organizations that define policy issues in terms of competition and conflict between young and old and warn of generational warfare. A new stereotype of the old emerged in the early 1980s, challenging the view of elderly persons as weak, ill, and poor with a new and equally false stereotype of elders as healthy and well-heeled (Binstock, 1983). Although neither stereotype accurately portrays the old (or even most of the old), the new stereotype—along with concerns about economic change, population aging, and federal spending—played a prominent role in the emergence of the generational equity and conflict theme. An example of the origins of this theme can be found in Jerry Flint's 1980 article in *Forbes* magazine. He observed, "The myth is they're sunk in poverty. The reality is they're living well. The trouble is that there are too many of them—God bless 'em" (Flint, 1980, p. 51). This article was followed by many others, some blaming expenditures on the elderly for increasing poverty among children and for declining expenditures on education (Chakravarty & Weisman, 1988; Longman, 1985), some saying that Social Security is gypping the young, some fingering expenditures on the elderly for rising federal deficits, declining national savings, economic stagnation, and placing the American dream at risk (Peterson, 1994).

As noted, the political drums of generational warfare have been beat by a series of organizations, each largely united by the goal of shrinking expenditures on the old to make more funds available for private savings and investment (Quadagno, 1996). Although mentioned, the well-being of children, especially those who are poor, is primarily window dressing and is used as a strategy to split those advocating social spending on the young from those concerned with spending on the old (Kingson et al., 1986; Minkler, 1986; Quadagno, 1996).

This approach, which arguably began 12 years ago with formation of Americans for Generational Equity, has now been carefully refined by the Concord Coalition, the National Taxpayers Union, and the Third Millennium. It has become the standard fare of attacks on Social Security and related programs and in discussions of the retirement of the baby boom cohorts. Moreover, the generational equity theme has been picked up as a primary strategy for advancing deficit reduction strategies. Consistent with that strategy, Republican pollster Frank Luntz circulated a memo in 1995 to the newly elected Republican members of the House warning them to present their political agenda in moral terms, that is, to talk in terms of "the American dream" and "our children's future" requiring a balanced budget and to turn the issue of fairness against the Democrats, by, for example, talking about Medicare being unfair because some elders get a better package of health care benefits than some of the workers who help pay for it. In other words, Luntz expressed little concern for extending protections to those who are without insurance but much concern for creating the rationale to pull apart the basic health insurance protections now provided for today's (and tomorrow's) old and the long-term severely disabled. Nor should it be surprising that the chairs of the Concord Coalition, Paul Tsongas and Warren Rudman, drew so heavily on this type of rhetoric. For example, in a foreword to a Concord Coalition pamphlet directed at people in their teens, 20s, and early 30s, they warned:

You are being robbed. Every second of every day, young Americans are the victims of a theft. Calling 911 won't help. This is not the type of crime that is reported nightly on the news. In fact, most people don't even know it is happening. But make no mistake, you are being robbed.

What is being stolen from you? Your future. Your chance to live as well as your parents and grandparents have lived throughout their lives. (Howe & Strauss, 1995)

Whatever the problem, it seems that there is now a genre of journalistic and political advocacy that finds fault with the old or at least with expenditures directed at today's and tomorrow's old. Overlooked, however, are factors such as the large tax cuts and defense build-ups of the early 1980s, which created the federal deficit. Similarly, important concerns are ignored such as the widening of the gaps between rich and poor and between the middle class and the very well-off during the 1980s and into the 1990s. It is not acknowledged (or even questioned) that "economic growth in itself" will not necessarily "benefit the average American family and solve the problems of poverty and economic hardship" for others (Danziger & Gottschalk, 1995, p. 10). Evidence that "demonstrates that economic, demographic, and policy changes have rendered obsolete the view that economic growth is the major factor in determining how many people are rich and how many are poor" is not explored (p. 10). In other words, the framing of contemporary policy debates in terms of generational conflict arguably emphasizes the wrong questions while distracting attention from more important concerns affecting the well-being of current and future generations. But, whether one likes the generational conflict analysis or not, this approach must be judged as influential.

Challenges and Opportunities
for an Intergenerational Approach to Policy

In contrast, no matter how effective and well intended, the voices of intergenerational advocates have been far less influential in shaping public policy agendas than those advancing the rhetoric of competition and conflict between generations. Advocacy groups for budget deficit reduction have developed and delivered a clear message and often receive financial support from the private sector competitors of Social Security and Medicare (for example, see Quadagno, 1996, and Wasik, 1996, for a discussion of Americans for Generational Equity's funding). The leadership of the 1994 Bipartisan Commission on Entitlement and Tax Reform picked up many of their themes (Kingson & Quadagno, 1995), and similar themes have been worked into Business Roundtables widely distributed resource book entitled *Fiscal Crossroads: Facing Up to the Budget Deficit,* which is designed to help member companies educate their 10 million employees.

Somewhat ironically, the success of the generational equity and conflict themes provides both incentives and opportunities for advancing more progressive and inclusive intergenerational themes (Kingson, 1988). Clearly, aging interest groups such as the American Association of Retired Persons and the National Council on the Aging have incentive—as part of their strategy to protect the basic retirement income and health benefits of the old—to recast some of their issues in terms that protect them from charges of "greedy-geezerism." Thus, we can anticipate more efforts to frame policy discussions in ways that indicate how the next generation of the old and even their children benefit from a sound Social Security and Medicare program. Although an element of symbolic politics is present here, there is also the reality that these benefits do flow through the entire family; for in assisting elder or disabled members to maintain their financial independence, considerable financial pressure is taken off other members of the family.

At one level elder interest groups also have incentive to build bridges to groups concerned with nonelderly issues. As noted, however, the difficulty here is that the categorical structure of many programs and short-term budgetary considerations—on local, state, and federal levels—often provide little reason for cooperation and sometimes actively mitigate against such cooperation among advocates of the old, the young, the disabled, or caregivers. Moreover, block grant strategies—especially those that might apply to Medicaid—that would shift responsibilities for programs from federal to state levels might exacerbate potential tensions between the advocates of various groups.

The advocates of the young and other groups, in turn, have an opportunity to encourage elder advocates to lend political and moral weight to some of their concerns, an argument likely to be particularly effective in situations of true mutual interest. For example, even though the Clinton Administration's health care reform failed, it is instructive that a largely federally financed, state-administered home and community-based long-term care program for all the disabled—regardless of age—was an important element of all of Clinton Administration's health care proposals.

As is often true in life, adversity creates potential for innovation and progress. Threats to the future of Social Security and Medicare provide reason and opportunity to advance public understanding of the value of the cross-generational benefits of maintaining such protections as basic rights of all citizens. Threats of block grants provide a rationale for the advocates of various groups to seek alternative policies. Moreover,

> *intergenerational programs and approaches to public policy provide two very positive ways of turning down this invitation to engage in divisive competition. First intergenerational programs promote understanding about issues affecting other generations. There is a need for forums that bring all the generations together to discuss important community topics such as school bond issues and maintaining tax bases. Senior centers and school systems ought to sponsor events that educate the elderly about the needs of schools in their communities and which serve to recruit the energies of the elderly. Similarly, youth and young adults need to understand the rationale behind social insurance programs (especially Social Security), why they pay payroll taxes, and the benefits and the issues that will confront them as citizens. Second, programs which bring the generations together in service to each other exemplify that, while tensions between age groups and generations may emerge and ought not be ignored, it is the strength of the bonds between generations which are most striking. (Kingson, 1989, p. 97)*

One challenge to overcome—internal to the advocates of intergenerational programs and politics—is the false choice between whether the intergenerational voice should emphasize the continued development of intergenerational programs or help to set a broader policy agenda. Plainly, both approaches to advocacy have implications for policy and intergenerational programs, for success in one area will likely spill over to the other. No doubt, the stakes are much higher and the politics more contentious in the policy arenas that address retirement income security, health care reform, and federal deficit issues. This makes the effort to reframe some of the policy discussions to reflect an intergenerational voice all that more effective. Yet there is parallel value in addressing the easier challenge of protecting and advancing gains in intergenerational programs. The victories are easier here, but more important, they may shape the lives of the people who participate in these programs and provide examples of what can be achieved through cooperative effort.

PROMOTING CITIZENSHIP AND COMMUNITY

Although there have been many significant intergenerational successes, much work remains to advance an intergenerational agenda. Although there is private and public support for intergenerational programs, more needs to be done if they are to assume the role of primary rather than secondary social service interventions. If intergenerational programs are to achieve their potential in addressing some of the social problems that affect families and society, they must continue to prove their significance, they must survive in a conservative political environment, and they must engage more people of all generations in intergenerational service. Although an intergenerational voice has begun to be heard in broader policy debates, the loudest expression of intergenerational thinking comes not from those who emphasize the interdependence between generations but from those who would paint a picture of generations pitted against each other in a competition for the same scarce resources.

Intergenerational approaches to programs and policy are badly needed as vehicles to counter the isolation, cynicism, competition, and self-interest that so often mark interaction in modern U.S. society. This chapter concludes with a discussion of how these approaches are embedded within and can promote ideals of citizenship and community.

Intergenerational programs and approaches to social policy are good for many reasons. Thinking about society's needs from an intergenerational perspective leads to policies that give consideration to the needs of all generations of families. Programs of exchange are good for children, who receive much needed nurturance, guidance, inspiration, and advocacy from the elders of their communities, who have such unique gifts to offer. They are good for youth, who through joint service or through providing or receiving assistance make strong connections with people who have learned from living and who have much to teach. They are good for the middle generation, who receive comfort in their children's nurture and in their parents' well-being. They are good for seniors as they provide opportunities for active and productive engagement with younger generations in their communities in ways that provide important meaning in later life. They provide for all generations a more accurate view of aging across the life span; reinforce mutual connection, respect, and affection between generations; and break down fears and stereotypes of aging. Finally, they are good for society. Intergenerational programs and approaches to social policy support a vision of community and citizenship in which all generations are valued, feel an obligation to contribute, and have opportunities to engage in community in ways that provide reciprocal support, connection and meaning, a community in which all generations truly share "a common stake" (Kingson et al., 1986) in their mutual well-being.

The vision of citizenship and community that is inherent in intergenerational programs and approaches to social policy is not a new vision. It has its roots in important national traditions. Alexis de Tocqueville (1900), in his classic study of early America, described Americans' unique tendency to join together in civil associations as one of the key elements of our democracy. Ellis and Noyes (1990) described the United States as a nation of joiners. In their study of the history of volunteerism in America, they described the rich tradition of citizens coming together in voluntary associations to work for the well-being of each other and their communities.

In more recent times, concern has arisen over the tendency in modern U.S. society for citizens to be consumed in a kind of individualism that erodes a sense of responsibility for the welfare of others. In response to those concerns, the communitarian movement (Bellah, 1991; Etzioni, 1993), with its emphasis on mutual responsibilities and on joining in community has stimulated and provided support for many programs through which people exercise their citizenship by becoming actively involved in their communities. Inherent in the communitarian approach is a vision of citizenship in which one feels a strong responsibility to contribute to the well-being of others. As noted earlier, in the modern era, the responsibility of all citizens to contribute to the well-being of society has been a common thread in appeals to volunteerism from Presidents Kennedy through Clinton. Finally, many elements of the rich religious traditions of the United States' diverse communities support a vision of individual and collective responsibility to contribute to the welfare of others.

Intergenerational programs and approaches to social policy build on these important traditions with an emphasis on the extra richness inherent in intergenerational connections and exchange. As they emphasize communal responsibility and active citizenship, they seek to recapture a vision of society in which the generations are linked together in reciprocal forms of exchange that provide important connection, support, resources, and meaning to all generations.

Moody and Disch (1989) place citizenship and communal responsibility at the heart of a rationale for intergenerational programs. Noting that rationales for these programs often focus on how they meet the needs and interests of the participants and service recipients, they argued that the most important rationale has to do with the obligations all generations have to their communities and their shared duties of citizenship.

In our view, both young and old are to be understood as members of an enduring historical community, a public world, existing before their birth and remaining after their departure from the scene. Each stage of the life course (youth, adulthood, old age) has its proper task of transmitting or assimilating the lessons of the past in order to create a better future: in short, to recreate the foundations of the common good. (Moody & Disch, 1989, p. 103)

Providing opportunities to exercise citizenship through intergenerational service for people of all generations, including "the very young and the very old" helps to change a view of those groups as only "consumers of services" to one of "change agents" and "valued community assets," contributing in rich and important ways to their communities (Scannell & Roberts, 1994, p. 3).

Although all generations benefit from this vision of a society, it can be argued that it has an especially rich meaning for older Americans. As much as older Americans benefit from being on the receiving end of intergenerational exchanges, they may actually benefit more from the opportunities provided for active contributive engagement with their communities and their society. Intergenerational programs provide older Americans with an opportunity to exercise their citizenship by making unique contributions to the well-being of other generations.

Many see seniors as the "elders" of American society and as having unique contributions to make. Eric Kingson (1989, p. 95) discussed a "special obligation" of the elderly to contribute to their communities:

Young and old and those in-between, have both an obligation and need to be part of a community: assisting others, sharing burdens (including taxation), and reaping the benefits of working with others. The elderly have a special opportunity and obligation to contribute to community institutions because they (a) have a very special relationship to the future, (b) have a unique role as conveyers of culture, and (c) have much leisure.

Moody (1988, p. 52), in his book *Abundance of Life: Human Development Policies for an Aging Society*, addressed the issue of the relationship between volunteering in later life and the use of leisure time. He used the term *abundance of life* to describe the many opportunities for older people, and for society, that are made possible by the demographic revolution described earlier in this text. He noted with concern, however, that living longer is not in itself enough, unless older people are provided with meaningful contributive roles. In short, he suggested that although people are living longer, are healthier, and have more discretionary time, for many older people time spent in later life (including leisure time) lacks important meaning.

His concern was for the qualitative aspects of how this extended leisure time is spent. He argued for social policy approaches that expand the scope of contributive roles for older people and advocated for lifelong education that would provide seniors with greater capacities for self-sufficiency and for contributing to society (Moody, 1988, p. 8). Focusing on policies that encourage self-development in later life will provide important meaning for seniors and will also allow them to contribute to the development of a better society. Intergenerational programs and policy that seeks to address the needs of all generations of families can do much to enhance meaning in later life.

Dychtwald and Flower (1989) alluded to a change in later life when seniors become more drawn to giving to others. They noted that national studies have consistently indicated that as people grow older, "they have a marked tendency to become more interested in what they give to others than what they get. Our elders are a vital national resource, with many wishing to give, not take" (Dychtwald & Flower, 1989, pp. 157–158). They saw seniors as having the unique opportunity to be a "living bridge between yesterday, today, and tomorrow—a critical evolutionary role that no other generation can perform" (p. 347). Quoting Monsignor Fahey, director of Fordham's Third Age Center, they argued that older people "should be the glue of society, not its ashes" (Dychtwald & Flower, 1989, p. 347).

Riley and Riley (1994, p. 19) used the phrase *opportunity structures* to represent the opportunities provided in society for older people to become actively and productively engaged. They argued that these opportunity structures are lacking and that society must make serious efforts to increase the number and types of contributive roles for older Americans that can provide meaningful ways to spend the extended leisure time in late life. Again, intergenerational programs provide one important form of opportunity structure for seniors to exercise their citizenship through active engagement with their communities.

Certainly, much about the current policy environment would suggest that expansion of intergenerational programs or a greater infusion of intergenerational thinking in current social policy debates faces many obstacles. A continued escalation of social problems, an emphasis on disinvesting in public social resources and an unrealistic view that private efforts will be able to make up for that disinvestment, a continuing tendency to think of need categorically rather than intergenerationally, and a political movement that emphasizes generationally divisive approaches to public social policy all serve as important practical barriers to the growth of intergenerational programs or policy initiatives that focus on meeting the needs of people across the life span (Kingson et al., 1986). Although those obstacles must be acknowledged and addressed, it is vitally important that intergenerational advocates be guided not by the current constraints in the policy environment but by a vision of how intergenerational approaches to community can help to shape American society.

Future is shaped by vision (Ilsley, 1990, pp. 138–140; Van Til, 1990, pp. 263–270). Although current constraints and future events will be involved in shaping what becomes of intergenerational approaches to community in the future, visions about what kind of society Americans will strive to become and what role all generations will play in that future will also have much to do with how the future is shaped. Values and vision, not just pragmatics, guide the future. It is essential that advocates for intergenerational approaches to community continue to focus on a vision of community in which all generations have rich and unique roles and the important potentials of all are recognized and realized. The traditional values of volunteerism that have been part of the United States' heritage, the rich values inherent in communitarian approaches to community and religious heritages, and the growing awareness of the rich interdependence among generations all enrich a vision of community in which programs of intergenerational exchange can thrive and contribute. Although intergenerational programs will need to deal with the realities and pragmatics of the times, how they choose to deal with those realities and pragmatics must be shaped fundamentally by a vision of what they need to become.

11

The Future

Sally Newman, PhD

Youth large, lusty living, youth full of grace, force and fascination. Do you know that old age will come after you with equal grace, force and fascination.
—Walt Whitman

This book has presented a picture of a social phenomenon in American society whose direction and impact are dynamic and far reaching. Intergenerational programs in the United States have been characterized as a movement, a social force, and a lens through which it is possible to view and begin to address many social issues confronting society. Their educational, social, philosophical, and political presence in society is beginning to shape the way individuals, groups, and systems resolve community problems that directly affect a community's young and old.

This book has described the many facets that currently characterize this phenomenon. It has established a theoretical context that undergirds intergenerational programs; reviewed the demographic, social, and economic environment in which they have developed; described the social issues addressed by intergenerational programs; and chronicled their history in the United States.

An overview of the types of models that constitute intergenerational programs have been presented and their outcomes in the context of evaluation and applied research have been examined. This book provides the reader with resources available to gain information on the many facets of intergenerational programs and has raised some of the crucial public policy issues that relate to the past and future of intergenerational programs as a social force in society. An examination of the multiple facets of intergenerational programming leads naturally to a discussion on the future of these programs. This discussion focuses on several key questions whose answers will shape this future:

- What is the status of intergenerational programs today?
- What are the projections for intergenerational programs in the next decade?
- How will intergenerational programs become a creditable human service field?
- How will intergenerational programs be integrated into American social structure?

CURRENT STATUS OF INTERGENERATIONAL PROGRAMS

Throughout the United States today there are millions of children, youth, and older adults who are participating in intergenerational programs. There are also

175

thousands of professionals involved in some aspect of the creation or implementation of these programs. These numbers reflect the need for intergenerational programs as a social model that is responding to a growing number of societal problems. Concomitant with this need is the question of who is responsible for the development, growth, maintenance, and sustainability of these programs.

The responsibility is shared among a group of professionals: program planners, developers, administrators, direct service providers, evaluators, researchers, and teachers, who are committed to the notion that there is a special synergy between the young and the old, that caring for each other is natural and appropriate, and that problems confronting these populations can be ameliorated by empowering these groups to help each other.

Those currently engaged in intergenerational work represent an array of human service fields such as aging, education, early childhood, developmental psychology, and community development. These practitioners are expanding their professional horizons to include intergenerational activities as part of their service delivery skills.

As this cadre of professionals involved in intergenerational work expands, there is a growing interest in the development of an intergenerational professional specialty that defines the nature of its work, the preparation and skills needed to succeed in this work, and the relationship between this work and other human service fields.

In considering the current status of intergenerational programs, it is important to note that an intergenerational field is emerging that will provide a link between the present and future of these programs. This emerging field has the following characteristics:

- a proliferation of structured programs in which professional practices are required;
- a growing body of knowledge that defines the structure and outcomes of programs and that examines some of the fundamental questions the programs address;
- an expanding interest in learning about the concepts, issues, and premises and theoretical paradigm that have given rise to this field; and
- a presence in public policy initiatives.

The existence of these characteristics, common also to other human service fields indicates a readiness for a new field.

However, one component fundamental to existing human service fields that is missing from the intergenerational field is a structure for professionalizing the field. This structure typically involves establishing procedures for certification, performance standards, and criteria that measure successful performance in the context of program outcomes.

AN INTERGENERATIONAL HUMAN SERVICE FIELD—
PROJECTIONS FOR THE NEXT DECADE

In the next decade, intergenerational programs will continue to proliferate throughout society and may become evident as a new social perspective to rebuild our communities. To reinforce and sustain this new perspective and in response to the mass of persons already working in intergenerational settings there will be a compelling need to develop competent professionals.

Focused initiatives should be directed toward professionalizing the intergenerational field. To this end, consensus among practitioners and academics needs to be reached on the following issues:

1. The basic definition of the intergenerational field:

   • What are the parameters and goals of the field?
   • What are the levels of work available within the field?
   • How does the field position itself in the context of other human service fields?

2. The determination of the competencies needed to be successful in the intergenerational field:

   • What are the unique skills knowledge, and insights needed for success at different levels of work in this field—direct service, management administrations, evaluation, teaching, and research?
   • What skills from other human service fields are applicable to the intergenerational specialist?

3. The creation of a credentialling system that validates professional competence:

   • How to certify professionals who complete training in preparation for job placement?
   • How to certify the level of work achievement in an intergenerational workplace?
   • How to integrate credentials for the intergenerational specialist with other human service credentials?

INTERGENERATIONAL PROGRAMS: BECOMING A CREDITABLE HUMAN SERVICE FIELD

Many of the questions posed in relationship to professionalizing the intergenerational field can be addressed by higher education. Academically trained human service professionals are becoming more aware of the necessity to enlarge their knowledge base related to intergenerational and interprofessional issues. Educators too are aware of the need to train students to become proficient intergenerational professionals who can successfully bridge service delivery systems and work collaboratively with others trained in a variety of disciplines (Newman & Larkin, 1997). Advocates for an intergenerational human service field are examining the level of readiness of higher education and professional organizations to establish a new field of study and practice that is based on solid theoretical frameworks, continued research, and high-quality professional preparation and practice. The response of universities to this examination is encouraging and is occurring parallel to considerations for restructuring by human service systems. Initiatives in some higher education institutions have already begun as they examine some of the following intergenerational options:

- Provide certificate-bearing training institutes in intergenerational areas, such as skill development, research opportunities, and public policy.
- Integrate intergenerational content into existing courses in early childhood, family and children, aging, education, lifelong learning, and nursing.
- Introduce multidisciplinary intergenerational courses.
- Develop an intergenerational continuing education certificate based on intergenerational work and study experience.
- Offer a minor within an existing degree track.
- Offer a degree in intergenerational studies.

THE INTERGENERATIONAL FIELD:
A PART OF AMERICAN SOCIAL STRUCTURE

The previous section presented the issues and strategies related to professionalizing the intergenerational field. However, to realize its status as a creditable human service field, the intergenerational concept must be integrated into American social structure and supported by social policy. Such integration has important long-term social, political, and academic implications.

The social and political implications are manifest in the report on the projected status and needs of children, youth, and older adults in the United States during the next decade (Edelman, 1996). These reports predict an escalation of the social, emotional, and economic needs of these two populations that portend the timeliness for a new approach to the issues that continue to confront young and old.

Advocates for an intergenerational societal perspective are lobbying local and federal governments in many areas of the United States for policies that bring new visions for social change. The segregated services and funding streams of the past are being challenged by innovative ideas and new social agendas. An intergenerational field that brings a vision of integrated services and integrated generations can become a catalyst to implement social change for the future (Larkin & Newman, 1997). The catalyst can be effective, however, only if the systems that currently provide segregated services recognize the urgency to integrate their services, to network their information, and to focus on the abundance of common issues that affect people across the life span. The need for comprehensive cross-family and cross-community services mandates that human service systems be ready to reorganize their mission and vision and to collaborate in a new turfless, comprehensive structure that recognizes the interdependence of the generations. Human service professionals must consider providing a linked continuum of social, educational, and health services designed to improve the quality of life for persons of all ages across the life span. A system that provides this for a family's very young and school-age children, its working parent or parents, and its elderly will be the integrated intergenerational system of the next decade. These systems will require a new kind of professional in both management and direct service.

The academic implications for this new human service field are challenging. To establish an effective strategy for preparing a new field of intergenerational professional, university faculties in a variety of human service disciplines will need to develop a variety of multidisciplinary credit-bearing options that focus on theory and practice and on intergenerational competence. These options will be examined, explored, and discussed at length in the next decade among many academics who are seeking the correct home for this new field of study. Intergenerational options may appear in a variety of venues, some more obvious than others, until they can be integrated into a multidisciplinary specialty.

A multidisciplinary university approach to intergenerational specialization at a variety of levels will prepare a new professional for work in the integrated social service agencies of the next decade and will prepare the scholar to further examine the issues and effects of this field and to develop an underlying uniform theory that will guide the future of the field.

CONCLUSION

The intergenerational field in the next decade should focus on the realization of a society in which all members recognize the value of all generations and are empowered to work together to enable all generations to live to their fullest with pride and dignity. This focus furthermore can produce a society that recognizes that "strength lies in its ability to integrate the wisdom of its elders with the spirit and vitality of its children and youth" (Mead, 1971). The future of the United States rests in its ability to integrate the strength, and the knowledge, of both the young and the old to create a society that is connected by all generations.

References

Aday, R., & Campbell, M. (1995). Changes in nursing students' attitudes and work preferences after a gerontology curriculum. *Educational Gerontology, 21*, 247–260.

Aday, R., Sims, C., & Evans, E. (1991). Youth's attitudes toward the elderly: The impact of intergenerational partners. *Journal of Applied Gerontology, 10*, 372–384.

Allis, J. M. (1989). *Child care programs for health care organizations.* Chicago: Health Administration Press.

American Association of Retired Persons. (1993). *Older worker child care employment survey: A survey by the American Association of Retired Persons and the University of Pittsburgh.* Washington, DC: Author.

American Association of Retired Persons. (1994). *Connecting the generations.* Washington, DC: Author.

American Association of Retired Persons. (1995). *A profile of older Americans: 1995.* Washington, DC: Author.

American Association of Retired Persons. (1996). Study examines employers' perceptions of older workers. *Working Age, 11*, 2–3.

Amir, Y. (1969). Contact hypothesis in ethnic relations. *Psychological Bulletin, 71*, 319–342.

Angelis, J. (1990). *Getting started now: A concise guide to developing effective intergenerational programs.* Carbondale, IL: Southern Illinois University, Illinois Intergenerational Initiative.

Angelis, J. (1992a). *Creating intergenerational coalitions: Bottom up . . . top down strategies.* Carbondale, IL: Southern Illinois University, Illinois Intergenerational Initiative.

Angelis, J. (1992b). The genesis of an intergenerational study. *Educational Gerontology, 18*, 317–327.

Angersbach, H., & Jones, S. (1996). *Intergenerational interactions: A descriptive analysis of elder/child interactions during a program in a campus-based child care center.* Unpublished thesis, Kean College, New Jersey.

Atchley, R. (1988). *Social forces and aging.* Belmont, CA: Wadsworth.

Becoming a school partner: A guidebook for organizing intergenerational partnerships in schools. (1992). Washington, DC: American Association of Retired Persons.

Bellah, R. (1991). *The good society.* New York: Knopf.

Bennett, R. (1976). Attitudes of the young toward the old: A review of the research. *Personnel and Guidance Journal, 5*, 126–129.

Biblarz, T. J. (1993). The effects of family disruption on social mobility. *American Sociological Review, 58*, 97–109.

Bi-Folkal Productions. (1991). *Learning from the past: A guide to using Bi-Folkal productions in schools and other intergenerational settings.* Madison, WI: Author.

Binstock, R. H. (1983). The aged as scapegoat. *The Gerontologist, 23,* 136–143.

Blancato, R. (1996, March). *Closing session: The future of the intergenerational movement.* Panel presentation at the Seventh National Conference of Generations United, Washington, DC.

Bocian, K., & Newman, S. (1989). Evaluation of intergenerational programs: Why and how? *Journal of Children in Contemporary Society, 29,* 147–163.

Botan, C. H. (1988). Communication and aging in organizational contexts. In C. Carmichael, H. Botan, & R. Hawkins (Eds.), *Human communications and the aging process* (pp. 21–28). Prospect Heights, IL: Waveland Press.

Boydston, J. A. (1970). *Guide to the works of John Dewey.* Carbondale, IL: Southern Illinois University Press.

Bredekamp, S. (Ed.). (1987). *Developmentally appropriate practice in early childhood programs serving children from birth through age 8.* Washington, DC: National Association for the Education of Young Children.

Brown, J. D. (1977). *Essays on Social Security.* Princeton, NJ: Princeton University Press.

Brudney, J. (1990). *Fostering volunteer programs in the public sector: Planning, initiating, and managing voluntary activities.* San Francisco: Jossey-Bass.

Buhler, C. (1968). The course of human life as a psychological problem. *Human Development, 11,* 184–200.

Butler, R. N., & Gleason, H. (Eds.). (1985). *Productive aging: Enhancing vitality in later life.* New York: Springer.

Butler, R. N., & Lewis, M. (1977). *Aging and mental health: Positive psychosocial approaches* (2nd ed.). St. Louis, MO: Mosby.

California State Department of Education. (1984). *Young and old together: A resource directory of intergenerational programs.* Sacramento, CA: Author.

Camp Fire Boys and Girls. (1992). *Friendship across the ages* (rev. ed.). Kansas City, MO: Author.

Campbell, H. M. (1971). *John Dewey.* New York: Twayne.

Camper, K. (1992). *SPICE: Intergenerational programs.* Seattle, WA: Seattle Public Schools, School Programs Involving Community Elders.

Caplow, T., Bahr, H., Modell, J., & Chadwick, B. (1991). *Recent social trends in the United States 1960–1990.* Frankfurt am Main, Germany: Campus Verlag.

Care Castle. (in press). *The grand connection: Senior volunteer manual.* Colorado Springs, CO: Author.

Carmel, S., Cwikel, J., & Galinsky, D. (1992). Changes in knowledge, attitudes, and work preferences following courses in gerontology among medical, nursing, and social work students. *Educational Gerontology, 18,* 329–342.

Carpenter, M. (1996, June 3). At the center of a philosophical firestorm. *Pittsburgh Post-Gazette,* p. A28.

Carstensen, L., Mason, S., & Caldwell, E. (1982). Children's attitudes toward the elderly: An intergenerational technique for change. *Educational Gerontology, 8,* 291–301.

Caspi, A. (1984). Contact hypothesis and inter-age attitudes: A field study of cross-age contact. *Social Psychology Quarterly, 47,* 74–80.

Chakravarty, S., & Weisman, K. (1988, November 14). Consuming our children? *Fortune,* 222–232.

Chambre, S. (1987). *Good deeds in old age: Volunteering by the new leisure class.* Lexington, MA: Lexington Books.

Chapman, N., & Neal, M. (1990). The effects of intergenerational experiences on adolescents and older adults. *The Gerontologist, 30,* 825–832.

Children's Defense Fund. (1992). *The state of America's children.* Washington, DC: Author.

Children's Defense Fund. (1995). *The state of America's children yearbook.* Washington, DC: Author.

Children's Defense Fund. (1996). *The state of America's children yearbook.* Washington, DC: Author.

Clark, R., & Spengler, J. (1980). *The economics of individual and population aging.* Cambridge, MA: Cambridge University Press.

Cohen, W. (1995). Volunteering for a better America. *Aging Network News, 12*(11/12), 5.

Cohon, D. (1989). Intergenerational program research to define theory and practice. *Journal of Children in Contemporary Society, 29*(3/4), 217–230.

Connecting the generations: A guide to intergenerational resources—An overview of intergenerational programming and selected listing of books, manuals, and media resources. (1994). [Janet O. Wilson, Compiler]. Washington, DC: American Association of Retired Persons.

Cook, A. (1993/1994). A case for research: Understanding the characteristics of potential volunteers. *Journal of Volunteer Administration, 12*(1/2), 27–29.

Cooledge, N., & Wurster, S. (1985). Intergenerational tutoring and student achievement. *The Reading Teacher, 39,* 343–346.

Corman, J., & Kingson, E. R. (1995). *Trends, issues, perspectives and values for the aging of the baby boom cohorts.* Background paper prepared for the Many Faces of Aging: Challenges for the Future conference at Fordham University, Graduate School of Social Services, New York.

Corporation for National Service. (1995). *Request for proposals: The Senior Corps Demonstration.* Washington, DC: Author.

Costello, C. (1991). Resourceful aging: Mobilizing older citizens for volunteer service. In R. Harootyan, A. Stowell, I. Takeuchi, W. Heil, L. Marks, W. Cater, A. Dixon, & S. Williams (Eds.), *Conference proceedings on resourceful aging: Today and tomorrow: Vol. 1. Executive summary* (pp. 41–56). Washington, DC: American Association of Retired Persons.

Couch, L. (1993). *Let us serve them all their days: Younger volunteers serving homebound elderly persons—A handbook of program ideas.* Washington, DC: National Council on the Aging.

Couper, D. (1992). *Schools in an aging society: Curriculum series.* Southington, CT: National Academy for Teaching and Learning about Aging.

Cumming, E., & Henry, W. E. (1961). *Growing old: The process of disengagement.* New York: Basic Books.

Dance, F. (1988). Introduction to communication. In C. Carmichael, C. H. Botan, & R. Hawkins (Eds.), *Human communications and the aging process* (pp. 9–19). Prospect Heights, IL: Waveland Press.

Danziger, S., & Gottschalk, P. (1995). *America unequal.* Cambridge, MA: Harvard University Press.

Delaware Valley Intergenerational Network. (1986, Spring). *Interchange,* p. 1.

de Tocqueville, A. (1900). *Democracy in America.* New York: Colonial Press.

Dewey, J. (1938). *Experience and education.* New York: Macmillan.

Doka, K. (1985/1986). Adolescent attitudes and beliefs toward aging in the elderly. *International Journal of Aging and Human Development, 22*(3), 173–187.

Dowd, J. J. (1980). *Stratification among the aged.* Monterey, CA: Brooks/Cole.

Dychtwald, K., & Flower, J. (1989). *Age wave: The challenges and opportunities of an aging America.* New York: St. Martin's Press.

Edleman, M. (1996, March). *Connecting communities to care for America's children.* Speech presented at the Generations United Conference, Washington, DC.

Ellis, S., & Noyes, K. (1990). *By the people: A history of Americans as volunteers.* San Francisco: Jossey-Bass.

Erikson, E. H. (1959). *Identity and the life cycle.* New York: Norton.

Erikson, E. H. (1963). *Childhood and society.* New York: Norton.

Erikson, E. H., Erikson, J. M., & Kivnick, H. Q. (1986). *Vital involvement in old age.* New York: Norton.

Estes, C. (1979). *The aging enterprise.* San Francisco: Jossey-Bass.

Etzioni, A. (1993). *The spirit of community: Rights, responsibilities, and the communitarian agenda.* New York: Crown.

Everline, D., & Schmitz, A. (1990). *GRANDCARE experience: Older adults as employees in childcare.* Kensington, MD: Interages.

Fein, E. (1994, July 19). Elderly find hardship in haven for young. *The New York Times,* pp. A1, A12.

Fink, D. (1985). *Intergenerational adventure: A training curriculum for older adult caregivers working with school age children during the hours after school.* Wellesley, MA: Wellesley College, Center for Research on Women.

Firman, J., Gelfand, D., & Ventura, C. (1983). Intergenerational service-learning: Contributions to the curriculum. *Educational Gerontology, 9,* 405–415.

Fischer, L. (1993, Spring). Recruiting older volunteers. *Journal of Volunteer Administration, 11*(3), 13–17.

Flint, J. (1980, February 18). The old folks. *Forbes,* 51–56.

Florida Department of Education. (1979). *Interlock, Florida school volunteer program directory, 1979–1980.* Tallahassee, FL: Author.

Fox, S., & Giles, H. (1993). Accommodating intergenerational contact: A critique and theoretical model. *Journal of Aging Studies, 7,* 423–451.

Franks, L., Hughes, J., Phelps, L., & Williams, D. (1993). Intergenerational influences on Midwest college students by their grandparents and significant elders. *Educational Gerontology, 19,* 265–271.

Freedman, M. (1993). *The kindness of strangers: Adult mentors, urban youth, and the new volunteerism.* San Francisco: Jossey-Bass.

Freedman, M. (1994). *Seniors in national and community service: A report prepared by the Commonwealth Fund's Americans Over 55 at Work program.* Philadelphia: Public/Private Ventures.

Generations United. (1993). *Public policy agenda: First session of the 102nd Congress.* Washington, DC: Author.

Generations United. (1994). *Public policy agenda: First session of the 103rd Congress.* Washington, DC: Author.

Generations United.(1995). *Public policy agenda: First session of the 104th Congress.* Washington, DC: Author.

Green, S. K. (1981). Attitudes and perceptions about the elderly: Current and future perspectives. *International Journal of Aging and Human Development, 13,* 99–119

Griff, M., Lambert, D., Fruit, D., & Dellman-Jenkins, M. (1996). *LinkAges: Planning an intergenerational program for preschool.* Menlo Park, CA: Addison-Wesley.

Gutmann, D. L. (1986). Oedipus and the aging male: A comparative perspective. *Psychoanlytic Review, 73,* 541–552.

Hammack, B. (1993). *Self-Esteem Through Service (S.E.T.S.): An intergenerational service-learning experience for at-risk students and isolated senior adults.* Kensington, MD: Interages.

Haslerud, G. (1972). *Transfer, memory and creativity: After-learning as perceptual process.* Minneapolis, MN: University of Minnesota Press.

Hegeman, C. (1985). *Child care in long-term care settings.* Albany, NY: Foundation for Long-Term Care.

Hegeman, C., & Linsider, R. (1992). *Coordinated student involvement in elder care.* Albany, NY: Foundation for Long Term Care.

Helfgott, K. P. (1992). *Older adults caring for children: Intergenerational child care.* Washington, DC: Generations United.

Henkin, N. (1996). *ABC's of program development.* Workshop presentation at the Seventh National Conference of Generations United, Washington, DC.

Henkin, N., Perez-Randall, C., & Rogers, A. (1993). *Elders as mentors: A training program for older adults.* Philadelphia, PA: Temple University, Center for Intergenerational Learning.

Henkin, N., Rogers, A., Lyons, M., & Charner, I. (1994). *Linking Lifetimes: A national intergenerational mentoring initiative—Summary report.* Philadelphia: Temple University, Center for Intergenerational Learning.

Henkin, N., & Sweeney, S. (1989). Linking systems: A systems approach to intergenerational programming. In S. Newman & S. Brummel (Eds.), *Intergenerational programs: Imperatives, strategies, impacts, trends* (pp. 165–172). Binghamton, NY: Haworth Press.

Herman, J. (1987). *Program evaluation kit* (2nd ed.). Newbury Park, CA: Sage.

Higgans, P., & Faunce, R. (1977, March). *Attitudes of Minneapolis elementary school students and senior citizens toward each other* (Report No. C-76-34). (ERIC Document Reproduction Service No. ED 139 823)

Hooyman, N. R., & Kiyak, H. A. (1991). *Social gerontology: A multidisciplinary perspective.* Boston: Allyn & Bacon.

Howe, N., & Strauss, B. (1995). *Get real about D's and E's (the deficits and entitlements that are trashing your future).* Washington, DC: The Concord Coalition.

Illinois Department of Aging. (1987, October). *Uniting the generations: Moving states toward family policies across the age spectrum.* Springfield, IL: Author.

Ilsley, P. (1990). *Enhancing the volunteer experience.* San Francisco: Jossey-Bass.

Information packet. (n.d.). (Available from the Center for Intergenerational Learning, Temple University Institute on Aging, 1601 N. Broad Street, Philadelphia, PA 19122)

Intergenerational Education Volunteer Act of 1985, H. R. 1587, 99th Cong., 1st Sess. (1985).

Intergenerational Education Volunteer Act of 1985, S. 1022, 99th Cong., 1st Sess. (1985).

Intergenerational mentoring: Roundtable discussion before the Special Committee on Aging, U. S. Senate, 102d Cong., 2d Sess. (Serial No. 102-26). (1992). (testimony of Marc Freedman).

Intergenerational programming development in Wisconsin. (1987). *Intergenerational Clearinghouse, 5*(2), 2–3.

Introducing Joining Together. (1986). *Joining Together, 1*(1), 1.

Isaacs, L., & Bearison, D. (1986). The development of children's prejudice against the aged. *International Journal of Aging and Human Development, 23*(3), 175–194.

Jantz, R. (1981). Children's attitudes towards the elderly: A look at Greek and American Children. *Theory and Research in Social Education, 9*(2), 1–22.

Johnson, S., & Siegel, W. (1980). *Bridging generations: A handbook for intergenerational child care.* Palm Springs, CA: Elder Press.

Kalish, R. (1969). The old and the new as generation gap allies. *Gerontologist, 9,* 83–89.

Kaplan, M. (1991). *An intergenerational approach to community education and action: A case study.* Unpublished doctoral dissertation, City University of New York, Graduate School and University Center.

Kaplan, M. (1994). *Side by side: Exploring your neighborhood through intergenerational activities: A curriculum guide.* Berkley, CA: MIG Communications.

Kasper, J. (1988). *Aging alone: Profiles and projections.* New York: The Commonwealth Fund.

Kimmel, D. C. (1990). *Adulthood and aging.* New York: Wiley.

Kingdon, J. (1994). *Agendas, alternatives, and public policies.* Boston: Little Brown.

Kingson, E. R. (1988). Generational equity: An unexpected opportunity to broaden the politics of aging. *The Gerontologist, 22,* 765–762.

Kingson, E. R. (1989). The social policy implications of intergenerational exchange. In S. Newman & S. Brummel (Eds.), *Intergenerational programs: Imperatives, strategies, impacts, trends* (pp. 91–99). Binghamton, NY: Haworth Press.

Kingson, E. R., Hirshorn, B. A., & Cornman, J. M. (1986). *The ties that bind: The interdependence of generations.* Cabin John, MD: Seven Locks Press.

Kingson, E. R., Hirshorn, B., & Harootyan, L. (1987). *The common stake: The interdependence of generations.* Washington, DC: Gerontological Society of America.

Kingson, E. R., & Quadagno, J. (1995). Social Security: Marketing radical reform. *Generations, 19*(3), 43–49.

Kingson, E. R., & Williamson, J. B. (1993). The generational equity debate: A progressive framing of a conservative issue. *The Journal of Aging and Social Policy, 5*(3), 31–53.

Kite, M., & Johnson, B. (1988). Attitudes toward older and younger adults: A meta-analysis. *Psychology and Aging, 3,* 233–244.

Knowles, M. (1978). *The adult learner: A neglected species* (2nd ed.). Houston, TX: Gulf.

Kolata, G. (1993, May 3). Strong family aid to elderly is found. *The New York Times,* p. A7.

Kramer, R. (1976). *Maria Montessori: A biography.* New York: Putnam.

Kramer, C., & Newman, S. (1986). *Senior Citizen School Volunteer Program: A manual for program implementation.* Albany, NY: Center for the Study of Aging.

Kuehne, V. (1989). "Younger friends/older friends": A study of intergenerational interactions. *Journal of Classroom Interaction, 24*(1), 14–21.

Kuehne, V. (1990). *A comparative study of children's extra-familial intergenerational relationships.* Unpublished doctoral dissertation, Northwestern University, Evanston, IL.

Kumpfer, K., Shur, G., Ross, J., Bunnell, K., Librett, J., & Millward, A. (1993). *Measurement in prevention: A manual on selecting and using instruments to evaluate prevention programs* (DHHS Publication No. 93-2041). Rockville, MD: U.S. Department of Health and Human Services, Center for Substance Abuse Prevention.

Kuypers, J. A., & Bengtson, V. L. (1973). Social breakdown and competence: A model of normal aging. *Human Development, 16,* 181–201.

La Belle, T., & Ward, C. (1994). *Multiculturalism and education.* Albany, NY: State University of New York Press.

Lambert, D., Dellmann-Jenkins, M., & Fruit, D. (1990). Planning for contact between the generations: An effective approach. *The Gerontologist, 30,* 553–556.

Larkin, E. (1995). *Intergenerational programs and curriculum development* (ED 560 K, course outline). Boston, MA: Wheelock College, Graduate School.

Laterza, T. (1995). *Intergenerational service learning: A guide for faculty.* Pittsburgh, PA: University of Pittsburgh, Generations Together.

Lawrence, B. S. (1988). New wrinkles in the theory of age demography, norms, and performance ratings. *Academy of Management Journal, 31,* 309–337.

Learning Corporation of America (Producer). (1980). *Close harmony* [Videotape]. (Available from Learning Corporation of America, 1350 Avenue of the Americas, New York, NY 10019)

Leon, K. (1990). *Linkage—Bringing together young and old.* Topeka, KS: Menninger Child Care Center.

Liederman, D., & Ossofsky, J. (1987). An open letter to members of Generations United. *Newsline, 1*(1), 1.

Longman, P. (1985). Justice between generations. *The Atlantic Monthly, 256,* 73–81.

Luks, A. (1988). Helper's high. *Psychology Today, 10*(3), 41–42.

Luntz, F. (1995, February 5). January 9, 1995 memorandum to the Republican Congress. *New York Times, 144,* pp. E7(N), E7(L).

Lutsky, N. (1981). Attitudes toward old age and elderly persons. In C. Eisdorfer (Ed.), *Annual review of gerontology and geriatrics* (Vol. 1, pp. 287–336). New York: Springer.

Lyons, E. (Ed.). (1982). *On growing older: Curriculum guides—Grades 1–6.* Pittsburgh, PA: University of Pittsburgh, Generations Together.

Mack, C., & Wilson, J. (1988). *Share it with the children: A preschool curriculum on aging instructional guide.* Pittsburgh, PA: University of Pittsburgh, Generations Together.

MacNeil, R. (1991). Attitudes toward the aged and identified employment preferences of therapeutic recreation students. *Educational Gerontology, 17,* 543–558.

Makin, J. H. (October 8, 1988). Social Security: Nothing but a Ponzi scheme. *The New York Times, 138*, pp. N15, L27.

Mannheim, K., & Stewart, W. (1962). *An introduction to the sociology of education.* New York: Humanities Press.

Marks, R. (1980). *Children's perception of the elderly: A quasi-experimental study of attitude change.* Unpublished doctoral dissertation, University of Pittsburgh, Pittsburgh, PA.

Marks, R., Newman, S., & Faux, B. (1993). *Children's Views on Aging (CVoA): A survey for children 8–12.* Unpublished manuscript, University of Pittsburgh, Generations Together.

Marks, R., Newman, S., & Onawola, R. (1985). Latency-aged children's views of aging. *Educational Gerontology, 11*(2/3), 89–99.

Marriott's senior volunteerism study [Survey commissioned by Marriott Senior Living Services and the United States Administration on Aging]. (1991). Washington, DC: Marriott Senior Living Services.

Marshall, M. (1985). *Development of intergenerational education in California.* Van Nuys, CA: Author. (Out of print)

Maryland names "SETS" model program for 1995. (1995, Winter). *Interages News,* 2.

Maryland State Board of Education Technical Team. (1992). *In the middle: Addressing the needs of at-risk students during the middle learning years* (Report to the Commission for Students At Risk of School Failure). Annapolis, MD: Author.

Massachusetts network formed. (1987). *Linkages, 2*(2), 1.

McCormick, E., & Tifflin, J. R. (1974). *Industrial psychology.* Englewood Cliffs, NJ: Prentice-Hall.

McCracken, A., Fitzwater, E., Lockwood, M., & Bjork, F. (1995). Comparison of nursing students' attitudes toward the elderly in Norway and the United States. *Educational Gerontology, 21*, 167–180.

McDonald, N. (1990). *How to organize and manage intergenerational partnership programs.* Alexandria, VA: National Association of Partners in Education.

McGowan, T. (1994). Mentoring–reminiscence: A conceptual and empirical analysis. *International Journal of Aging and Human Development, 39*, 321–336.

McTavish, D. (1971). Perceptions of old people. A review of research methodologies and findings. *The Gerontologist, 11*, 90–101.

Mead, M. (1971). *Coming of age in Samoa.* New York: Morrow.

Meany, D. (1982). *Curriculum on aging: An intergenerational program for grades K–6.* San Diego, CA: San Diego County Superintendent of Schools.

Medicaid: What's at stake in the budget negotiations? [White House policy briefing]. (1996, January 23). Washington, DC: White House.

Medicare: What's at stake in the budget negotiations? [White House policy briefing]. (1996, January 23). Washington, DC: White House.

Melcher, J. (1990). *Caring is the key: Building a school-based intergenerational service program with training modules.* Pittsburgh, PA: University of Pittsburgh, Generations Together.

Mersereau, Y., & Glover, M. (1990). *A guide to community: An intergenerational friendship program between young people and nursing home residents.* Madison, WI: Bi-Folkal Productions.

Miller, P. (1993). *Theories of developmental psychology.* New York: Freeman.

Miller, S., Blalock, J., & Ginsburg, H. (1984). Children and the aged: Attitudes, contact, and discriminative ability. *International Journal of Aging and Human Development, 19,* 47–53.

Minkler, M. (1986). "Generational equity" and the new victim blaming: An emerging public policy issue. *International Journal of Health Services, 16,* 539–551.

Minkler, M., & Roe, K. (1993). *Grandparents as caregivers: Raising children of the crack cocaine epidemic.* Newbury Park, CA: Sage.

Moody, H. (1988). *Abundance of life: Human development policies for an aging society.* New York: Columbia University Press.

Moody, H., & Disch, R. (1989). Intergenerational programming in public policy. In S. Newman & S. Brummel (Eds.), *Intergenerational programs: Imperatives, strategies, impacts, trends* (pp. 101–110). Binghamton, NY: Haworth Press.

Morris, R., & Caro, F. (1995). The young-old, productive aging, and public policy. *Generations, 19*(3), 32–37.

Murphy, M. (1984). *A guide to intergenerational programs.* Washington, DC: National Association of State Units on Aging.

Murphy-Russell, S., Die, A., & Walker, J. (1986). Changing attitudes toward the elderly: The impact of three methods of attitude change. *Educational Gerontology, 12,* 241–251.

Myths and reality of aging in America. (1975). New York: Louis Harris & Associates.

Nathanson, P. (1989). The intergenerational movement: A sound imperative. In S. Newman & S. Brummel (Eds.), *Intergenerational programs: Imperatives, strategies, impacts, trends* (pp. 111–118). Binghamton, NY: Haworth Press.

National Academy on Aging. (1994). *Old age in the 21st century.* Washington, DC: Author.

The National and Community Service Trust Act [Memorandum]. (1994, January 13). Washington, DC: Generations United.

National Center for Children in Poverty. (1991). *Five million children: 1991 update.* New York: Author.

National Center for Service-Learning. (1980). *Planning by objections: A manual for student community service program coordinators* (ACTION Pamphlet #4000, 15, 10/80). Washington, DC: U. S. Government Printing Office.

National Council on the Aging. (1981). *Strategies for linking the generations.* Washington, DC: Author.

National Council on the Aging. (1992a). *Jobstart: The road to independence—Family Friends training curriculum.* Washington, DC: Author.

National Council on the Aging. (1992b). *Rural family friends replication manual: A project of the National Council on the Aging and Save the Children Federation.* Washington, DC: Author.

National School Volunteer Program. (1983). *Annual report for 1982.* Alexandria, VA: Author.

National Senior Corps Programs. (1995, March/April). *Aging Network News, 12*(11/12), 4.

Nee, D. (1989). The intergenerational movement: A social imperative. In S. Newman & S. Brummel (Eds.) *Intergenerational programs: Imperatives, strategies, impacts, trends* (pp. 79–90). Binghamton, NY: Haworth Press.

Neugarten, B., Havighurst, R., & Tobin, S. (1961). The measurement of life satisfaction. *Journal of Gerontology, 16*, 134–143.

Newman, S. (1980). *Linking the generations: A consideration for the 1981 White House Conference on Aging.* Speech presented at the National Council on the Aging Mini-Conference, University of Georgia, Athens.

Newman, S. (1986). *Creating effective intergenerational programs.* Unpublished manuscript, University of Pittsburgh, Generations Together.

Newman, S. (1989a). Connections. *Generations Together Exchange, Issue 5*, 1.

Newman, S. (1989b). A history of intergenerational programs. In S. Newman & S. Brummel (Eds.) *Intergenerational programs: Imperatives, strategies, impacts, trends* (pp. 1–16). Binghamton, NY: Haworth Press.

Newman, S. (1992). *Innovative models and promising practices for older adults in child care.* Unpublished manuscript, University of Pittsburgh, Generations Together.

Newman, S. (1994, Fall). Generations Together celebrates its 15th anniversary [special issue]. *Generations Together Exchange,* p. 1.

Newman, S., Baum, M., & Vasudev, J. (1983). *The experience of senior volunteers in intergenerational programs in schools and the relationship to their life satisfaction* (Final report to the NRTA–AARP Andrus Foundation). Pittsburgh, PA: University of Pittsburgh, Generations Together.

Newman, S., & Brummel, S. (Ed.). (1989). *Intergenerational programs: Imperatives, strategies, impacts, trends.* Binghamton, NY: Haworth Press.

Newman, S., Karip, E., & Faux, R. (1995). Everyday memory function of older adults: The impact of intergenerational school volunteer programs. *Educational Gerontology, 21*, 569–580.

Newman, S., & Larimer, B. (1995). *Senior Citizen School Volunteer Program: Report on cumulative data for 1988–1995.* Pittsburgh, PA: University of Pittsburgh, Generations Together.

Newman, S., & Larkin, E. (in press). Intergenerational studies: A multidisciplinary field. *Journal of Gerontological Social Work.*

Newman, S., & Riess, J. (1992). Older workers in intergenerational child care settings. *Journal of Gerontological Social Work, 19*(2), 45–66.

Newman, S., & Ward, C. (1993). An observational study of intergenerational activities and behavior change in dementing elders at adult day care centers. *The International Journal of Aging and Human Development, 36*, 253–265.

Nishi-Strattner, M., & Myers, J. (1983). Attitudes toward the elderly: An intergenerational examination. *Educational Gerontology, 9*, 389–397.

Northern Virginia Planning District Commission. (1992). *Let's link ages in Northern Virginia: Intergenerational resource guide.* Annandale, VA: Author.

Oriol, W. (1982). *Aging in all nations* (Special report on the United Nations World Assembly on Aging, Vienna, Austria, July 26–August 6). Washington, DC: National Council on the Aging.

Palmore, E. B. (1977). Facts on Aging: A short quiz. *The Gerontologist, 17*, 315–320.

Palmore, E. B. (1980). The Facts on Aging quiz: A review of the findings. *The Gerontologist, 20*, 669–672.

Palmore, E. B. (1988). *The Facts on Aging quiz: A handbook of uses and results.* New York: Springer.

Pennsylvania Department of Aging. (1984). *Reaching across the years: Selected intergenerational programs in Pennsylvania.* Harrisburg, PA: Author.

Peterson, P. G. (1994, April 7). Entitlement reform: The way to eliminate the deficit. *New York Review of Books, 41*(7), 3–19.

Phillips, C. (1992). The personnel crisis in child care. *Generations Together Exchange,* Issue 7, 2.

Piers, E., & Harris, D. (1969). *"The way I feel about myself": The Piers–Harris Children's Self-Concept Scale.* Los Angeles: Western Psychological Services.

Powell, J., Wisenbaker, J., & Connor, R. (1987). Effects of intergenerational tutoring and related variables on reading and mathematics achievement of low socioeconomic children. *Journal of Experimental Education, 55*, 206–211.

Pratt, C., Miksis, J., & Trapp, J. (1986). *Perspectives on aging: Bridging the generation gap.* Corvalles, OR: College of Home Economics.

Prosper, V. (1987). *Intergenerational programming: Overview and sample programs.* New York: New York State Office for the Aging.

Quadagno, J. (1996). Generational equity and the politics of the welfare state. In J. Quadagno & D. Street (Eds.), *Aging for the twenty-first century: Readings in social gerontology* (pp. 398–418). New York: St. Martin's Press.

Reinke, B., Holmes, D., & Denney, N. (1981). Influence of a "friendly visitor" program on the cognitive functioning and morale of elderly persons. *American Journal of Cognitive Psychology, 9*, 491–506.

Reville, S., & Adams, J. (Eds.). (1988). *Public/private national intergenerational initiative.* Washington, DC: U.S. Department of Health and Human Services.

Riegel, K. F. (1976). The dialectic of human development. *American Psychologist, 31*, 689–700.

Riley, J., & Riley, M. (1994). Beyond productive aging. *Aging International, 21*(2), 15–19.

Romero, C. (1986). The economics of volunteerism: A review. In Committee on an Aging Society (Ed.), *Productive roles in an older society* (pp. 23–50). Washington, DC: National Academy Press.

Romney, G. (1991). Volunteers in the 1990s: Commitment to serve others. In R. Harootyan, A. Stowell, I. Takeuchi, W. Heil, L. Marks, W. Cater, A. Dixon, & S. Williams (Eds.), *Conference Proceedings on Resourceful Aging: Today and tomorrow: Vol. 1. Executive summary* (pp. 35–38). Washington, DC: American Association of Retired Persons.

Roosevelt, F. D. R. (1934, June 8). *Broad objectives and accomplishments of the Administration* [Message to Congress].

Rose-Colley, M., & Eddy, J. (1988). Interactions of university students with elderly individuals. *Educational Gerontology, 14*, 33–43.

Rosen, B., & Jerdee, T. (1976). The nature of job-related stereotypes. *Journal of Applied Psychology, 61*, 428–432.

Rosenbaum, W., & Button, J. (1993). The unquiet future of intergenerational politics. *Gerontologist, 33*, 481–490.

Rosenmayr, L. (1980). Achievements, doubts and prospects of the sociology of aging. *Human Development, 23*, 46–62.

Rothstein, E. (1996, February 18). The tribulations of the not-so-living arts. *The New York Times,* Sec. 4, pp. 1, 14.

Ryan, E., Hamilton, J., & See, S. (1994). Patronizing the old: How do younger and older adults respond to baby talk in the nursing home? *International Journal of Aging and Human Development, 39,* 21–32.

Sainer, J., & Zander, M. (1971). *SERVE: Older volunteers in community service.* New York: Community Service Society of New York.

Saltz, R. (1970). *Effects of a Foster Grandparent Program on the intellectual and social development of young children in institutions.* Unpublished doctoral dissertation, Wayne State University, Detroit, MI.

Saltz, R. (1971). Aging persons as child-care workers in a Foster Grandparent Program: Psycho-social effects and work performance. *Aging and Human Development, 2,* 314–340.

Scannell T., & Roberts, A. (1994). *Young and old serving together: Meeting community needs through intergenerational partnerships.* Washington, DC: Generations United.

Schaie, K. W., & Willis, S. (1986). *Adult development and aging.* Boston: Little, Brown.

Schreter, C. (1989). *Intergenerating America: The final report on the Administration on Aging Public/Private National Intergenerational Initiative.* La Quinta, CA: Elvirita Lewis Foundation.

Schuetz, J. (1988). Communication and lifelong learning. In C. Carmichael, C. H. Botan, & R. Hawkins (Eds.), *Human communications and the aging process* (pp. 205–219). Prospect Heights, IL: Waveland Press.

Seefeldt, C. (1984). Children's attitudes toward the elderly: A cross-cultural comparison. *International Journal of Aging and Human Development, 19,* 319–328.

Seefeldt, C. (1987). The effects of preschoolers' visits to a nursing home. *The Gerontologist, 27,* 228–232.

Seefeldt, C., Bredekamp, R., & Serock, K. (1982). How older people view children. *Children Today, 11,* 16–20.

Seefeldt, C., Jantz, R. K., Galper, A., & Serock, K. (1976). *Children's Attitudes Toward the Elderly (CATE): Final Report.* College Park, MD: University of Maryland. (ERIC Document Reproduction Services No. ED 181 081)

Seefeldt, C., Jantz, R., Galper, A., & Serock, K. (1977). Using pictures to explore children's attitudes toward the elderly. *The Gerontologist, 17,* 506–512.

Seefeldt, C., Jantz, R., Serock, K., & Bredekamp, S. (1982). Elderly persons' attitudes toward children. *Educational Gerontology, 8,* 493–506.

Seefeldt, C., & Warman, B. (1990). *Young and old together.* Washington, DC: National Association for the Education of Young Children.

Shamas, E. (1979). Social myth as hypothesis: The case of the family relations of old people. *The Gerontologist, 19,* 3–9.

Sheehan, R. (1975). Young children's contact with the elderly. *Journal of Gerontology, 33,* 567–574.

Simmons, R. G. (1987). The impact of cumulative change in early adolescence. *Child Development, 58,* 1220–1234.

Smith, T., Mack, C., & Tittnich, E. (1993). *Generations Together: A job training curriculum for older adults in child care.* Syracuse, NY: Syracuse University Press.

Standing, E. M. (1959). *Maria Montessori, her life and work.* Fresno, CA: Academy Library Guild.

The state of America's children. (1996). Washington, DC: Children's Defense Fund.

Stearns, P. (1989). Historical trends in intergenerational contacts. In S. Newman & S. Brummel (Eds.), *Intergenerational programs: Imperatives, strategies, impacts, trends* (pp. 21–32). Binghamton, NY: Haworth Press.

Steitz, J., & Verner, B. (1987). What adolescents know about aging. *Educational Gerontologist, 13*, 357–368.

Sterngold, J. (1995, July 30). The budget knife boomerangs home. *The New York Times,* p. E3.

Stout, B., Boyd, S., & Volanty, K. (1993). *Y.E.S. project training guide.* Lubbock, TX: Texas Tech University, Home Economics Curriculum Center.

Thesaurus of aging terminology: AgeLine database on middle age and aging (4th ed.). (1991). Washington, DC: American Association of Retired Persons.

Thomas, E., & Yamamoto, K. (1975). Attitudes toward age: An exploration in school-age children. *International Journal of Aging and Human Development, 6,* 117–129.

Thorp, K. (1985). *Intergenerational programs: A resource for community renewal.* Madison, WI: Wisconsin Positive Youth Development Initiative.

Tice, C. (1982). *Linking the generations—Intergenerational programs: A Wingspread report.* Racine, WI: The Johnson Foundation.

Tice, C. (1993). *A guide to mentoring.* Ann Arbor, MI: Lifespan Resources.

Tice, C., & Warren, B. (1986). *T-LC coordinators handbook teaching-learning communities.* Ypsilanti, MI: Eastern Michigan University, Institute for the Study of Children and Families.

Treas, J. (1995). Older Americans in the 1990s and beyond. *Population Bulletin, 50,* 1–43.

University of the State of New York. (1986). *Educational elements of a comprehensive state policy on aging.* Albany, NY: Author.

U.S. Bureau of the Census. (1992). *Sixty-five plus in America* (Current populations reports, special studies, P23-178). Washington, DC: U.S. Government Printing Office.

U.S. Bureau of the Census. (1993). *Current population reports* (Series No. P20-478). Washington, DC: U.S. Government Printing Office.

U.S. Bureau of the Census. (1995). *Statistical abstract of the United States: 1995* (115th ed.). Washington, DC: U.S. Government Printing Office.

U.S. Department of Health and Human Services. (1991). *Aging America: Trends and projections* (DHHS Publication No. FCOA 91-28001). Washington, DC: U.S. Government Printing Office.

Update on the intergenerational program network. (1985, Spring). *Project Joy: Joining Older and Younger Newsletter,* p. 7.

Van Til, J. (1990). *Critical issues in American philanthropy.* San Francisco: Jossey-Bass.

Ventura-Merkel, K., & Lidoff, L. (1983). *Program innovation in aging: Volume VIII. Community planning for intergenerational programming.* Washington, DC: National Council on the Aging.

Ventura-Merkel, K., & Parks, E. (1984). *Intergenerational programs: A catalog of profiles.* Washington, DC: National Council on the Aging.

Vincent, L. J. (1988). Changing economic and social influences on family involvement. *Topics in Early Childhood Special Education, 8*(1), 48–59.

Volunteer centers are an important local resource. (1995). *Aging Network News,* *12*(11/12), 6.

Vujovich, J. E. (1987). *Child care in nursing homes: Creating an intergenerational program.* Steamboat Springs, CO: Author.

Wallace, R. (1995). *Ethical spectacle* [on-line]. Retrieved October 1995 from World Wide Web: http//www.spectacle.org.

Ward, C., Los Kamp, L., & Newman, S. (1996). The effects of participation in an intergenerational program on the behavior of residents with dementia. *Activities, Adaptation, and Aging, 20*(4), 61–76.

Ward, C., & McCrea, J. (1996). Evaluation of a collaborative intergenerational community service project. In J. Eby (Ed.), *Service-learning: Linking academics and the community* (pp. 53–60). Harrisburg, PA: Pennsylvania Campus Compact, Pennsylvania Association of Colleges and Universities.

Ward, C., Newman, S., Engel, R., & Karip, E. (1994a). *Older workers in child care: A longitudinal study of their experiences and impact* (Final report for the Retirement Research Foundation). Pittsburgh, PA: University of Pittsburgh, Generations Together.

Ward, C., Newman, S., Engel, R., & Karip, E. (1994b). *A time series study of factors associated with retention and attrition of older adult child-care workers* (Final report to the AARP–Andrus Foundation). Pittsburgh, PA: University of Pittsburgh, Generations Together

Ward, C., & Smith, T. (1992). Community college training of older adults for child care employment. *Community Services Catalyst, 22,* 3–6.

Ward, C., & Smith, T. (1993). *Older adults in child care: A job-training model.* Pittsburgh, PA: University of Pittsburgh, Generations Together.

Ward, C., & Streetman, H. (1995). *Evaluation of GENERATIONS.* Pittsburgh, PA: University of Pittsburgh, Generations Together.

Wasik, J. (1996, March/April). Will Social Security be there for you? *Consumer's Digest,* 49–54.

Weatherford, C., & Seoane, M. (1992). *Evaluation guide for tutoring programs.* Clemson, SC: National Dropout Prevention Center.

Weinsberg, E. J. (1974). *High school volunteers' attitudes about the elderly: The short-term effects of contact with aged residents of nursing homes.* Unpublished doctoral dissertation, Columbia University, New York.

Wertsch, J. V. (1985). *Vygotsky and the social formation of mind.* Cambridge, MA: Harvard University Press.

Whitbourne, S. K. (1985). The psychological construction of the life span. In J. E. Birren & K. W. Schaie (Eds.), *Handbook of the psychology of aging* (2nd ed., pp. 594–618). New York: Van Nostrand Reinhold.

White House Conference on Aging. (1981a). *Challenging age stereotypes in the media* (GPO 720-019/6927). Washington, DC.: U.S. Government Printing Office.

White House Conference on Aging. (1981b). *Intergenerational cooperation and exchange* (GPO 720-019/6929). Washington, DC: U.S. Government Printing Office.

White House Conference on Aging. (1981c). *Older Americans as a growing national resource* (GPO 720-019/6886). Washington, DC: U.S. Government Printing Office.

White House Conference on Aging. (1995). *Adopted resolutions: Official 1995 White House Conference on Aging.* Washington, DC: Author.

Whitley, E., Duncan, R., McKenzie, P., & Sledjecki, S. (1976). *From time to time: A record of young children's relationships with the aged.* Gainesville, FL: University of Florida, College of Education, P. K. Yonge Laboratory School.

Wilson, J. (1994). *Intergenerational readings/resources 1980–1994: A bibliography of books, book chapters, journal articles, manuals, papers/reports/studies, curricula, bibliographies, directories, newsletters, data bases, and videos* (3rd ed.). Pittsburgh, PA: University of Pittsburgh, Generations Together.

Wilson, L., & Simson, S. (1991). The role of social work in intergenerational programming. *Journal of Gerontological Social Work, 16*(1/2), 87–96.

Wilson, L., & Simson, S. (1993). Senior volunteerism policies at the local level: Adaptation and leadership in the 21st century. *The Journal of Volunteer Administration, 11*(4), 15–23.

Wood, J. (1992). *Life spectrum programming bringing generations together: A library guide to supporting community-wide intergenerational programming.* Pekin, IL: Pekin Public Library.

Yamazaki, T. (1994). Intergenerational interaction outside the family. *Educational Gerontology, 20*, 453–462.

Yaroshevsky, M. (1989). *Lev Vygotsky* (S. Syrovatkin, Trans.). Moscow: Progress Publishers.

Zandi, T., Mirle, J., & Jarvis, P. (1990). Children's attitudes toward elderly individuals: A comparison of two ethnic groups. *International Journal of Aging and Human Development, 30*, 161–174.

Zastrow, C., & Kirst-Ashman, K. (1994). *Understanding human behavior and the social environment.* Chicago, IL: Nelson-Hall.

Appendix

Section 1: Finding and Assessing Intergenerational Program Resources

Janet O. Wilson, MLS

Any field or profession is largely defined by a body of collected information that describes the practices associated with the field and provides the theoretical justification for those practices. Access to this information enables practitioners to learn about the field, replicate appropriate practices, and design new research efforts, which in turn add to the basic body of knowledge. *Intergenerational program resources* contain the information that is needed by persons who are working within, or learning about, the emerging intergenerational field.

To be of value, of course, intergenerational program resources must be identified and available. The fact that an intergenerational field has not been formally established poses problems for practitioners, students, and other researchers in need of information. Much of the information that is relevant to intergenerational professionals has not been designated as such, nor has it been organized or catalogued in a consistent fashion.

Intergenerational program resources currently consist largely of print materials, drawn from or found in a wide variety of locations. Other programmatic information can be found in videotapes, which are usually either descriptive (depicting actual intergenerational activities) or educational (training tools illustrating the basic concepts of the field).

Recent years have seen the growth of the Internet as an important tool for practitioners and researchers in many fields, for both locating and retrieving relevant information. The Internet is as youthful as the intergenerational field, however, and its value to those seeking intergenerational information is currently somewhat limited. For various reasons (e.g., budget considerations, access to technology, and the lack of a clear need), intergenerational practitioners have been slow to take advantage of new electronic information-related resources.

As both the Internet and the intergenerational field continue to grow and evolve, this situation is certain to change, although the nature and direction of that change is difficult to predict. As more and more intergenerational professionals begin to disseminate information via the World Wide Web, for example, the Internet is likely to become an increasingly important source of information.

Finally, in this new, steadily evolving field, the practitioners themselves represent an additional, often-overlooked source of primary intergenerational information, and of assistance in locating relevant print, media, and electronic materials.

At this point in the development of an intergenerational field, then, finding and

197

retrieving intergenerational program resources remain something of a challenge. In this Appendix, the predominant sources of intergenerational information and their relationship to each other are discussed. The information in this discussion, combined with the list of reference materials used in the preparation of this book, will enable individuals or organizations to meet the challenge of identifying, locating, and retrieving intergenerational program resources.

SPECIAL SEARCH PROBLEMS

Even experienced information seekers find "intergenerational" searching to be a challenging process, involving some creativity and much guesswork. As a basis for approaching this task, it is helpful to understand the complexities of searching for—and acquiring—information about intergenerational programs, research and evaluation, and policy development. These complexities arise from the unique characteristics of this rapidly evolving field.

Diversity of Contributing Fields

Intergenerational program resources are not collected or catalogued under a specific subject or category. Rather, they reflect the wide variety of human service fields that have provided service to children, youth, and older adults for the last 30 years. The multidisciplinary composition of this field and the diversity among the individuals who create programs, their agencies, the clients, and the programs' locations all contribute to the unique nature of intergenerational program information.

For seekers of intergenerational information, then, the first decisions involve where to start. Not unexpectedly, a majority of intergenerational information is found in the literature of the education, human service, and social service disciplines, such as

- gerontology,
- sociology,
- psychology,
- political science,
- criminal justice, and
- anthropology.

Intergenerational information can also be found in the literature of health-related fields such as

- hospital administration,
- nursing,
- physical and occupational therapy, and
- physician training.

A searcher's quest for intergenerational information, then, necessarily involves a careful assessment of the data he or she is seeking, particularly in identifying any logical links to one or more of these fields.

Self- or In-house Publishing

Another challenge facing an intergenerational researcher is the current nature of the relevant print materials. A common characteristic of these materials—books, manuals, papers and reports, curricula, and media from the 1970s to the present—is the in-house or self-published nature of the documents. The commitment of professionals in the field to sharing program information has prompted individuals and agencies to formally document their efforts, creating valuable intergenerational program resources. These self-published materials are then made available primarily through the authoring agencies or sponsoring individuals themselves (see Section 2).

The efforts of these individuals are certainly appreciated, but such informal distribution methods prevent much of their work from reaching libraries, databases, and other places where information seekers normally find reference material. Listings of these publications are most effectively located by contacting specific individuals or agencies or through newsletters from intergenerational organizations (both of these approaches are discussed later).

SOURCES OF INFORMATION

An understanding of the nature of this informal field and the information it generates, then, is crucial to the development of successful search strategies. Also necessary is a basic understanding of the materials in which this information can be found and the location of the materials themselves.

Publications

In the early 1970s, magazine articles and manuals describing intergenerational program efforts began to appear. The late 1970s brought an information explosion to the intergenerational world, with nearly 400 publications appearing by 1989 (Wilson, 1994). During this 10- to 12-year period, intergenerational information appeared in a wide range of professional journals, such as *The Gerontologist* and *Illinois Libraries*, as well as in popular magazines such as *Modern Maturity* and *Children Today*. This information explosion has continued into the 1990s; in fact, the most significant and concentrated growth in intergenerational publications has occurred in the past 5 or 6 years. The number of publications appearing since 1990 is well over 350 and growing (Wilson, 1994). As a help to the searcher, the following is a list of magazines and journals in which intergenerational information has regularly been found:

Activities, Adaptations, Aging
American Health Care Association Journal
American Libraries
Childhood Education
Contemporary Longterm Care
Continuing Care
Educational Gerontology

Generations
The Gerontologist
Gerontology and Geriatrics Education
International Journal of Aging and Human Development
Journal of Applied Gerontology
Journal of Classroom Interactions
Journal of Clinical Psychology
Journal of Gerontological Nursing
Journal of Gerontological Social Work
Journal of Home Economics
Journal of Physical Education, Recreation, and Dance
Language Arts
Modern Maturity
Perspectives on Aging
Parents
Parks and Recreation
Phi Delta Kappan
Public Health Reports
Public Library Quarterly
Southwestern: The Journal of Aging for the Southwest
Today's Nursing Home
Young Children

No single journal covers the intergenerational field in depth, but, generally speaking, journals for aging professionals carry the largest amount of information.

In addition to journal articles, a small but growing number of intergenerational books have been published. Commercial publishing companies such as Haworth Press, MIG Communications, Syracuse University Press, and Addison-Wesley (and of course Taylor & Francis) have become interested in intergenerational topics. Terra Nova Films not only distributes but also creates videotapes on intergenerational topics. Such commercial publishing of intergenerational program materials is a significant benchmark for the field. Because these items can be found in bibliographic resources such as *Books In Print,* commercial publishing of intergenerational program resources permits this intergenerational information to be easily located and thus shared by a wider audience. As intergenerational programs are increasingly crafted to address pressing social issues, and as professionals become certified in intergenerational competencies, it is expected that more publishing will occur on a commercial basis.

Beginning with the *Intergenerational Clearinghouse Newsletter* from the Dane County, Wisconsin, Retired Senior Volunteer Program, many intergenerational professionals have published informational newsletters. For almost 20 years, such newsletters have gathered and dispensed information on intergenerational programs at local, regional, state, and national levels. Their editors are knowledgeable persons who represent the cutting edge of the field. The work, the publications, the people who are part of the programs, their successes and failures—the nitty-gritty of intergenerational programs can be found in these newsletters. Some of these newsletters are free on request; others are available for a nominal fee (see Section 2).

People

As noted earlier, the people who engage in intergenerational programming represent one of the most valuable sources of useful information for intergenerational professionals. Through direct contact with these experienced individuals, researchers and practitioners may obtain valuable information relating to many facets of the intergenerational field, including

- program model development,
- program management,
- program research and evaluation,
- program policy development,
- curriculum development,
- college and university teaching,
- training of trainers,
- network creation and maintenance,
- funding of programs,
- publishing and information dissemination, and
- public policy implications.

A practitioner who knows the field can provide valuable information, such as appropriate journal citations or the names of other contacts. These contacts can often provide information on successful program design, grant proposal writing, or ideas for research initiatives.

As indicated earlier, many of these practitioners have expressed a commitment to the dissemination of intergenerational information by self-publishing a wide variety of materials. Such efforts have made these individuals themselves a significant resource to the intergenerational field, especially because direct contact is often the only way to locate their materials. Contact information for many of these valuable people can be found in the resource lists at the end of this appendix. Entries in the lists often include individual's names as well as organization or agency addresses.

HOW TO SEARCH
FOR INTERGENERATIONAL INFORMATION

There will be times when personal contacts are not feasible or do not yield sufficient relevant information. In such cases, a more exhaustive search of the literature is needed to answer questions about intergenerational programs. The next section of this appendix provides assistance in conducting such a search by

- examining the language used by indexers and abstracters to describe intergenerational programs,
- describing successful search strategies, and
- reviewing bibliographic search tools, including on-line databases, CD-ROMs, and the Internet.

Terminology

When speaking about their intergenerational programs, individuals working in the field use language that indexers and abstractors may not recognize as program descriptors. Practitioners use words such as the following.

friendly visiting
telephone reassurance
colocated facilities
intergenerational staff training
generating
intergenerational caregiving
friendly listener
senior citizen school volunteer
intergenerational music
intergenerational child care
intergenerational service-learning
older adults in child care
older volunteers
teaching–learning communities
elders service
coalition building
intergenerational partners
intergenerating

The process of discovering what words are used in indexes and abstracts to describe intergenerational programs is often time consuming. The researcher needs to find words that describe the program by using alternative descriptors for children, youth, and older adults, the primary clients in intergenerational programs, and combine them with the physical location of the program. There will be occasions when adding words to the search (e.g., *attitudes, perceptions, behaviors, life satisfaction,* and *beliefs)* will produce intergenerational program information. Once a researcher has successfully located two or three citations in an index or abstract, he or she should examine the descriptors chosen by the indexer or abstractor to describe the intergenerational information. By using those terms, the searcher can then tailor new searches within that particular bibliographic source to find additional relevant information.

Databases publish searchable terms in a thesaurus, such as the Ageline database's *Thesaurus of Aging Terminology* (1991). By initially examining a thesaurus of terms, the user can save time by selecting appropriate searchable terms with which to create a search strategy for a specific database.

Experience suggests a note of caution to those who are planning a search for literature on intergenerational programs. It is not unusual to find the phrase *intergenerational relationships* as a listed descriptor in a human service database thesaurus, but its value in finding intergenerational program information is limited. Intergenerational programs are certainly about creating or enhancing intergenerational relationships, but this specific term is used by indexers and abstractors to describe relationships within and sometimes between genders (e.g., women's studies), ethnic groups (e.g., Hispanic households), and families (e.g., multigenerational studies). When this phrase is used as a primary search term to find intergenerational program information, therefore, it usually generates results that have little to do with the kind of intergenerational programs under discussion here.

Developing a Search

The recommended first search term is simply *intergenerational program*, using a truncation symbol on the word *program*. The truncation symbol and rules are designated by each database, and the use of truncation allows the searcher to access multiple forms of a word. For example, in many databases a search for the word *program?* (the question mark is a frequently used symbol for truncation) will produce citations containing the words *program, programs, programming, programmer, programmed,* and so forth. This symbol is remarkably useful in developing good search strategies.

To find intergenerational information when searching databases, a searcher must also think creatively about alternative terms to describe intergenerational programs and about ways to combine them in search strategies. Combinations of search terms, such as those in the following example, will save the researcher time and produce effective results.

To find information on *intergenerational colocated facilities* or *shared sites* (i.e., information that would describe the joint care of young children and older adults in day care or day-care programs for young children in older adult residential facilities), the following combinations of terms can be useful:

(preschool age children) and elders
(nursing homes) and (children & youth)
(child care) and (adult day care)

Note that most database searching requires nesting, that is, placing several terms together as a unit in parentheses, combined with another term or terms. Occasionally, long descriptive terms are treated as a whole term and do not require parentheses, for example, *child care in long-term care facilities*.

The following are some helpful hints for selecting search terms:

- Choose alternate terms for *children*, such as *preschool-age children, early childhood, infants, youth, elementary school students, boys, girls, child care, children & youth, teenagers.*
- Choose alternate terms for *youth*, such as *adolescence, childhood, young adults, students, middle school students, high school students, boys, girls.*
- Choose alternate terms for *older adults*, such as *elders, elderly, aged, old age, senior citizens, mentors, older people.*
- Choose clarifying descriptors to go with the term *students*, such as *elementary school students, middle school students, junior high school students, high school students, college and university students, secondary school students.*
- Choose alternate terms for *attitudes*, such as *attitudes toward aging, ageism, perceptions.*

In some cases, terms related to a specific topic may assist the searcher in finding intergenerational information:

- *Recreation* may lead to information on intergenerational gardening programs.
- *Correspondence* may lead to information on pen-pal programs.
- *Perceptions* may lead to information on attitudes between older adults and children and youth.
- *Role models* may lead to information on mentors or mentoring.
- *Social programs* or *social conditions & trends* may lead to information on policy development on intergenerational programs.
- *Community services* may lead to information on intergenerational community service or intergenerational service-learning.

Searching first for the term *intergenerational program?* (? = truncation) in a database will ideally produce several citations, from which the researcher can then develop more in-depth search strategies.

Bibliographic Search Tools

As discussed throughout this book, intergenerational programs are found in myriad disciplines, many of which have their own indexes in database form. A thorough search might therefore require the use of several bibliographic search tools.

The databases are mounted either on large computer servers or on CD-ROM discs, which must be read using smaller desktop machines. These indexes are accessible to researchers and practitioners in public libraries, college and university libraries, the Internet, and through fee-based commercial services. An individual's choice of access point will be determined by a number of factors, including the availability of particular services and his or her willingness to pay any necessary fees.

The following is a list of bibliographic tools that experience suggests will be most useful in finding intergenerational information. The information industry is booming as this book is being written; therefore, this list is not a complete inventory of available databases. It does include those tools that are commonly used to find information on intergenerational programs, as well as brief descriptions.

Social Science Citation Index—indexes 1,400 journals in the social sciences and related disciplines. Beginning in 1992, abstracts are included.
ABI/Inform—a very comprehensive database that covers the literature in every aspect of business, management, and related areas.
ERIC—the Educational Resources Information Center (ERIC) is a national information system designed to provide users with ready access to an extensive body of education-related literature. It contains over 850,000 abstracts of documents and journal articles on education research and practice.
MEDLINE—contains all references found in the *Index Medicus,* plus the citations from the *International Nursing Index* and the *Index to Dental Literature* and the related topics of health care administration, biomedical research, and medicine.
OCLC—the Online Computer Library Center (OCLC) is the world's largest library

database, with catalog holdings from over 21,000 libraries. This service is available in most libraries and can be used through the librarian.

Periodical Abstracts—lists references to articles from a broad spectrum of social sciences, humanities, and general science journals.

PsycInfo—covers the literature in psychology, mental health, biomedicine, and related disciplines.

The following list contains related indexes and abstracts, most of which are in database form:

American Statistical Index
Anthropological Literature
Bibliographic Index
Child Development Abstracts and Bibliography
Criminal Justice Periodical Index
Current Contents
Dissertation Abstracts International
Expanded Academic Index (general and scholarly periodicals from 1988)
GPO Database (U. S. Superintendent of Documents Monthly Catalog)
Index to U.S. Government Periodicals
Sage Urban Studies Abstracts

As noted earlier, the amount of specific intergenerational information available on the Internet is somewhat limited, largely because the intergenerational field is still in its youth. This situation will almost certainly change rapidly over the years to come. To find what is currently available, researchers can use one of the readily available Internet search engines (e.g., Lycos, Magellan, or Alta Vista). When using most of these search engines, the recommended search strategies resemble those used for a CD-ROM or online database.

However, the search engines themselves are currently undergoing rapid development and improvement, and each has its own characteristics and methodologies. As a result, it is difficult to offer specific instruction here regarding their use, and information seekers are best advised to try several different search engines when exploring the Internet. When using any of these, the recommended starting term is *intergenerational program*, although in some cases the single word *intergenerational* will yield better results. A successful search on these terms consists of a large number of hits, but it is not necessary to read each one. Usually the hits listed on the first few pages will provide valuable information and lead the researcher in other useful directions.

As more practitioners, academics, and students are able to utilize the services of the Internet both professionally and personally, more information will become available. Already, some intergenerational organizations have created home pages that include programmatic or basic intergenerational information (or both):

Generations Together at the University of Pittsburgh (http://www.pitt.edu/~gti)
The Illinois Intergenerational Initiative at Southern Illinois University (http://www.siu.edu/offices/iii/)

The Center for Intergenerational Learning at Temple University (http://www.temple.
   edu/departments/CIL/)
The Retirement and Intergenerational Studies Laboratory at Clemson University
   (http://strom.clemson.edu/risl/risl.html)
Generations United of Central Pennsylvania (http://ourworld.compuserve.com/home-
   pages/intergen_info/)
Let's Link Ages in Virginia—The Virginia Intergenerational Network (http://users.aol.
   com/intergen01/index.html)

These home pages can be also found by searching for the name of the sponsoring
agency.
   There is also a great deal of information available through the Internet that,
although it is not specifically intergenerational, may be quite useful to researchers.
Currently, for example, ERIC is available for searching via the Internet, as are almost
all government documents. In addition, there are sites devoted to specific aspects of
intergenerational programming, such as evaluation, aging, or early childhood.

CONCLUSION

   For the practitioner, academic, student, or policy analyst who wants to research
the intergenerational field, the process of finding information is challenging. As the
field grows and more is written about intergenerational experiences, the potential for
an explosion of intergenerational materials is an exciting prospect. There is an especially exciting challenge in the idea that an expanding body of intergenerational
program resources, when gathered together, will ultimately provide definition and
shape for the new intergenerational field.
   Until the existence of an organized central body of information related to the
intergenerational concept becomes a reality, though, the multidisciplinary aspect of
intergenerational information will keep researchers in this field thinking critically and
creatively. The following sections open the intergenerational world to the reader.

Section 2: Organizations

The following organizations are either wholly devoted to intergenerational programming or maintain an office dedicated to intergenerational programs. Newsletters are listed at the end of some organizations.

American Association of Retired Persons
Intergenerational Programs
601 E Street, NW, Room B5-270 PC&DD
Washington, DC 20049

Association for Gerontology in Higher Education
1001 Connecticut Avenue, NW, Ste. 410
Washington, DC 20036

Bi-Folkal Productions, Inc.
809 Williamson Street
Madison, WI 53703
Newsletter: *Insight*

Care Castle
An Intergenerational Day Care Center
1430 N. Hancock
Colorado Springs, CO 80903-2621

Center for Intergenerational Learning
Temple University
1601 N. Broad Street
Philadelphia, PA 19122
Newsletter: *Interchange*

The Community Intergenerational Program
c/o Bi-Folkal Productions, Inc.
809 Williamson Street
Madison, WI 53703

Corporation for National and Community Service
1100 Vermont Avenue, NW
Washington, DC 20525

Elders Share the Arts, Inc.
57 Willoughby Street
Brooklyn, NY 11201

Newsletter: *Cultural Connections*
Fairhill Center for Aging
12200 Fairhill Road
Cleveland, OH 44120
Newsletter: *Intergenerational Connections*

Foster Grandparent Program
1100 Vermont Avenue, NW, Room 6100
Washington, DC 20525

The Full Circle Theater Group
Center for Intergenerational Learning
Temple University
1601 N. Broad St., Room 206
Philadelphia, PA 19122

Generations
A Program of Intergenerational Care
1185 E. Broad Street
Columbus, OH 43215

Generations Together
University of Pittsburgh
121 University Place, Suite 300
Pittsburgh, PA 15260
Newsletter: *Generations Together Exchange*

Generations United
A National Coalition on Intergenerational Issues and Programs
c/o Child Welfare League of America
440 First Street, NW, Suite 310
Washington, DC 20001
Newsletter: *Newsline*

Generations United of Michigan
c/o Waterford Senior Center
6455 Harper
Waterford, MI 48329
Newsletter: *LINKages*

Illinois Intergenerational Initiative
Southern Illinois University
Mail Code 4341
Carbondale, IL 62901
Newsletter: *Continuance*

Interages
9411 Connecticut Avenue
Kensington, MD 20895

Newsletter: *Interages News*
Kansas Intergenerational Network, Inc.
132 South Main
Ottawa, KS 66067
Newsletter: *KINections*

Lifespan Resources, Inc.
Intergenerational Education, Service, Research
1212 Roosevelt
Ann Arbor, MI 48104

Massachusetts Intergenerational Network (MINS)
c/o Elder Services
360 Merrimac Street, Building 5
Lawrence, MA 01843
Newsletter: *MINews*

Mill Street Loft
12 Vassar Street
Poughkeepsie, NY 12601
Newsletter: *Mill Street Loft Newsletter*

National Academy for Teaching and Learning About Aging
(formerly Center for Understanding Aging)
Northeast Office
200 Executive Boulevard, Suite 202
P.O. Box 246
Southington, CT 06489-0246
Newsletter: *Linkages*

National Academy for Teaching and Learning About Aging
Southwest Office
University of North Texas
P.O. Box 13438
Denton, TX 76203

National Association for the Education of Young Children
1509 16th Street, NW
Washington, DC 20036

National Association of Partners in Education
209 Madison Street, Suite 401
Alexandria, VA 22314

National Council on the Aging, Inc.
Intergenerational Programs
409 Third Street, SW

Washington, DC 20024
National Council on the Aging, Inc.
Family Friends Resource Center
409 Third Street, SW
Washington, DC 20024
Newsletter: *Newsline*

National Recreation and Park Association
Leisure and Aging Section
2775 S. Quincy Street, Suite 300
Arlington, VA 22206
Newsletter: *Bridges*

National Service-Learning Cooperative
The K–12 Serv-America Clearinghouse
University of Minnesota
Vocational & Technical Education Building
1054 Buford Avenue, R-290
St. Paul, MN 55108

Neighborhoods 2000
c/o MIG Communications
1802 Fifth Street
Berkeley, CA 94710

New York State Intergenerational Network (NYSIGN)
c/o Brookdale Center on Aging
425 E. 25th Street, Room 806
New York, NY 10010

The Points of Light Foundation
1727 H Street, NW
Washington, DC 20006

Roots & Branches
40 West 68th Street
New York, NY 10023
Newsletter: *Roots & Branches*

RSVP of Dane County, Inc.
517 North Segoe Road, Suite 210
Madison, WI 53715
Newsletter: *Intergenerational Clearinghouse Newsletter*

Self-Esteem Through Service (SETS)
c/o Interages
Montgomery County Intergenerational Resource Center
9411 Connecticut Avenue

Kensington, MD 20895
The Senior Citizen School Volunteer Program (SCSVP)
Generations Together: An Intergenerational Studies Program
University Center for Social and Urban Research
University of Pittsburgh
121 University Place, Suite 300
Pittsburgh, PA 15260

Virginia Intergenerational Network
Northern Virginia Community College
3001 North Beauregard Street
Alexandria, VA 22311
Newsletter: *Let's Link Ages*

Section 3: Intergenerational Program Resources

This listing of intergenerational program resources reflects a systematic effort to gather print and media materials on intergenerational programs of the 1990s. Because many of these materials are self-published, a contact person and address is included at the end of each entry. The abstracts are brief, intended only to provide a sense of what the publication is about. The subject categories used are listed below:

- Arts
- Children and Youth Serving Older Adults
- Coalition Building
- College Students and Older Adults
- General Information on Intergenerational Programs
- Library Programming
- Mentoring
- Older Adults and Young Children Being Cared for Together
- Older Adults Serving Children and Youth
- School-Based Programs
- Young and Old Serving the Community

ARTS

Clark, P. (1991). Intergenerational arts in the nursing home: A handbook. New York: Greenwood, ISBN 0-313-25965-8, 180 pages

> This book encourages interaction between younger and older people through creative use of arts in painting, sculpture, and language arts. It details key elements of the successful programs and has four plays in appendix.

Contact: Greenwood Press, 99 Post Road W., Westport, CT 06881.

Creating a spark. ½" VHS/9 min/1993

> Highlighting four intergenerational arts programs, this videotape shows youth and elders engaging in theater, folk dancing, quilt making, and cross-cultural exchange programs.

Contact: Temple University, Center for Intergenerational Learning, 1601 North Broad Street, Room 206, Philadelphia, PA 19122.

Davis, S., & Ferdman, B. (1993). *Nourishing the heart: A guide to intergenerational arts projects in the schools.* New York: City Lore, 116 pages

> This is an intergenerational activity book, free on request, with an emphasis on folklore, for use with school students and senior center participants in the classroom. Activities range from youngsters interviewing seniors for class projects to bringing classes together with senior centers to produce collaborative works of art.

Contact: City Lore, Inc., 72 East First Street, New York, NY 10003.

Intergenerational music manual. (1993). Upper Arlington, OH: Upper Arlington Senior Center, 41 pages

> Focusing on the arts, this guide explains how to combine elementary school age children and older adults to create a musical production.

Contact: Susan Drenning, Upper Arlington Senior Center, 1945 Ridgeview Road, Upper Arlington, OH 43221.

Mill Street Loft Intergenerational Chorus. ½" VHS/7 min/1992

> This videotape showcases the Mill Street Loft Intergenerational Chorus, which brings together a culturally diverse group of young people and older adults to sing, share stories, and perform throughout the community.

Contact: Carole Wolf, Mill Street Loft, 12 Vassar Street, Poughkeepsie, NY 12601-3021.

Perlstein, S., & Bliss, J. (1994). *Generating community: Intergenerational partnerships through the expressive arts.* New York: Elders Share The Arts, 126 pages

> A resource to help community leaders from senior centers, hospitals, nursing homes, schools, and colleges and universities create and establish intergenerational arts programs. The guide includes approaches to agency partnerships, icebreakers for intergenerational exchange, ways to turn interviews into public presentations, an intergenerational curriculum, issues to watch for, and troubleshooting situations.

Contact: Elders Share The Arts, 57 Willoughby Street, Brooklyn, NY 11201.

Shared visions. ½" VHS/20 min/1993

> This videotape documents a lively exchange between 3 older artists and 10 high school art students. It reveals the insights of their meeting together.

Contact: Terra Nova Films, Inc., 9848 S. Winchester Avenue, Chicago, IL 60643.

Wilder, R. (1996). *Life drama with youth and elders—Come, step into my life.* Charlottesville, VA: New Plays, ISBN 0-932720-11-0, 159 pages

> This book engages participants in life explorations using story-telling, narrative, movement, sound and song, role play, and improvisation. This guide,

with practical workshop suggestions, is for use with older adults and school-age children from the 4th grade up.

Contact: New Plays Incorporated, P.O. Box 5074, Charlottesville, VA 11905.

CHILDREN AND YOUTH SERVING OLDER ADULTS

Adopt a nursing home: Caring is ageless—Adoption handbook. (1993). Austin: Texas Department of Human Services, 47 pages

This handbook is designed to guide adopters and adoptees through the establishment and maintenance of adoption partnerships. It offers suggestions and models for volunteer services and recommendations for orientation, training, and recognition of adopters.

Contact: Sharon S. Rowley, APR, Adopt-A-Nursing Home Program Manager, Texas Department of Human Services, 701 W. 51st Street, P.O. Box 149030, Mail Code W-404, Austin, TX 78714-9030.

Best Friends handbook. (nd). Indianapolis, IN: Indianapolis Public Schools, loose-leaf binder

The Best Friends Program provides students with the opportunity to develop a close relationship with residents of health care facilities during the school year. This manual is a complete guide for teachers and administrators and includes an additional packet with information and a videotape; annotated bibliographic references; school curricula; music; evaluation forms; sample letters; and awards and certificates.

Contact: Indianapolis Public Schools, 120 East Walnut Street, Room 504C, Indianapolis, IN 46204.

Best Friends health care facility handbook. (nd). Indianapolis, IN: Indianapolis Public Schools, 38 pages

This manual is a complete guide for administrators and program directors on how to start a Best Friends program in care facilities. It provides students with the opportunity to develop a close relationship with residents of health care facilities during the school year.

Contact: Indianapolis Public Schools, 120 East Walnut Street, Room 504C, Indianapolis, IN 46204.

Between friends: Creating intergenerational work/study programs for youth at-risk and older adults—A guide for concerned communities. (1990). New York: New York City, Department for the Aging, 64 pages

A step-by-step guide for program replication that includes an overview of the work/study program linking high school students with nursing homes.

Contact: New York City Department for the Aging, Intergenerational Programs, Intergenerational Work-Study Program, 2 Lafayette Street, 15th Floor, New York, NY 10007-1392.

Programs that work: NYC Department for the Aging intergenerational work/ study program. ½" VHS/12 min/1992

A documentary of the work/study program, the video highlights the program's value through interviews with staff, students, and seniors.

Contact: New York City Department for the Aging, Intergenerational Programs, Intergenerational Work-Study Program, 2 Lafayette Street, 15th Floor, New York, NY 10007-1392.

Caring for each other. . . a way of life. ½" VHS/7 min/1990, with question and answer guide. Producer: Lucy Jones, Video Difference, Pittsburgh, PA

This videotape shows planned interactions between frail elderly and high school students, third graders, and preschool children.

Contact: Generations Together, University of Pittsburgh, 121 University Place, Suite 300, Pittsburgh, PA 15260.

Couch, L. (1994). *Young and old serving together meeting community needs through intergenerational partnerships.* Washington, DC: Generations United, 109 pages

A replication manual for combining youth and elders in service programs in a community setting.

Contact: Generations United, c/o CWLA, 440 First Street, NW, Suite 310, Washington, DC 20001-2085.

Couch, L. (1993). *Let us serve them all their days: Younger volunteers serving homebound elderly persons—A handbook of program ideas.* Washington, DC: National Council on the Aging, ISBN 0-910883-66-1, 170 pages

A how-to book for intergenerational programs in which high school students provide services for homebound elders. It includes an extensive listing of program descriptions and case studies of exemplary programs.

Contact: National Council on the Aging, 409 Third Street, SW, Suite 200, Washington, DC 20024.

Feroldi, N. J. (1988). *Building Bridges Project program manual.* Providence, RI: Alliance for Better Nursing Home Care, 33 pages

This program manual is designed to assist administrators of nursing homes in providing quality intergenerational programming. The Building Bridges Program brings together nursing home residents and a class of preschoolers in the nursing home setting.

Contact: Alliance for Better Nursing Home Care, 1213 Elmwood Avenue, Providence, RI 02907.

Gentle Connections. ½" VHS/20 min/1989. Produced by Oakton Community College, Oakton, Illinois

This video shows an intergenerational program in which preschool children are helped to understand the process of aging by interacting with and giving hand massages to older adults in nursing homes and in adult day-care centers.

Contact: Terra Nova Films, Inc., 9848 S. Winchester Avenue, Chicago, IL 60643.

Isabella Geriatric Center's Health Careers Partnership: A program guidebook —Isabella's award-winning program including successful models for intergenerational and mentoring programs. (1995). New York: Isabella Geriatric Center, 98 pages

This workbook for replication describes the relationship between a high school and a nonprofit facility serving seniors. The program pioneered a collaborative school-to-work health career partnership.

Contact: Director of Community Services, Isabella Geriatric Center, 515 Audubon Avenue, New York, NY 10040.

McCrea, J. M. (1992). *Talking with children and teens about Alzheimer's disease: A question and answer guidebook for parents, teachers, and caregivers.* Pittsburgh, PA: University of Pittsburgh, Generations Together, 73 pages

This guidebook provides age-appropriate answers to questions frequently asked by children and teens about Alzheimer's disease and includes recommended intergenerational activities. It also includes an annotated bibliography of books for children and youth that focus on Alzheimer's disease.

Contact: Generations Together, University of Pittsburgh, 121 University Place, Suite 300, Pittsburgh, PA 15260.

Melcher, J. (1990). *Caring is the key: Building a school-based intergenerational service program*, with McCrea, J. (1993). *Training modules.* Pittsburgh, PA: University of Pittsburgh, Generations Together, 127 pages

A manual for adult and student leaders to plan and implement an intergenerational service project. The 10 training modules supplement the training components of the manual.

Contact: Generations Together, University of Pittsburgh, 121 University Place, Suite 300, Pittsburgh, PA 15260.

Mersereau, Y., & Glover, M. (1992). (rev. ed.). *A guide to community: An intergenerational friendship program between young people and nursing home residents.* Madison, WI: Bi-Folkal Productions, 119 pages

This manual, with companion videotapes, is designed for administrators and coordinators in schools to be used as a guide for friendship programs that encourage relationships between school-age children and older adults in nursing homes. It includes information on how to sell the idea, what to do at the first visit, ongoing activities, curriculum plans, and evaluation.

Contact: Bi-Folkal Productions, Inc., 809 Williamson Street, Madison, WI 53703.

Community: An intergenerational friendship program. ½" VHS/20 min/1989

This video introduces the community intergenerational visiting project.

Contact: Bi-Folkal Productions, Inc., 809 Williamson Street, Madison, WI 53703.

Orientation for youth: Aging and nursing homes. ½" VHS/40 min/nd

This video prepares children to visit nursing home residents and can be used as a training tool for teachers or group leaders.

Contact: Bi-Folkal Productions, Inc., 809 Williamson Street, Madison, WI 53703.

Building community: Tips for teachers and activity directors. ½" VHS/30 min/ 1994

Administrators and practitioners who currently direct an intergenerational friendship program based on the community model talk about what they were most afraid of their first year, the importance of staff support, the logistics and strategies of planning, and the techniques they learned to help bring students and elders together.

Contact: Bi-Folkal Productions, Inc., 809 Williamson Street, Madison, WI 53703.

Stout, B., Boyd, S., & Volanty, K. (1993). *Y.E.S. project training guide.* 200 pages; Stout, B., Boyd, S., & Volanty, K. (1993). *Y.E.S. service kit* (job order forms, business cards, certificates); Stout, B., Boyd, S., & Volanty, K. (1992). *Y.E.S. youth service provider guide,* 20 pages

These publications and the following videos guide practitioners through a program for youth who provide assisted-living services to help the elderly live independently. Y.E.S. is Youth Exchanging With Seniors, helping to regenerate rural America.

Contact: Home Economics Curriculum Center, Texas Tech University, Box 41161, Lubbock, TX 79409.

Y.E.S. video series. Three videos per case/1992–1993. Produced by Phillips Productions, Dallas, TX

The woman who remembered and the boy who dreamed. ½" VHS/17:25 min/1993

This videotape shows how the Y.E.S. project was initiated to breathe new life, self-determination, and interdependence into the town by bringing together youth and seniors.

The fires of earth. ½" VHS/11:40 min/1993

This videotape introduces effective communication techniques, identifies aging-related career opportunities, and illustrates the positive outcomes of intergenerational exchanges.

Linking lifetimes/spanning generations. ½" VHS/18:30 min/1993

A Y.E.S. project youth team in an ongoing service/friendship relationship with their senior client reviews Y.E.S. project training principles, learns employability skills, shares life stories, experiences aging-related concerns, and discovers that intergenerational understanding and bonding can promote dignity and respect.

Contact: Home Economics Curriculum Center, Texas Tech University, Box 41161, Lubbock, TX 79409.

Tunick, S. (1994). *A helping hand: Outreach to community elders*. Atlanta, GA: Boys & Girls Clubs of America, 30 pages

This program development manual is designed to assist leaders in the Boys & Girls Clubs of America in establishing outreach services to the elderly. It includes lists of resources, sensitivity to aging activities, training materials, a statement of understanding, evaluation materials, and publicity materials.

Contact: Boys & Girls Clubs of America, Program Services, 1230 West Peachtree Street, Atlanta, GA 30309.

COALITION BUILDING

Angelis, J. (1992). *Creating intergenerational coalitions: Bottom up . . . top down strategies*. Carbondale, IL: Southern Illinois University, Illinois Intergenerational Initiative, 30 pages

This manual is designed to help in creating intergenerational coalitions by engaging in a simultaneous bottom-up/top-down organizational model. The bottom-up strategy focuses on local coalition development by educators, service providers, and older adults, and the top-down strategy develops endorsement and support from high-level administrators.

Contact: Jane Angelis, Illinois Intergenerational Initiative, Southern Illinois University, Mail Code 4341, Carbondale, IL 62901.

Angelis, J. (1990). *Intergenerational service-learning: Strategies for the future*. Carbondale, IL: Southern Illinois University, Illinois Intergenerational Initiative, 59 pages

This report summarizes the seven Circle of Helping meetings facilitated by the Illinois Intergenerational Initiative and suggests a future based on a tradition of younger and older generations serving and learning together.

Contact: Jane Angelis, Illinois Intergenerational Initiative, Southern Illinois University, Mail Code 4341, Carbondale, IL 62901.

Angelis, J. (1995). *Putting our heads together*. Carbondale, IL: Southern Illinois University, Illinois Intergenerational Initiative, 42 pages

This report is a composite of recommendations and essays generated by the participants of meetings held by Generations Connect in 1995 in preparation for the 1995 White House Conference on Aging. The essays cover topics such as building community coalitions, communication between young and old, and working to improve community.

Contact: Jane Angelis, Illinois Intergenerational Initiative, Southern Illinois University, Mail Code 4341, Carbondale, IL 62901.

Scannell, T., & Roberts, A. (1995). *State and local intergenerational coalitions and networks: A compendium of profiles.* Washington, DC: Generations United, 88 pages

> This guide describes 20 state and local intergenerational coalitions and networks and includes summaries of activities, services, and resources. It lists Generations United organizational members.

Contact: Generations United, c/o CWLA, 440 First Street, NW, Suite 310, Washington, DC 20001.

Ventura-Merkel, C. (1990). *Strategies for change: Building state and local coalitions on intergenerational issues and programs.* Washington, DC: Generations United, 42 pages

> The model described in this guide is useful for organizations interested in developing state or local coalitions to promote intergenerational understanding, awareness, and cooperation. The model may be used by any state or local agency that works with or serves children, youth, older persons, and their families.

Contact: Generations United, c/o CWLA, 440 First Street, NW, Suite 310, Washington, DC 20001.

COLLEGE STUDENTS AND OLDER ADULTS

Manuals and Media

Delaney, B., & Marinko, C. *Time-out program development manual.* (1990). Philadelphia, PA: Temple University, Center for Intergenerational Learning, 135 pages

> Recruiting and training manual for college students providing in-home respite for caregivers of impaired older adults. It includes trainer's guide and respite worker handbook.

Contact: Temple University, Center for Intergenerational Learning, 1601 N. Broad Street, Room 206, Philadelphia, PA 19122.

Hegeman, C., & Linsider, R. (1992). *Coordinated student involvement in elder care.* Albany, NY: Foundation for Long-Term Care, 100 pages

> Details the concept of service learning for both elder-care agencies and colleges, describing it as a project in which students perform service to elderly while simultaneously taking a credit-bearing course on elder issues.

Contact: Foundation for Long-Term Care, 150 State Street, Suite 301, Albany, NY 12210.

Weinstein-Shr, G., & Henkin, N. (1988). *Project LEIF (Learning English Through Intergenerational Friendship) program development manual.* Philadelphia, PA: Temple University, Center for Intergenerational Learning, 75 pages

A how-to guide that describes the planning and implementing of a successful intergenerational literacy program using college students to teach English as a second language to elderly immigrants and refugees.

Contact: Temple University, Center for Intergenerational Learning, 1601 N. Broad Street, Room 206, Philadelphia, PA 19122.

Westacott, B., & Hegeman, C. (1996). *Service learning in elder care.* Albany, NY: Foundation for Long-Term Care, 173 pages

This implementation manual outlines steps for establishing service learning programs linking college students with nursing homes and elder care facilities. Students from eight colleges participated in a credit-bearing seminar in which they kept logs detailing their volunteer experiences, participated in reflection activities, and completed related course work.

Contact: The Foundation for Long-Term Care, 150 State Street, Suite 301, Albany, NY 12207.

Curriculum

The social context and organizational framework for successful intergenerational programming: A course study for educators and human services personnel. (1990). Toronto, Ontario, Canada: Ryerson Polytechnic Institute, 69 pages

This curricular package for faculty and students is designed to explore issues of aging, ageism, and intergenerational programming from a curricular, activation, and community development perspective that can be readily implemented at the college and university level.

Contact: Ryerson Polytechnic Institute, 360 Victoria Street, Toronto, Ontario, Canada M5B 2K3.

GENERAL INFORMATION ON INTERGENERATIONAL PROGRAMS

Books

Berkowitz, L., & Benderly, B. (1989). *Building bridges to citizenship: How to create successful intergenerational citizenship programs.* Washington, DC: Close Up Foundation, 87 pages

This book outlines intergenerational programs that stimulate citizen action, including the benefits and characteristics of successful programs and program suggestions.

Contact: Close Up Foundation, Program for Older Americans, 44 Canal Cnt. Plaza, Alexandria, VA 22314.

Cram, M., & VanDerveer, B. (Eds.). (1996). *Proceedings from the 1995 NRPA regional and national intergenerational institutes.* Arlington, VA: National Recreation and Park Association, ISBN 0-9603540-4-2, 153 pages

This book is divided into three sections: texts from institute presentations; intergenerational model descriptions; and discussions providing information on intergenerational philosophy and funding. It is of value to practitioners, educators, and researchers in parks and recreation.

Contact: National Recreation and Park Association, Leisure and Aging Section, 2775 S. Quincy Street, Suite 300, Arlington, VA 22206.

Intergenerational projects: Idea book. (1993). Washington, DC: American Association of Retired Persons, 66 pages, Stock #D15087

A listing of 74 programs and resources for people involved with intergenerational organizations. It gives a contact person (with their address and phone number) for each entry, along with a description of the program.

Contact: American Association of Retired Persons, 601 E Street, NW, Washington, DC 20049.

Newman, S., & Brummel, S. (Eds.). (1989). *Intergenerational programs: Imperatives, strategies, impacts, trends.* Binghamton, NY: Haworth, ISBN 0-86656-773-9, 258 pages

A collection of papers written by various experts in the intergenerational field. It discusses intergenerational cooperation, the history of interaction between young and old in Western culture, cross-cultural issues, the status of research, intergenerational programming, and links with public policy.

Contact: Haworth Press, 10 Alice Street, Binghamton, NY 13904-1580.

Bibliography

Connecting the generations: A guide to intergenerational resources—An overview of intergenerational programming and selected listing of books, manuals, and media resources. (1994). [Janet O. Wilson, Compiler]. Washington, DC: American Association of Retired Persons, 19 pages, Stock #D15596

This brief bibliography done in cooperation with Generations Together, University of Pittsburgh; Generations United; National Council on the Aging, Inc.; Center for Intergenerational Learning, Temple University; and the American Association of Retired Persons provides a short overview of what intergenerational programs are and an annotated listing of available print and media resources.

Contact: American Association of Retired Persons, 601 E Street, NW, Washington, DC 20049.

Wilson, J. (Compiler). (1994). *Intergenerational readings/resources 1980–1994: A bibliography of books, book chapters, journal articles, manuals, papers/reports/ studies, curricula, bibliographies, directories, newsletters, databases, and videos* (3rd ed.). Pittsburgh, PA: University of Pittsburgh, Generations Together, 71 pages

A bibliographic listing of 658 items specific to the field of intergenerational program development and implementation, policy, research and evaluation, and studies.

Contact: Generations Together, University of Pittsburgh, 121 University Place, Suite 300, Pittsburgh, PA 15260.

Manuals

McNeill, A. (1995). *How to succeed in fundraising while really trying: A funding guide for intergenerational programs.* Washington, DC: National Council on the Aging, 78 pages

This handbook serves a guide through the maze of fundraising for non-profit organizations planning and implementing intergenerational programs. It identifies steps to take to get a program funded and describes specific funding sources.

Contact: National Council on the Aging, 409 Third Street, SW, Washington, DC, 20024.

LIBRARY PROGRAMMING

Rubin, R. (1993). *Intergenerational programming: A how to do it manual for librarians.* New York: Neal-Schuman, ISBN 1-55570-157-4, 198 pages

Intended as a practical guide, the manual describes and discusses the what and why of intergenerational programming, presents planning and evaluation suggestions, details successful library-based programs, and gives ideas of how to start "intergenerating" quickly and easily.

Contact: Neal-Schuman Publications, 100 Varick Street, New York, NY 10013.

Wood, J. (1992). *Life spectrum programming bringing generations together: A library guide to supporting community-wide intergenerational programming.* Pekin, IL: Pekin Public Library, 12 pages

A replication guide that provides guidelines for libraries that want to examine their collection to find items that may pertain to intergenerational programming.

Contact: Joan Wood, Pekin Public Library, 301 S. 4th Street, Pekin, IL 61554.

MENTORING

Manuals and Media

Elders as mentors: A training program for older adults (with facilitator's guide). ½" VHS/10 min/1993

Typical mentor scenarios are presented through short dramatic skits that can be used separately in mentor training. The guide presents process questions and activities related to the issues presented in each skit.

Contact: Temple University, Center for Intergenerational Learning, 1601 N. Broad Street, Room 206, Philadelphia, PA 19122.

Freedman, M. (1993). *The kindness of strangers: Adult mentors, urban youth, and the new voluntarism.* San Francisco, CA: Jossey-Bass, ISBN 1-555425-57-7, 182 pages

Based on 300 interviews with mentors, the manual reveals how caring adults in cities across America are trying to turn young lives around. It also tells of the much-celebrated mentoring movement they have created. This book takes a hard look at mentoring and asks some critical questions.

Contact: Jossey-Bass, 350 Sansome Street, San Francisco, CA 94104.

Henkin, N., Perez-Randall, C., & Rogers, A. (1993). *Elder mentor handbook.* Philadelphia, PA: Temple University, Center for Intergenerational Understanding, 30 pages

This basic handbook contains information about roles as elder mentors, the needs of at-risk youth today, and tips on effective mentoring. It can be used as a resource at different points in relationships with youth.

Contact: Temple University, Center for Intergenerational Learning, 1601 N. Broad Street, Room 206, Philadelphia, PA 19122.

Henkin, N. Z., Perez-Randall, C., & Rogers, A. M. (1993). *Elders as mentors: A training program for older adults.* Philadelphia, PA: Temple University, Center for Intergenerational Learning, 20 pages

This guide, with companion videotape, contains information about the roles of elder mentors, the needs of at-risk youth today, and tips on effective mentoring. It can be used as a training manual by professionals as well as a resource for older adults interested in becoming a mentor.

Contact: Temple University, Center for Intergenerational Learning, 1601 N. Broad Street, Room 206, Philadelphia, PA 19122.

Linking Lifetimes: A national intergenerational mentoring initiative. ½" VHS/ 12:20 min/1993

Mentor/youth pairs from several Linking Lifetimes sites share their mentoring experiences in a video narrated by film star Ossie Davis.

Contact: Temple University, Center for Intergenerational Learning, 1601 N. Broad Street, Room 206, Philadelphia, PA 19122.

Henkin, N., Perez-Randall, C., & Rogers, A. (1993). *Linking Lifetimes program development manual.* Philadelphia, PA: Temple University, Center for Intergenerational Learning, 237 pages

This manual, developed from the Linking Lifetimes national initiative, provides guidance for developing in-depth mentor–youth relationships and includes extensive evaluation forms and evaluation materials.

Contact: Temple University Center for Intergenerational Learning, 1601 N. Broad Street, Room 206, Philadelphia, PA 19122.

A mentoring manual on intergenerational substance use prevention models. (1993). Alexandria, VA: Let's Link Ages in Virginia, 82 pages

This intergenerational manual provides a framework for elementary school teachers, counselors, principals, and others in the aging network and educational fields, which will assist them in replicating drug prevention models. It includes bibliographic references, audiovisual resources, a release form, survey forms, questionnaires, assessments, evaluations, and a certificate of appreciation.

Contact: Sheila Craig, Let's Link Ages in Virginia, Northern Virginia Community College, Counseling Services, 3001 North Beauregard Street, Alexandria, VA 22311-5097.

Mines, H. (1993). *Intergenerational bridges: A manual for intergenerational mentoring*. Kensington, MD: Interages, 33 pages

This manual focuses on a mentoring program established by Interages that utilizes older adults as mentors for newly arrived immigrant youth. It includes a mentoring evaluation questionnaire, job descriptions, forms, guidelines, agreements, and letters.

Contact: Interages, 9411 Connecticut Avenue, Kensington, MD 20895.

Tice, C. (1993). *A guide to mentoring.* Ann Arbor, MI: Lifespan Resources, 19 pages

This brief manual is an outline that can be used as a guide for mentoring programs that utilize elder mentors to help children and teenagers at risk of dropping out of school. It discusses children's right to privacy and potential liability issues.

Contact: Lifespan Resources, 1212 Roosevelt, Ann Arbor, MI 48104.

Reports and Studies

Freedman, M. (1988). *Partners in growth: Elder mentors and at-risk youth.* Philadelphia, PA: Public/Private Ventures, 82 pages

The intent of this study is a fuller understanding of what really happens when elders and at-risk youth are brought together. It sought to answer several questions, such as, will intergenerational relationships form? what do the relationships look like? do they result in benefits for the youth? are there benefits for the elders? why do intergenerational bonds form? and can program factors stimulate intergenerational bonding?

Contact: Public/Private Ventures, One Commerce Square, 2005 Market Street, Suite 900, Philadelphia, PA 19103.

Freedman, M. (1994). *Seniors in national and community service: A report prepared for the Commonwealth Fund's Americans Over 55 at Work Program.* Philadelphia, PA: Public/Private Ventures, 88 pages

> The study explores the current and potential contributions of older adults to mentoring and providing services to youth and their communities.

Contact: Public/Private Ventures, One Commerce Square, 2005 Market Street, Suite 900, Philadelphia, PA 19103.

OLDER ADULTS AND YOUNG CHILDREN
BEING CARED FOR TOGETHER

Manuals and Media

Cottage Hill: An intergenerational community of caring. (1994). Baldwinville, MA: Protestant Youth Center, 20 pages

> This manual reports on a colocated facility that houses physically handicapped and emotionally disturbed children in grades K–12 and a nursing home for frail elders. It includes architectural plans.

Contact: Protestant Youth Center, Hospital Road, P.O. Box 23, Baldwinville, MA 01436-0023.

Griff, M., Lambert, D., Fruit, D., & Dellman-Jenkins, M. (1996). *LinkAges: Planning an intergenerational program for preschool.* Menlo Park, CA: Addison-Wesley, ISBN 0-20149427-2, 98 pages

> This manual is designed to help preschool teachers and/or eldercare staff set up an intergenerational program that would combine preschoolers and elders in either a child-care center or a senior center. Included are lesson plans and curriculum activities section; benefits tables for children and elders; and benefits and concerns for caregivers in intergenerational programs.

Contact: Addison-Wesley, 1 Jacob Way, Reading, MA 01867.

Hegeman, C. R. (1985). *Child care in long-term care settings.* Albany, NY: Foundation for Long-Term Care, 103 pages

> This manual is written for professionals interested in the management and development of programs that combine the care of healthy young children with care of frail older adults. It is the outcome of a national study of 51 preschool child-care programs in long-term care settings, including nursing homes, independent housing facilities, and adult day-care settings.

Contact: Carol Hegeman, Research Associate, Foundation for Long-Term Care, 150 State Street, Suite 301, Albany, NY 12210.

Vujovich, J. E. (1987). *Child care in nursing homes: Creating an intergenerational program*. Steamboat Springs, CO: Author, 84 pages

This book gives clearly written instructions on how to start a child-care center and an intergenerational activities program in a nursing home or similar health-care facilities.

Contact: Jane E. Vojovich, P.O. Box 882503, Steamboat Springs, CO 80488.

Curricula

Interactions between children and the elderly: Intergenerational curriculum and training modules. (1994). Lubbock, TX: Texas Tech University, loose-leaf binder

A curriculum to train individuals who desire to work in an intergenerational care setting that provides care to children and older adults. Includes a train-the-trainer guide with the curriculum.

Contact: Home Economics Curriculum Center, Box 41161, Texas Tech University, Lubbock, TX 79409-1161.

Intergenerational professions instructional guide. (1994). Lubbock, TX: Texas Tech University, Home Economics Curriculum Center, 399 pages

This is a curriculum guide for a 2-year secondary course of study entitled Intergenerational Professions I and II. It is to be used with persons seeking employment in occupations that provide care and services for children, elders, and dependent adults.

Contact: Home Economics Curriculum Center, Box 41161, Texas Tech University, Lubbock, TX 79409-1161.

OLDER ADULTS SERVING CHILDREN AND YOUTH

Manuals and Media

Because you have so much to share: A guide to using older volunteers. (1990). Philadelphia, PA: Big Brothers/Big Sisters of America, 54 pages

This manual can be used as a planning and implementation tool by Big Brothers/Big Sisters agencies that wish to expand existing efforts or to begin inter-generational programming. It is a compilation of important topics to consider, necessary steps to take, and methods for targeting a valuable resource—the older adult.

Contact: Big Brothers/Big Sisters of America, 230 North 13th Street, Philadelphia, PA 19107.

Bring Family Friends to your community: A replication manual. (1994). Washington, DC: National Council on the Aging, 87 pages

A guide to developing a Family Friends project that offers suggestions and discusses problems and their solutions. Family Friends is an intergenerational elder volunteer program that matches mature men and women with children and families at risk.

Contact: Family Friends Resource Center, National Council on the Aging, 409 Third Street, SW, Suite 200, Washington, DC 20024.

Family Friends: Intergenerational support for families who have children with disabilities and chronic illnesses. ½" VHS/9 min/1996

This video profiles Family Friends, a unique family support program that can be adapted for vulnerable families of any kind. The volunteers and families themselves describe their experiences and what the program has meant to them.

Contact: Temple University, Center for Intergenerational Learning, 1601 N. Broad Street, Room 206, Philadelphia, PA 19122.

Friendly Listener Intergenerational Program (FLIP) procedure manual. (1985). Madison, WI: Dane County, Retired Senior Volunteer Program, 20 pages

The Friendly Listener Intergenerational Program (FLIP) is a telephone reassurance check-in program that matches older persons with 3rd through 5th graders who are home alone after school. This manual provides all the necessary administrative materials for a school system to conduct a FLIP program.

Contact: RSVP of Dane County, 517 N. Segoe Road, Madison, WI 53705.

Grandma, Please. (1991). A replication packet, volunteer training manual, screening tool, video (*Grandma Please!* ½" VHS/15 min/nd), and technical assistance

An instructional packet of how-to information and program descriptive videotape that will assist organizations and communities in creating and developing an intergenerational telephone help-line. This program is designed to link elementary school latchkey children with older adult volunteers during after school hours.

Contact: Monica Glaser, Grandma Please, Uptown Center Hull House, 4520 N. Beacon Street, Chicago, IL 60640.

Helfgott, K. (1992). *Older adults caring for children: Intergenerational child care.* Washington, DC: Generations United, 119 pages

An intergenerational child-care program guide that includes 35 summary descriptions of intergenerational child-care programs, with their names, addresses, and telephone numbers. The guide offers recommendations for planning, developing, and implementing successful intergenerational child-care programs.

Contact: Generations United, c/o CWLA, 440 First Street, NW, Suite 310, Washington, DC 20001.

McDuffie, W., & Whiteman, J. (Eds.). (1989). *Intergenerational activities program handbook* (3rd ed.). Binghamton, NY: Broome County Child Development Council, 132 pages

> This handbook contains essays by 30 early childhood professionals familiar with integrating older adults as volunteers into child-care centers. It includes staff training and activity plans for linking preschoolers with older adult volunteers.

Contact: Broome County Child Development Council, 29 Fayette Street, P.O. Box 880, Binghamton, NY 13902-0880.

Intergenerational Activities Program Training Video. ½" VHS/30 min/1989

> This video demonstrates how to develop an intergenerational child-care program, how to train a child-care center's staff, and how to train older adult volunteers in the program.

Contact: Broome County Child Development Council, 29 Fayette Street, P.O. Box 880, Binghamton, NY 13902-0880.

Newman, S., VanderVen, K., & Ward, C. R. (1991). *Guidelines for the productive employment of older adults in child care.* Pittsburgh, PA: University of Pittsburgh, Generations Together, 29 pages

> The purpose of the guidelines is to help child-care programs effectively integrate older adults into child care while respecting their interests in productive work, appropriate preparation, suitable working conditions, and proper compensation. It may be used for volunteer programs also.

Contact: Generations Together, University of Pittsburgh, 121 University Place, Suite 300, Pittsburgh, PA 15260.

Newman, S., VanderVen, K., & Ward, C. R. (1992). *Practitioner's manual for the productive employment of older adults in child care.* Pittsburgh, PA: University of Pittsburgh, Generations Together, 96 pages

> This book covers all aspects of older adults as child-care workers, from recruitment to supervision, and shows how older adults can enhance the quality of programming for children, staff, and parents alike. It is a detailed, idea rich resource for early childhood and older adult administrators, teachers, program developers, and staff.

Contact: Generations Together, University of Pittsburgh, 121 University Place, Suite 300, Pittsburgh, PA 15260.

Roberts, A. (1996). *The Retired and Senior Volunteer Program, a catalyst for intergenerational partnerships: A report describing how thirteen RSVP projects developed intergenerational partnerships in their communities.* Washington, DC: Generations United, 118 pages

> This report describes 13 RSVP projects that implemented high-quality intergenerational programs that developed long-standing community partnerships.

It includes useful and practical strategies for partnership building and discusses the project's successes and lessons learned.

Contact: Generations United, c/o CWLA, 440 First Street, NW, Suite 310, Washington, DC 20001.

Rural Family Friends replication manual: A project of the National Council on the Aging and Save the Children Federation. (1992). Washington, DC: National Council on Aging, 128 pages

A replication manual designed to help a community organization establish, maintain, and expand a local community-based program that deals with rural communities and families with an emphasis on child abuse and neglect prevention.

Contact: Family Friends Resource Center, National Council on the Aging, 409 Third Street, SW, Suite 200, Washington, DC 20024.

Curriculum and Media

LaVilla, S., & Otis, D. (1992). *Child care training for senior adults.* Miami, FL: Little Havana Activities and Nutrition Centers of Dade County, 63 pages

This manual provides guidelines for conducting in-service and ongoing training program for senior participants serving as senior child-care aides in an intergenerational child-care program.

Contact: Little Havana Activities & Nutrition Centers of Dade County, 700 SW 8th Street, Miami, FL.

Mack, C., & Wilson, J. (Eds.). (1988). *Share it with the children: A preschool curriculum on aging.* Pittsburgh, PA: University of Pittsburgh, Generations Together, 152 pages

This manual contains six curriculum units and a "how to develop intergenerational linkages" section. The curriculum has 45 field-tested, developmentally appropriate preschool activities for children and older volunteers to share.

Contact: Generations Together, University of Pittsburgh, 121 University Place, Suite 300, Pittsburgh, PA 15260.

Share it with the children. ½" VHS/17 min/1989. Producer: Lucy Jones, Video Difference, Pittsburgh, PA

This companion videotape to the above manual illustrates the implementation of the curriculum activities in three child-care settings and demonstrates successful interactions between young children and frail elderly, grandparents, and older volunteers.

Contact: Generations Together, University of Pittsburgh, 121 University Place, Suite 300, Pittsburgh, PA 15260.

Mack, C., & Smith, T. *Separation and loss: A handbook for early childhood professionals.* (1991). Pittsburgh, PA: University of Pittsburgh, Generations Together, 179 pages

> The handbook and accompanying videotape offer specific suggestions for supporting children during a loss crisis. Throughout the handbook, older adults are recognized as an important natural resource to children, parents, and teachers, and their unique contributions are described and encouraged.

Contact: Generations Together, University of Pittsburgh, 121 University Place, Suite 300, Pittsburgh, PA 15260.

Learning to say goodbye. ½" VHS/17 min/1991. Producer: Lucy Jones, Video Difference, Pittsburgh, PA

> This video helps workshop participants visualize the concepts and activities contained in the handbook *Separation and loss: A handbook for early childhood professionals.*

Contact: Generations Together, University of Pittsburgh, 121 University Place, Suite 300, Pittsburgh, PA 15260.

Seefeldt, C., & Warman, B. (1990). *Young and old together.* Washington, DC: National Association for the Education of Young Children, ISBN 0-93598934-x, 88 pages

> This book offers teachers a rationale and concrete suggestions for bringing the generations together in the classroom. Comprehensive, constructive, and optimistic, this manual will help ease the growing gap between these natural allies—young children and their elders.

Contact: National Association for the Education of Young Children, 1509 16th Street, NW, Washington, DC 20036.

Smith, T., Mack, C., & Tittnich, E. (1993). *Generations Together: A job training curriculum for older workers in child care.* Syracuse, NY: Syracuse University Press, ISBN 0-8156-2590-1, 195 pages and a packet of handouts

> The first of its kind, this curriculum handbook is designed to capitalize on potential child-care workers who are over 55 years old. An innovative and valuable resource for educators, trainers, job developers, government agencies, and other professionals training or serving older citizens.

Contact: Generations Together, University of Pittsburgh, 121 University Place, Suite 300, Pittsburgh, PA 15260.

SCHOOL-BASED PROGRAMS

Manuals and Media

Bagby, B., & Snyder, J. (nd). *Youth and seniors: The dynamic duo.* Urbana, IL: University of Illinois at Urbana-Champaign, 67 pages

This manual describes how youth can learn from or help older adults. The older adults serve as teachers or receivers of services.

Contact: College of Agriculture, University of Illinois at Urbana-Champaign, Cooperative Extension Service, 535 Bevier Hall, 905 South Goodwin Avenue, Urbana, IL 61801.

Barret, D., Myers, R., Kramer, C., Newman, S., & Mullins, I. (1983). *Intergenerational volunteer program in special education: A manual for implementation*. Pittsburgh, PA: University of Pittsburgh, Generations Together, 95 pages

This training manual has been developed as a tool to assist special education administrators, teachers, and other interested people in the development of an intergenerational school volunteer program. It includes general information pertaining to the background, benefits, and outcomes of an intergenerational program as well as specific procedures for implementation.

Contact: Generations Together, University of Pittsburgh, 121 University Place, Suite 300, Pittsburgh, PA 15260.

Bear Care: Middle school initiatives in youth service-learning. (1991). Upper Arlington, OH: Upper Arlington Schools, 113 pages

This handbook is designed to assist others in planning and developing service-learning projects at the middle-school level. Definitions and rationale for service-learning are provided along with a theoretical framework based on moral, intellectual, and personality development.

Contact: Ellen Erlanger, Career Education Coordinator, Upper Arlington City Schools, 1950 North Mallway, Upper Arlington, OH or Kathy Fickell, Director, UA, Community Involvement Program, Burbank School, 4770 Burbank Drive, Upper Arlington, OH 43220.

Becoming a school partner: A guidebook for organizing intergenerational partnerships in schools. (1992). Washington, DC: American Association of Retired Persons, 36 pages, Stock #D13527

This free guidebook offers guidance for those interested in planning an intergenerational school partnership program using a 12-step process developed by the National Association of Partners in Education.

Contact: American Association of Retired Persons, 601 E Street, NW, Washington, DC 20049.

Becoming a School Partner. ½" VHS/13:30 min/1992, Stock #D14864

This videotape program is intended to illustrate the benefits of involving older volunteers in schools and how such involvement can benefit the schools, the teachers, the students, and the volunteers.

Contact: American Association of Retired Persons, A/V Programs, Program Resources Department (B4), P.O. Box 1040, Station R, Washington, DC 20013-1040.

The best of you . . . the best of me. ½" VHS/27 min/1986, with manual. Producer: Lucy Jones, Video Difference, Pittsburgh, PA

A sampler of six intergenerational programs in Pennsylvania, this motivational videotape provides information on program development procedures and highlights the impact of these programs. The programs include school-based programming, community-based programming, and older workers in child care.

Contact: Generations Together, University of Pittsburgh, 121 University Place, Suite 300, Pittsburgh, PA 15260.

Charnow, S., Nash, E., & Perlstein, S. (1988). *Life review training manual.* Brooklyn, NY: Elders Share The Arts, 68 pages

This project manual is based on Erik Erikson's developmental theory of human behavior and the final task or life crisis engaged in by older adults. By creating projects that utilize reminiscence therapy with older adults in the school environment, which include theater and story-telling, older adults are able to bring a rich and rewarding experience to both the children and themselves.

Contact: Elders Share The Arts, 57 Willoughby Street, Brooklyn, NY 11201.

A circle of helping: How intergenerational programs help achieve the six national education goals. (1992). Carbondale, IL: Southern Illinois University, Illinois Intergenerational Initiative, 48 pages

Outlined in this publication are the six national education goals along with a collection of essays dealing with intergenerational subjects. Each essay includes background information on the authors and the projects they are affiliated with.

Contact: Jane Angelis, Illinois Intergenerational Initiative, Mail Code 4341, Southern Illinois University, Carbondale, IL 62901.

Closing the gap: An intergenerational discussion model guide for replication. (1989). Kensington, MD: Interages, 52 pages

This replication guide is intended for use by teachers and program coordinators who want to replicate "Closing the Gap." The guide contains activities, forms, and guidelines necessary to begin and sustain a model intergenerational discussion program.

Contact: Interages, 9411 Connecticut Avenue, Kensington, MD 20895.

Computer ease: Intergenerational computer literacy. (1990). Upper Arlington, OH: The Upper Arlington Senior Center, 60 pages

This manual's focus is on computer literacy. It describes the use of elementary school resources, such as available computer hardware and software, staff, and students to enhance the natural curiosity and eagerness to learn of seniors age 60 and over.

Contact: Upper Arlington Senior Center, City of Upper Arlington, Parks and Recreation Department, 1945 Ridgeview Road, Upper Arlington, OH 43221.

Education projects idea book: A guide for volunteers. (1992). Washington, DC: American Association of Retired Persons, 39 pages

> This manual is a practical guide for older adult volunteers working with children. There are a number of suggested activities and resources geared toward aiding the volunteers in providing better service.

Contact: American Association of Retired Persons, 601 E Street, NW, Washington, DC 20049.

Friedman, S. (Ed.). (1990). *Closing the gap: An intergenerational discussion model guide for replication.* Kensington, MD: Interages, 69 pages

> This guide describes a project for replication that links older adults with high school students in a classroom setting.

Contact: Interages, 9411 Connecticut Avenue, Kensington, MD 20895.

A guide for older volunteers: Becoming a school partner. (1989). 35 pages, Stock #D14863

> This free guide describes the opportunities open to older volunteers in local elementary and secondary schools, discusses the rewards of school volunteer activities, and presents some of the challenges facing students and schools.

Contact: American Association of Retired Persons, 601 E Street, NW, Washington, DC 20049.

Illinois READS (Retirees Educating and Assisting in the Development of Students): Program guide. (1993). Springfield, IL: Illinois Department on Aging, 46 pages

> This manual overviews Illinois READS, a statewide program that utilizes retired individuals as volunteers through reading and other activities targeted at the elementary school age population. The guide includes information on program planning, recruitment, implementation, and evaluation. There is a companion videotape.

Contact: Illinois Department on Aging, 421 East Capitol Avenue, #100, Springfield, IL 62701-1789.

Kramer, C., & Newman, S. (1986). *Senior Citizen School Volunteer Program: A manual for program implementation.* Albany, NY: Center for the Study of Aging, 101 pages

> This guide will enable schools to implement an older volunteer program by adapting the procedures detailed in this manual to individual school needs and interests. It provides how-to information on Generations Together's Senior Citizen School Volunteer Program and pre- and postprogram evaluation questionnaires for teachers and volunteers.

Contact: Generations Together, University of Pittsburgh, 121 University Place, Suite 300, Pittsburgh, PA 15260.

Laterza, T. (1995). *Intergenerational service learning: A guide for faculty.* Pittsburgh, PA: University of Pittsburgh, Generations Together, 18 pages

This manual reviews the components for development of an intergenerational service-learning program. It is composed of materials adapted from the service-learning field to assist program coordinators, teachers, and college and university faculty in developing an intergenerational service-learning program.

Contact: Generations Together, University of Pittsburgh, 121 University Place, Suite 300, Pittsburgh, PA 15260.

McDonald, N. (1990). *How to organize and manage intergenerational partnership programs: A self-guide workplan of 12 steps to a successful intergenerational partnership program.* Alexandria, VA: National Association of Partners in Education, 269 pages

A guidebook for planners who want to create intergenerational school volunteer and partnership programs that respond to local school and community priorities.

Contact: National Association of Partners in Education, 209 Madison Street, Suite 401, Alexandria, VA 22314.

One to One. ½" VHS/24 min/1987

Through a series of dialogues, the interactions between teens and older people explore many issues, including self-esteem, death, parenting, the aging process, and the role of both older people and teens in society.

Contact: Terra Nova Films, Inc., 9848 S. Winchester Avenue, Chicago, IL 60643.

SPICE Intergenerational programs. (1992). Seattle, WA: Seattle Public Schools, School Programs Involving Community Elders (SPICE), 35 pages; *Everybody's Coming To School,* ½" VHS/14 min/1992

A brief program manual and videotape describe a cooperative project between schools, elders, the city of Seattle, and the federal government. By combining nutrition and social services in an intergenerational setting, students who have special needs and older adults are served in a school setting. The videotape depicts the projects activities, and the participants tell the viewer of their experiences.

Contact: Kenneth Camper, Director, SPICE, 3311 N.E. 60th Street, Seattle, WA 98115-7318.

Woodward, K. (1994). *Intergenerational service-learning: A handbook for intergenerational service-learning programs.* Ottawa, KS: Kansas Intergenerational Network, 67 pages

This guide discusses how to design, implement, and evaluate school-based programs that combine intergenerational community service and academic learning.

Contact: Kansas Intergenerational Network, 132 South Main, Ottawa, KS 66067.

Zuccolotto, D., & Scott, T. (1993). *Guided memories: An intergenerational program for youth and seniors*, 60 pages; *Guided memories: Your personal autobiography on video or audio cassette*, instructor's workbook, 96 pages; Scotts Valley, CA: R & Z Publishing, ISBN 0-9634378-0-1

The first book help adults organize their autobiographical material and prepare it for recording on video or audio cassette, and the instructor's workbook guides young people as they help adults record their autobiographies.

Contact: R & Z Publishing Co., 245-M. Mt. Hermon Road., #280, Scotts Valley, CA 95066.

Bibliographies

Newman, S., & Wilson, J. (1992). *Teaching about aging to children and youth.* Washington, DC: Association for Gerontology in Higher Education, 11 pages

Prepared by Generations Together of the University of Pittsburgh, this annotated bibliography lists available curricula, books, journal articles, and ERIC documents for teachers and community service practitioners.

Contact: Association for Gerontology in Higher Education, 1001 Connecticut Avenue, NW, Suite 410, Washington, DC 20036.

McGuire, S. (nd). *Non-ageist picture books for young readers: An annotated bibliography for preschool to third grade.* Southington, CT: National Academy for Teaching and Learning about Aging, 15 pages

This annotated bibliography lists early children's literature that contains positive portrayals of older adults.

Contact: National Academy for Teaching and Learning about Aging, 200 Executive Boulevard, Suite 202, P.O. Box 246, Southington, CT 06489-0246.

Wilson J. (1988). *Intergenerational stories for children and youth: A selected annotated bibliography, 1980–1988.* Pittsburgh, PA: University of Pittsburgh, Generations Together, 34 pages

This annotated bibliography of over 135 titles covers intergenerational issues such as friendship, death and dying, grandparenting, divorce, and multicultural relationships.

Contact: Generations Together, University of Pittsburgh, 121 University Place, Suite 300, Pittsburgh, PA 15260.

Curricula

Barkman, D., Jenkins, C., & Freeman, S. (1992). *Learning from the past: Using Bi-Folkal productions in schools and intergenerational settings.* Madison, WI: Bi-Folkal Productions, loose-leaf binder

A curriculum enhancement for kindergarten through 12th grade on intergenerational activities. It contains Bi-Folkal's 16 multimedia, multisensory program kits for use in schools and intergenerational settings.

Contact: Bi-Folkal Productions, 809 Williamson Street, Madison, WI 53703.

Brown, M., Masatani, K., Daniels, J., & McCullough, M. (1992). *Roots and shoots: An intergenerational garden curriculum guide for grades 2–4* (rev. ed.), 55 pages

This curriculum pairs third graders with older adults in an outdoor classroom where elders teach the students gardening techniques. Curriculum includes 17 lesson plans and sections on program implementation, cooking projects, and garden chores.

Contact: Elizabeth F. Gamble Garden Center, 1431 Waverly Street, Palo Alto, CA 64301.

Couper, D. (1992). *Schools in an aging society: Curriculum series.* Southington, CT: National Academy for Teaching and Learning About Aging

Six interrelated guides that promote education for, with and about older adults at the middle and high school levels. The titles are *Strengthening the school–community connection,* 38 pages; *Elders as resources,* 30 pages; *Guide for pupil personnel specialists,* 64 pages; *Social studies classroom activities for secondary schools* (20 lessons), 110 pages; *Health/home economics classroom activities for secondary schools* (21 lessons), 104 pages; and *Language arts classroom activities for secondary schools* (13 lessons), 64 pages.

Contact: National Academy for Teaching and Learning about Aging, P.O. Box 246, Southington, CT 06489-0246.

Growing together: An intergenerational curriculum. (1989). Providence, RI: Alliance for Better Nursing Home Care, 38 pages

This curriculum is part of the Building Bridges Program that encourages friendly visiting between preschool children and the elderly. It is designed to teach preschool children about aging and the aged through specific lesson plans.

Contact: Alliance for Better Nursing Home Care, 1213 Elmwood Avenue, Providence, RI 02907.

Hammack, B. (1994). *Dialogues across the ages: An intergenerational discussion model for high school social studies classes.* Kensington, MD: Interages, 52 pages

This replication guide includes lesson plans designed by several social studies teachers from Montgomery County, Maryland. The purpose of this curriculum is to bring senior adults and high school students together to discover both the similarities and the differences in how the generations feel about a variety of social problems, historical events, and other social studies issues of interest to both generations.

Contact: Interages, 9411 Connecticut Avenue, Kensington, MD 20895.

Hammack, B. (1992). *Shared lives: An intergenerational discussion model,* 50 pages

> This is a guide for use by teachers bringing senior adults and students together to share life memories for use as enhancement in existing school curricula.

Contact: Interages, 9411 Connecticut Avenue, Kensington, MD 20895.

Lyons, C. (Ed.). (1982). *On growing older: Curriculum guides—Grades 1–6.* Pittsburgh, PA: University of Pittsburgh, Generations Together

> These curriculum enhancement guides (one for each grade level) are designed to help children develop a deeper awareness, understanding, and acceptance of the aging process and an appreciation of the contributions made to American society by the elderly.

Contact: Generations Together, University of Pittsburgh, 121 University Place, Suite 300, Pittsburgh, PA 15260.

Mississippi's curriculum on aging for secondary schools (Grades 7–12). (1991). Jackson: Mississippi State Department of Education, 120 pages

> A curriculum enhancement designed to teach secondary school students about the aging process through an existing health curriculum. It can be used to enhance collaborative efforts between local school districts and community aging organizations

Contact: Felix A. Okojie, Office of Research, Policy, and Development, Mississippi State Department of Education, P.O. Box 771, Jackson, MS 39205.

Promoting aging awareness among youth: Establishing intergenerational linkages. (1992). Columbia, MO: Missouri Education Center

> The resource materials and activities in this curriculum series (21 titles, designed to be used along with existing curricula) were developed for the 3rd, 7th, and 10th grades to enhance awareness and understanding of the aging process.

Contact for specific titles and pricing: The Missouri Education Center, 105 Waugh Street, Columbia, MO 65201.

Tice, C. (1994). *Developing a curriculum of caring: A guide to intergenerational programs in schools.* Ann Arbor, MI: Lifespan Resources, 60 pages

> This guide has been developed for teachers, administrators, and community volunteers who desire to work toward a curriculum of caring through intergenerational programs in schools. It is largely based on experiences in the Teaching–Learning Communities (T-LC) Program of the Ann Arbor public schools.

Contact: Lifespan Resources, Intergenerational Education, Service, Research, 1212 Roosevelt, Ann Arbor, MI 48104.

Woodward, C. (1994). *Grandpals program: A model elementary school-based adopted grandparent program,* guidebook, 30 pages; *Aspects of aging: An annotated bibliography of children's literature for aging education,* 94 pages; Ottawa, KS: Kansas Intergenerational Network

> The guidebook outlines a week-by-week activity-based program for use by teachers who wish to engage in adopting nursing home grandpals, to investigate opportunities for living history visits, and to teach weekly aging education topics. The bibliography designed for use with the guidebook contains children's book titles with summaries and aging application suggestions that can be integrated into regular elementary classroom curricula.

Contact: Kansas Intergenerational Network, 132 South Main, Ottawa, KS 66067.

YOUNG AND OLDER ADULTS SERVING THE COMMUNITY

Bagby, B., & Snyder, J. (1992). *Youth and seniors: The dynamic duo.* Urbana: University of Illinois, Cooperative Extension, 47 pages

> This manual discusses planning and implementation of intergenerational programs, including how to identify community needs, program goals, resources, volunteers, and funding. Program and project ideas are included.

Contact: Adult Life and Aging Specialist, University of Illinois Cooperative Extension Service, 535 Bevier Hall, 905 S. Goodwin Avenue, Urbana, IL 61801.

Hammack, B. (1993). *Self-Esteem Through Service (S.E.T.S.): An intergenerational service-learning experience for at-risk students and isolated senior adults.* Kensington, MD: Interages, 28 pages

> This guide describes an intergenerational service-learning intervention program targeted to involve at-risk middle school students with isolated and often frail adults. The activities used in this intervention are designed to enhance the self-esteem of both groups, provide supportive relationships, change stereotypes, and give both groups the opportunity to engage in community service projects to help other needy populations.

Contact: Interages, 9411 Connecticut Avenue, Kensington, Maryland 20895.

Kaplan, M. (1994). *Side by side: Exploring your neighborhood through intergenerational activities: A curriculum guide.* Berkeley, CA: MIG Communications, ISBN 0-944661-21-1, 120 pages

> Side by Side is a program of activities designed to help youth and elders have input into what their neighborhoods will look like in the future. A program manual contains 9 curriculum enhancement units that captures the interest of young people, teaching them skills and disciplines.

Contact: MIG Communications, 1802 Fifth Street, Berkeley, CA 94710-1915.

McCrea, J. M., & Crisafio, D. (1995). *CareSharing: A mutual service exchange program: Guidelines for replication.* Pittsburgh, PA: University of Pittsburgh, Generations Together, 52 pages

> This replication manual is based on Generation Together's successful credit-sharing program in partnership with the University of Pittsburgh Medical Center's Living at Home Program. It provides step-by-step instructions on how to design and implement an intergenerational service credit program in a low-income urban neighborhood.

Contact: Generations Together, University of Pittsburgh, 121 University Place, Suite 300, Pittsburgh, PA 15260.

Project EASE (Exploring Aging Through Shared Experiences). (1993). Ithaca, NY: Resource Center

> Project EASE brings groups of young adolescents together with senior citizens through joint service, shared group activity, and/or one-on-one matching at the discretion of the program director. This manual contains a leader's guide (36 pages), member's guide (6 pages), warm-up activities (6 pages), and a polarity activity (loose-leaf pages in pockets).

Contact: Resource Center, 7 Cornell Business & Technology Park, Ithaca, NY 14850.

Scannell, T., & Roberts, A. (1994). *Young and old serving together: Meeting community needs through intergenerational partnerships.* Washington, DC: Generations United, 115 pages

> This handbook contains state-of-the-art program development techniques, tips from experts, best practice criteria, funding options, anecdotes, program profiles, and real-life illustrations and examples for maximizing the potential of intergenerational community service programs.

Contact: Generations United, c/o CWLA, 440 First Street, NW, Suite 310, Washington, DC 20001.

Index